A HISTORY OF THE INDIAN NATIONALIST MOVEMENT

A HISTORY OF THE INDIAN NATIONALIST MOVEMENT

SIR VERNEY LOVETT, K.C.S.I.

GYAN

Published by

Gyan Publishing House
5, Ansari Road
Daryaganj, New Delhi-110002
Phone: 011-47034999, 9811692060
E-mail: books@gyanbooks.com

Distribution Network
gyanbooks.com
India, USA, Canada, UK, Australia, France

ISBN : 978-81-212-9671-7 (PB)
First Published, 1920

2nd Impression 2023

Printed at: Gyan Press, Delhi.

A HISTORY OF THE INDIAN NATIONALIST MOVEMENT
Author: SIR VERNEY LOVETT

A HISTORY OF THE INDIAN NATIONALIST MOVEMENT

BY SIR VERNEY LOVETT, K.C.S.I.
(LATE OF THE INDIAN CIVIL SERVICE)

1920

PREFACE

I LEFT India in April, 1919, and in the following October completed thirty-five years of service passed in direct contact with Indians of all classes. I have enjoyed considerable facilities for observing from close quarters various phases of the Indian Nationalist movement.

In this book I have tried to trace its history and to summarise political conditions in India as they were when I left the country. My object has been to render some slight assistance toward a clear understanding of the difficult problems which India offers, and will continue to offer, to the British people.

Throughout I have felt the extreme difficulty of appraising and setting forth fairly the ideals and mental processes of men not of my own race. I have, therefore, aimed at explaining these, as far as possible, in the words of Indian Nationalists themselves. My book may be held to contain an excessive number of quotations; but the quantity of these is due to my anxiety to throw as accurate a light as possible on causes, motives, and events.

Another object has been present to my mind. British rule in India has been, and is constantly slandered and vilified in India, in England, and in other countries. I have taken care to show what has been said of its character and policy by prominent founders and leaders of Indian Nationalism.

My story is one of my own time, and ends with the day of my departure from India. My last chapter was written before publication of the amended Government of India Bill, which has since become law. I have endeavoured to write what I believe to be the truth in a fair and considerate spirit.

I wish to acknowledge my obligations to a large variety of authorities, to the published reports of the Indian National Congress, from 1885 to the present time, to the newspapers *India*, *The Times of India*, the *Pioneer*, the *Leader*, and other Indian journals, to the writings of the late Sir Alfred Lyall, to Mr. Vincent Smith's *Early History of India*, to the *Life of Saiyid Ahmad Khan, C.S.I.*, by Colonel Graham, to the Speeches of Lord Curzon of Kedleston edited by Sir Thomas Raleigh, to Lord Morley's *Recollections and Indian Speeches*, to the Speeches of the late Mr. Gokhale, to Papers on Indian Social Reform, edited by Mr. C. Y. Chintamani, to Mr. William Archer's *India and the Future*, to the Montagu-Chelmsford Reforms Report, to various reports published by the Government of India, and to other sources of information too numerous to detail.

Lastly, I would express the hope that the importance and interest of the subject, especially at the present time, may lead my readers to forgive the shortcomings of the book; and I would express my gratitude to the people of the United Provinces, and to my brother officers of the Indian Civil Service, with whom I have passed many happy years.

H. V. L.

December 31*st*, 1919.

CONTENTS

CHAPTER I

INTRODUCTORY

CHAPTER II

POLITICAL MOVEMENTS—FIRST STAGE

CHAPTER III

POLITICAL MOVEMENTS—SECOND STAGE

CHAPTER IV

POLITICS FROM THE OUTBREAK OF THE WAR TO THE END OF 1916

CHAPTER V

THE DECLARATION OF AUGUST 20TH, 1917

CHAPTER VI

THE REFORMS REPORT

CHAPTER VII

THE SEDITION BILLS AND THE "PASSIVE RESISTANCE" RIOTS

CHAPTER VIII

A SUMMARY OF EXISTING CONDITIONS

APPENDICES

A HISTORY OF THE INDIAN NATIONALIST MOVEMENT

CHAPTER I

INTRODUCTORY

"An accurate knowledge of the conditions of the past is necessary for a right understanding of the problems of the present."

SOME time ago, in the well-known book *J'accuse,* I read the following passage:

"National movements in fact cannot be suppressed. The practical politician must deal with them as facts; and if he hopes to conduct them in the desired direction, he must endeavour, as far as possible, to satisfy their demands, which rest on community of race, of language, and often of religion—demands which are thus healthy and justifiable. Therein lies the skill of the English, and the true basis of their colonial greatness."

These words, written by a German, and inspired by observation of stirring incidents in the recent War, are a well-deserved tribute to the success of the colonial policy of Great Britain. Her Indian policy has been declared to be based on the same principles, but must be adapted to far more complex circumstances; for in this great continent, or collection of countries, diverse in soil and physical characteristics, she has to deal with, not community, but numerous varieties of race, language, and religion. Yet she must recognise that "although Indians are broken up into diversities of race and language, they are, as a whole, not less distinctly marked off from the rest of Asia by certain material and moral characteristics than their country is by the mountains and the sea. The component parts of that great country hang together morally and politically. There is no more room for two irreconcilable systems of government than there is in Persia, China, or Asiatic Turkey."[1]

The British Government has decided to accede to the demand of Indian Nationalists that India shall tread the paths that lead to parliamentary government. This decision calls for, and will call for the solution of very difficult questions. We shall explore these to small purpose unless we make some study of the past, unless we observe the course of events which introduced democratic politics into the most rigidly conservative country in the world. The formal introduction took place thirty-four years ago; but the India of 1885 was, like the India of to-day, heir to a former time.

In view of perversions of Indian history which have lately become too common, it will be convenient to describe briefly the nature of the political inheritance to which Britain succeeded. The Moghal Empire, the product of a great Muhammadan invasion from Central Asia, had previously swept away all indigenous political institutions and shattered all semblance of Hindu nationality except in the States of Rajputana. When, after two centuries, that Empire itself fell gradually into decay, Sikhs, Jats, Afghans, Marathas disputed and fought over its territories. The Marathas were showing signs of consolidating their acquisitions when British intervention turned the scale; but history does not show that their Government represented any pan-

[1] Sir Alfred Lyall.

Hindu nationality. In its later days it was described by Sir Thomas Munro, a high contemporary authority, as "one of the most destructive that ever existed in India." He went on: "Their work was chiefly desolation. They did not seek their revenue in the improvement of the country, but in the exaction of the established *chaut*[1] from their neighbours and in predatory incursions to levy more."

Province after province fell to the East India Company because the Moghal Empire could no longer withstand the attacks of its enemies, and in each the company's servants found no stable or organised political institutions. Everywhere the strongest ruled, or tried to rule, by purely despotic methods. Everywhere the lives and property of the people were at the arbitrary disposal of their rulers. Everywhere armies, or hosts of marauders, marched frequently over the country, supplied their wants by plunder and left ruin in their train. Sir Alfred Lyall writes, in *Asiatic Studies*:

> "The character and consequences of the events which preceded British supremacy in India have, perhaps, been seldom adequately estimated. There intervened a period of political anarchy greater and more widespread than India had experienced for centuries. It was a mere tearing and rending of the prostrate carcass, a free fight with little definite aim or purpose beyond plunder or annexation of land revenue."

Let those who are prone to undervalue the advantages of British government remember the miseries which it brought to an end.

Endeavouring to achieve peace and security, first for their commerce and then for their territories, constantly seeking for a permanent frontier, the East India Company as constantly lost it in receding vistas, until at

[1] Impost.

last they found themselves supreme over the whole of India south-east of the Punjab. Such rapid extension would have been impracticable had not their rule been generally welcome for reasons explained by Abbé Dubois, a French missionary who worked in Southern India early in the last century:

"Nevertheless," he wrote, "the justice and prudence which the present rulers display in endeavouring to make these people less unhappy than they have been hitherto; the anxiety they manifest in increasing their material comfort; above all, the inviolable respect which they constantly show for the customs and religious belief of the country; and, lastly, the protection they afford to the weak as well as to the strong, to the Brahman, to the Pariah, to the Christian, to the Muhammadan; all these have contributed more to the consolidation of their power than even their victories and conquests."

But now other considerations began to claim the attention of thinking men. Perhaps the most noteworthy utterances on the subject were those of Sir Thomas Munro, who, arriving in India in 1780 as a military cadet at the age of nineteen, died as Governor of Madras in 1827. Not only did he consider

"how we can raise the character and material condition of our people, how by better organisation we can root out needless misery of mind and body, how we can improve the health and intelligence, stimulate the sense of duty and fellowship, the efficiency and patriotism of the whole community;" but, going further, he struck an altogether new note. "The strength of the British Government enables it to put down every rebellion, to repel every foreign invasion, and to give to its subjects a degree of protection which those of no Native Power enjoy. Its laws and institutions also afford them a security from domestic oppression unknown in Native States; but these advantages are dearly bought. They are purchased by the sacrifice of independence, of national character, and of whatever renders a people respectable. The natives of British provinces may, without fear, pursue their different occupations as traders or husbandmen and enjoy the fruits of their labours in tranquillity; but none of them can look forward to any share in the civil or military government of their country. It is from men who either hold or are eligible for public life that nations take their character; where no such men exist, there can be no energy in any other class of the community. No elevation of character can be expected among men who in the military line cannot attain to any rank above that of a subadar, where they are as much below an ensign as an ensign is below the commander-in-chief, and who in the civil line can hope for nothing beyond some petty judicial or revenue office in which they may by corrupt means make up for their slender salary."

On another occasion he wrote:

"Our great error in this country, during a long course of years, has been too much precipitation in attempting to better the condition of the people with hardly any knowledge of the means by which it was to be accomplished, and indeed without seeming to think that any other than good intentions were necessary. It is a dangerous system of government to be constantly urged by the desire of settling everything permanently; to do everything in a hurry and in consequence wrong, and in our zeal for permanency to put the remedy out of our reach. The ruling vice of our Government is innovation; and its innovation has been so little guided by a knowledge of the people, that though made after what was thought by us to be mature discussion, it must appear to them as little better than the result of mere caprice."

Munro overlooked an important condition of the future, as I shall subsequently show; but he was regarded as an official of exceptional ability, and his ideas were to some extent shared by other prominent men of his day. Thus it was that broad and liberal principles guided the statesmen who were responsible for that important Act of Parliament—the Government of India Bill of 1833—which asserted the sovereignty of the Crown over the Company's territories, and declared that these were held in trust for His Majesty. It formulated definitely the principles of British rule. It declared that no person by reason of his birth, creed, or colour should be disqualified from holding any office in the East India Company's service. It also forbade the Company to engage in any kind of trade, thus terminating the association of Government with profit-making, and it converted the Governor-General of Fort William in Bengal into the "Governor-General of India in Council." There were to be four ordinary members of Council, three servants of the Company, and the fourth a legal member appointed with the approbation of the Crown, but only entitled to sit and vote at meetings convened for legislative purposes. The first legal member was the great Macaulay. Great Britain thus declared her determination that her Empire in India should rest on freedom and fair opportunity, and took a further important step in the process of transforming the East India Company from what was originally a purely mercantile association into a special agency for the government of a great dependency. The Directors of the Company endeavoured to give effect to this generous policy by a despatch dated December 10th, 1834. Natives of India were to be admitted to places of trust as freely and extensively as a regard for the due discharge of the functions attached to such places would permit. Fitness was henceforward to be the criterion of eligibility. And in order that the natives of India might become fit, and able to compete with a fair chance of success, every design tending to their improvement was to be promoted, "whether by conferring on them the advantages of education or by diffusing on them the treasures of science, knowledge, and moral culture." At the same time the Governor-General was to remember that

"it is not by holding out incentives to official ambition, but by repressing crime, by securing and guarding property, by ensuring to industry the fruits of its labour, by protecting men in the undisturbed enjoyment of their rights and in the unfettered exercise of their faculties, that governments best minister to the public wealth and happiness."

Democratic political ideals in India owe their origin largely to the decision of Lord William Bentinck, then Governor-General, who in pursuance of the "liberal and comprehensive policy" laid down by the despatch from which I have quoted, announced, on March 7th, 1835, that "the great object of the British Government ought to be the promotion of European literature and science among the natives of India." Up to that time the pioneers of Western education had been mainly Christian missionaries, but now the advancement of such teaching was declared to be a part of State policy. As has often been told, this announcement was largely influenced by Macaulay, and closed a controversy in which the question at issue was whether the instruction to be subsidised by public money should be English or Oriental; whether the language, the philosophies, and science of the West or the East should be encouraged by the State. The settlement arrived at was in principle right, for it was clearly the duty of the British Government to attempt the intellectual enlightenment of India on Western lines; but in carrying out this settlement the Government made one mistake perceptible to after-experience—it promoted literature far above science; it also necessarily offended conservative communities with sensitive prejudices, the Brahmans, who were depositaries of orthodox Hindu tradition, and the higher classes of Muhammadans, who were attached to their own books and philosophy. Nevertheless, for the first time in India, State-aided instruction was established on a firm foundation. In the words of the last Census of India Report "the country had been for centuries in an unsettled condition, and the common people were sunk in deepest ignorance. Under the caste system, the learned professions were the monopoly of a few castes, and in the law books the imparting of knowledge to Sudras (low castes) was forbidden." But now a new system was introduced. English and vernacular education were opened to all, although years elapsed before the former penetrated beyond an extremely limited number of persons belonging to the already lettered classes. In 1854 the directors of the East India Company in a memorable despatch accepted the systematic promotion of general education as one of the duties of the State, and emphatically declared their desire for the diffusion of European knowledge in India. Shortly afterwards a University was established at Calcutta which devoted its entire energies to literary and theoretical instruction.

It must be remembered that in 1835 neither the Punjab nor Oudh belonged to Great Britain, also that throughout the whole of British India communications were still primitive and adverse to a rapid spread of the new learning. Hindus formed and form the great majority of the population. Their higher castes represent, generally, the early Aryan invaders. Their lower castes are the descendants of the original inhabitants of the country, who lost their independence by the imposition of the caste system. Sir R. G. Bhandarkar, late Vice-Chancellor of the Bombay University, tells us that each Aryan tribe that invaded India in the remote past had a king of its own, and a family or families of priests.

"There were among them," he says, "three social grades. To the first belonged priests, who composed Brahmans, *i.e.*, songs or hymns to the gods, knew how to worship them, and were called Brahmans. The second grade was occupied by those who acquired political eminence and fought battles, and were called Rajans. All the other Aryas were referred to the third grade, and were distinguished by the name of Visas, or people, generally. These three classes formed one community, and such of the aborigines as had yielded to the Aryas were tacked on to it as a fourth grade under the name of Dasas, slaves, or servants."

As the Aryans spread eastward over the vast continent of India, subjugating or pushing back the earlier inhabitants, they developed the religious and social system known as Hinduism, which is founded on the original Aryan beliefs, but has adopted certain additional doctrines which are generally accepted among Hindus and are likely to influence the future materially, if less profoundly than they have influenced the past. That here and there they have been modified or largely rejected by particular sects or classes does not alter the fact that they are the basis of the working creed of the great majority of Hindus, and form the mental windows through which these many millions look out upon the things of life. The first of these doctrines is that the cleavages between the four main castes were divinely ordained, that these castes alone are within the pale of Hinduism; and that outside that pale are barbarians or outcastes, descendants of the aborigines who never intermingled with the lowest caste of Hindus. The second doctrine is that every soul passes through a variety of bodies. At each birth the caste or outcasting of the body is determined by the deeds of the soul in its previous body. This doctrine is named "karma," or action. In effect it implies, and is understood to imply, that persons who are so fortunate as to be born Brahmans have won their position by merit and spirituality; that members of the lowest caste and outcastes are paying a just penalty for transgressions in a previous existence, and must be content to accept this unpleasant fact. To this belief was added another, that the high castes, and notably the Brahmans, must be most careful to preserve their spirituality and position; that for this reason they must, as far as possible, avoid contact with lower castes.

As the centuries rolled on, the original four castes expanded into many sub-castes; but although the law and the scriptures were by no means always observed, and modifications of caste practices resulted from migrations and changes of occupation, the basic principles of "karma" and caste-organisation hardened. Even the outcastes largely accepted them, together with vague varieties of Hindu theology, and are at the present day classed as Hindus in census returns. And thus it is that, in spite of the political disintegration which prevailed in India at the time of the Muhammadan inroads from central Asia, there was a Hindu social and religious system combining external unity with internal cleavages. This system remained intact during the period of Muhammadan domination, although the temptations of a militant religion, which taught that all true believers were equal before God, proved irresistible with many Hindus of the lower castes. It was, indeed, not until the establishment of British rule and the introduction of English education, often imparted by Christian European missionaries, that the rooted ideas engendered by the caste system and the pessimism implanted among the lowest castes by the doctrine of "karma" weakened in the slightest degree; and even now these ideas, although partially dissolving among the English-educated, are very strong among the generality of Hindus, and necessarily imply rigid social distinctions, assuring Brahman supremacy and supporting it by the teaching that the presence of Brahmans is indispensable for the religious family ceremonies to which orthodox Hindus attach supreme value. Caste distinctions are now enforced by strict rules and penalties, even though such rules and penalties are here and there lapsing into disuse. Brahman ascendancy has been largely temporal as well as spiritual. Brahmans were the councillors of early Hindu monarchs, and have often been the ministers of Muhammadan rulers. Neither foreign conquest nor domestic dissensions have materially impaired a religious and social position which is buttressed by the sanction of ages. Such a supremacy has necessarily developed an intense pride of place, and has produced restrictions and exclusions of the most arbitrary kind.

British rule had followed closely on the fall of Muhammadan sovereignty, and had inherited the autocratic system of administration which the Muslim conquerors from Central Asia had themselves received from earlier rulers of India. No other system had ever been known in the country from time immemorial. In the gradual dissolution of their own empire, many Muhammadans freely assisted in establishing British authority. Not only did they enlist in the army of the East India Company, but, in the years which immediately preceded the Mutiny, they considerably outnumbered Hindus in the best offices which could be held by Indians under the British Government. The majority of their upper classes, however—adventurers by descent and soldiers by tradition—clung to their own history and literature, and turned their faces away from the new learning, failing to realise that, in course of time, under Western rule, Western education must necessarily become the channel to office and power. The Parsis, on the other hand, descendants from Persian exiles who settled in India some centuries ago and form a strong commercial section in Bombay, and the Hindu clerical and trading castes, as well as those families of Brahmans who, by tradition, inclined to Government employ, quickly availed themselves of opening opportunities, especially in the capital province of Bengal and in the seaports of Bombay and Madras. The Rajputs or Thakurs, the great Hindu fighting caste, at first held entirely aloof from English education. Their ambitions were military or territorial. They lived in the interior of Upper India, and were slightly represented elsewhere.

The India of the East India Company's days ended with the Mutiny. Lord Roberts has pointed out that this was a military revolt, but that the revolt would not have taken place had there not been considerable discontent through that part of the country from which the Hindustani sepoy chiefly came, and had not powerful persons borne the British a grudge. He states that the discontent was largely due to the antagonism of the Brahmans to our innovations and to Western education, which was sapping their influence. He points out that we had spread among the ruling chiefs uncertainty and discontent; that we had recently annexed Oudh and Jhansi, and had informed the titular King of Delhi that on his death his title would cease and his court would be removed from the Imperial city.

It is also important to notice that for various reasons, the more sensitive Hindu and Muhammadan classes had conceived the idea that their religions were losing their exclusive privileges and were being steadily undermined. The proclamations issued from Delhi and Lucknow appealed to the multitude with the cry of religion in peril.

The arena of the Mutiny was the United Provinces of Agra and Oudh, which then included Delhi, and a large part of Central India. There was little fighting anywhere else, and no popular trouble in Bengal proper, although there was some fighting in Bihar. Unlike the Punjab, neither Agra nor Oudh had been disarmed. In the Agra Province there were very few British troops, and those few either were drawn off to the siege of Delhi or were themselves for the first four or five months hopelessly beleaguered. At Agra itself the Lieutenant-Governor was, until after the fall of Delhi, supported against 42,000 rebel soldiers by one company's regiment of 655 effectives and one battery of six guns manned by Indian drivers. It was indeed fortunate for our cause that in this province, which contains so much that is most national and most sacred in Hindu eyes, and has moreover been the centre of Muslim empire, the rebellion, although animated largely by racial and religious sentiment, was not a great patriotic or religious combination. Here is a contemporary description of ordinary district occurrences away from the great centres of population: "The villages and towns generally side with some neighbouring potentate, or more generally they side with no one at all. They are delighted at being relieved from all government whatsoever, and instantly set to work fighting among themselves. Every man of enterprise and a little influence collects his clan, and plunders all the weaker villages round him."

In Oudh, recently annexed, and the chief recruiting-ground of the old sepoy army, the landed aristocracy, who are now our good friends the talukdars, were boiling with rage and discontent. In our recent settlement of the land revenue we had inclined to the principle of pushing them aside as grasping middlemen devoid of right or title, and, when the sepoys mutinied, most of the talukdars naturally joined them. In the whole province we had not 1,000 British soldiers, but those whom we had, assisted by some loyal Indian troops, gave a remarkably good account of themselves. The rebellion in Oudh was more national than in Agra, but here, too, the fighters were generally more concerned to make as much as they could out of unusual opportunities for licence and plunder than to oppose a persistent and determined front to the enemy.

Later on I shall have occasion to quote the remarks of a loyal and competent Indian observer on the events of the Mutiny. But what struck the late Sir Alfred Lyall, at that time a young civilian in the Agra Province, was the fierce hatred borne to us by the Muhammadans, and he put the whole rebellion down to them. This was an off-hand expression of opinion. But more weight attaches to his later views, expressed many years after his early adventures, that after the Mutiny the British turned on the Muhammadans as their real enemies "so that the failure of the revolt was much more disastrous to them than to the Hindus. They lost almost all their remaining prestige of traditionary superiority over the Hindus; they forfeited for the time the confidence of their foreign rulers; and it is from this period that must be dated the loss of their numerical majority in the higher subordinate ranks of the civil and military services."

When the revolt had been suppressed, the Crown took over the government of India from the East India Company. Queen Victoria's Proclamation of November 1st, 1858, which is frequently referred to by educated Indians as the Magna Charta of their liberties, declared that the rights, dignity, and honour of Indian ruling princes were to be preserved as Her Majesty's own, and that, so far as might be, all Her Majesty's subjects, of whatever race and creed, were to be freely and impartially admitted to offices in the public service, the duties of which they might be qualified by their education, ability, and integrity duly to discharge. The peaceful industry of India was to be stimulated; works of public utility and improvement were to be promoted; and the Government was to be administered for the benefit of all Her Majesty's subjects resident in India. "In their prosperity will be our strength, in their contentment our security, and in their gratitude our great reward." Three years later, an important step was taken in the first association of Indians with the Government for legislative purposes. By the Councils Act of 1861 the Governor-General's Executive Council was to consist of five members, three of whom had been in the Indian service of the Crown for ten years at least. The Commander-in-Chief was to be an extraordinary member; and for the purpose of making laws and regulations the Governor-General could nominate to his Council not less than six or more than twelve persons, not less than half of whom must be non-officials.

The Governors of Bombay and Madras, who were also assisted by Executive Councils, could similarly nominate a few persons to aid in legislation, not less than half of whom must be non-officials.

The Governor-General in Council could, with the approval of the Home Government, extend to the Lieutenant-Governors of Bengal, the North-Western Provinces,[1] and the Punjab, who ruled without Executive Councils, the power to convoke small Legislative Councils and to appoint persons thereto, not less than one-third of whom would be non-officials.

Prominent Indians were to be associated henceforward with the Government in legislation. The association was to be extremely limited, but marked the beginning of a more liberal policy.

At this time about two-thirds of the country was under direct British administration. The rest was, and is now, ruled by its hereditary chiefs, all owing allegiance to the British Crown. The area under British administration now consists of seven provinces, each under a Governor or Lieutenant-Governor, and seven under Chief Commissioners. Four of the major provinces exceed the United Kingdom in area, and two exceed it in population.

All classes of the population were now led into the ways of peace, and the whole edifice settled down. Starting badly as usual in the recent conflict, the British had vindicated their supremacy, and now rapidly re-established peace and order throughout the country. Means of correspondence and communication rapidly improved; British capital poured in; railways and commerce developed; schools and colleges grew and

[1] Now the United Provinces of Agra and Oudh.

multiplied, until at last the Muhammadans yielded to the general impulse and began to enter the English educational arena. The India of to-day gradually came into being. It was, in an important respect, a different country from that foreseen by Sir Thomas Munro. It involved more complex interests. He had not anticipated the part which European capital would play in the development of an India no longer "standing before her captors like some beautiful stranger," but traversed by railways, served by steamships, and brought into the bustling consolidation of the modern world. So blind was his augury of this side of the future that he defended the monopoly of the East India Company on the ground that it was doubtful whether or not trade with India could be greatly increased.

"No nation," he wrote, "will take from another what it can furnish cheaper and better itself. In India almost every article which the inhabitants require is made cheaper and better than in Europe. . . . Their simple mode of living renders all our furniture and ornaments for the decoration of the house and table utterly unserviceable to the Hindus." He saw no prospect of any considerable number of Europeans being able to make a livelihood in the country. "The trading disposition of the natives induces me to think it impossible that any European trader can long remain in the interior of India, and that they must all sooner or later be driven to the coast."

Those were easy days for the rulers of India, for their superior efficiency was taken for granted, and opposition was scarce and insignificant. The ruling chiefs were less apprehensive and more contented than they had ever been before, and their content was reflected in our own territories. These were administered by British officers,[1] assisted by a host of improving Indian subordinates. The officers themselves for the most part did their work, as it came, with zeal and energy, liking the people and holding generally that, in the words of a distinguished lieutenant-governor, "Good administration was like good digestion. It did its work and you heard no more about it." And indeed to the simple and docile masses of India, who desire only strong and sympathetic protection, good administration must always be the best of blessings.

Mainly peasants living in mud-built huts and cultivating small holdings, at times absorbed in pilgrimages or religious observances, they are generally preoccupied

[1] "The easiest way of understanding the organisation of a province is to think of it as composed of districts, which in all provinces, except Madras, are combined, in groups of usually from four to six, into divisions, under a commissioner. The average size of a district is 4,430 square miles, or three-fourths the size of Yorkshire. Many are much bigger. Mymensingh district holds more human souls than Switzerland. Vizagapatam district, both in area and population, exceeds Denmark. In the United Provinces, where districts are small and the population dense, each collector is, on the average, in charge of an area as large as Norfolk and of a population as large as that of New Zealand. The commissioner of the Tirhut division looks after far more people than the Government of Canada.

"The district, which is a collector's charge, is the unit of administration, but it is cut up into sub-divisions under assistants or deputy collectors, and these again into revenue collecting areas of smaller size. The provincial Government's general authority thus descends through the divisional commissioner in a direct chain to the district officer. The district officer has a dual capacity; as collector he is head of the revenue organisation, and as magistrate he exercises general supervision over the inferior courts and, in particular, directs the police work. In areas where there is no permanent revenue settlement, he can at any time be in touch, through his revenue subordinates, with every inch of his territory. This organisation in the first place serves its peculiar purpose of collecting the revenue and of keeping the peace. But, because it is so close-knit, so well-established, and so thoroughly understood by the people, it simultaneously discharges easily and efficiently an immense number of other duties."—*Montagu-Chelmsford Report, paragraphs* 122–3.

with the prospects of the weather, the humours of their moneylenders and landlords, frequent litigation with these powerful persons or with other neighbours, and perhaps the exactions of some petty subordinate official. As was truly said in the Montagu-Chelmsford Report: "the physical facts of India, the blazing sun, the enervating rains, have coloured their mental outlook"; and it is difficult to suppose that the day will ever come when these facts will cease largely to dominate their lives. Ignorant and credulous, industrious and frugal, but, in spite of frequent inroads of epidemics, breeding to the very margin of subsistence, they form with their landlords 90 per cent. of the population, and have always contributed by far the larger share of Indian revenues. The greatest natural asset of India is and must be its soil. It is, too, from those agricultural castes which are martial by tradition that the Army has always drawn its recruits. The importance in the body politic of the people who live on and by the land has been often overshadowed in these latter days, but things were not so formerly. It was to them and their affairs, to the ascertainment and codifying of their rights and tenures, to the adjustment and readjustment of their relations with their landlords and with Government, it was to the protection of their interests, to the settlement of their feuds, that some of our most famous administrators, men who are remembered in their provinces as the salt and justification of British rule, devoted years of unremitting energy. British administration could never have prospered as it did, had they not done so. It is with the rural masses that district officers are still mostly concerned. In this untroubled period the rights of the people of India and the rights of their rulers agreed together in a silence that was seldom broken, and the foundations of comprehensive revenue and tenancy legislation, which had been well and truly laid by the East India Company, were examined, improved, and consolidated. Things worked on laborious but broad and simple lines in the interior of the country.

But at the great seaports, with which the majority of English officials were seldom in personal contact, among those middle or professional classes which had originally embraced English education, thought was beginning to enter fresh channels and new problems were coming into dim outline. With some members of these the Hindu ideas of the unimportance of life, as a mere link in a chain of existences, of the desirability of rigid adherence to caste and family customs, as well as the ancient belief that the course of the four ages of the world was a continuous process of deterioration, were rapidly weakening. They were yielding to the allurements of a world of greater material comfort and of growing interest. Western education, English history, English literature, the works of Milton, Burke, Macaulay, were inspiring ideas of liberty, nationality, self-government. From England were returning Indian visitors with accounts of unusual consideration conceded there. These and a commencing contact with the British democracy were producing the idea that Anglo-Indian social and political exclusiveness was humiliating and unjustifiable. Things should be changed; power and high place should cease to be a preserve from which educated Indians were mainly shut out. In 1859 the late Sir Alfred Lyall, then a young civil officer, had written from the seclusion of an up-country district:

"I am always thinking of the probable future of our Empire, and trying to conceive it possible to civilise and convert an enormous nation by establishing schools and missionary societies. Also having civilised them and taught them the advantage of liberty and the use of European sciences, how are we to keep them under us and persuade them that it is for their good that we hold all the high offices of Government?"

The time was nearing when questions of this kind would call for answer. It is true that Act XXXIII of 1870, while laying down the principle that "it is one of our first duties toward the people of India to guard the safety of our dominion," had provided for more extended employment of Indians in the uncovenanted civil service, and for promotion therefrom to the covenanted service "according to tried ability." But such promotions were rare and merely whetted rising ambitions. Education was expanding not only Indian capacities, but Indian desires. What if, after all, life could offer a more exciting prospect? After some preliminary indications of discontent, the position became more fully disclosed. It contained a sinister element.

The Mutiny had shown the ease with which the British could establish their supremacy, but had bequeathed a legacy of bitter memories to persons on both sides. Fear had, for some years, stifled expression of these; but, as time went on, a section of the Indian Press began to display malignant hostility to the existing state of things.

The tendency of some vernacular newspapers, especially in Calcutta, to excite popular feeling against the British Government had for some time attracted attention. In 1873, Sir George Campbell, then Lieutenant-Governor of Bengal, and subsequently for many years a Liberal member of the House of Commons, had expressed the opinion that special legislation was required; and in 1878 an Act was passed by Lord Lytton's Legislative Council for the better control of the vernacular press.

The following extracts from the speech of the Legal Member of the Government, who introduced the bill, explains clearly the mischief which was brewing:

"But there is a large and increasing class of native newspapers which would seem to exist only for the sake of spreading seditious principles, of bringing the Government and its European officers into contempt, and of exciting antagonism between the governing race and the people of the country. This description of writing is not of very recent growth, but there has been a marked increase in it of late, and especially during the last three or four years. During the past twelve months it has been worse than ever, the writers gaining in boldness as they find that their writings are allowed to pass unpunished. Their principal topics are the injustice and tyranny of the British Government, its utter want of consideration towards its native subjects, and the insolence and pride of Englishmen in India, both official and non-official. There is no crime however heinous, and no meanness however vile, which according to these writers is not habitually practised by their English rulers."

The Honourable Member then proceeded to illustrate his argument with examples, and continued:

"The extracts which I have read, are specimens, extracted haphazard from a great number, of the manner in which the British Government and the English race are habitually aspersed and held up to the contempt and hatred of the people of India. Of late, however, a further step has been taken, and a beginning has been made in the direction of inciting the people to upset the British Raj by denunciations, sometimes open and sometimes covert, of the alleged weakness and timidity of the English and their inability to maintain their present position in India."

The bill became Act IX of 1878. But it was denounced in England by Mr. Gladstone, who was then in opposition, and after his return to office it was repealed in 1882 by Lord Ripon's Government, who considered that circumstances no longer justified its existence. The evil which had brought it into being forthwith revived. Close on the repeal of the Vernacular Press Act followed the Ilbert Bill controversy. But before describing this melancholy episode, we must turn back a few years to incidents of wide and healthful importance in India's political history.

She had recently been brought into touch with the Royal Family of England through the visit of the late King Edward, then Prince of Wales, and on January 1st, 1877, a strong and abiding tie was forged when Her Majesty Queen Victoria, in recognition of the transfer of Government made in 1858, was at Delhi proclaimed Empress of India. As in 1858, so in 1877 there was a real and living personal note in Her Majesty's message which evoked warm response.

"We Victoria by the Grace of God, of the United Kingdom, Queen, Empress of India, send through our Viceroy to all our Officers, Civil and Military, and to all Princes, Chiefs and Peoples now at Delhi assembled, our Royal and Imperial greeting, and assure them of the deep interest and earnest affection with which we regard the people of our Indian Empire. We witnessed with heartfelt satisfaction the reception which they have accorded to our beloved son, and have been touched by the evidence of their loyalty and attachment to our House and throne. We trust that the present occasion may tend to unite in bonds of yet closer affection ourselves and our subjects; that from the highest to the humblest all may feel that under our rule the great principles of liberty, equity, and justice are secured to them; and that to promote their happiness, to add to their prosperity, and advance their welfare, are the ever present aims and objects of our Empire."

The response of the Ruling Chiefs expressed a sentiment which has never since varied.[1] It was voiced by His Highness the Maharaja Scindia after the delivery of the Viceroy's address:

"Shah-in-shah Padishah, may God bless you! The princes of India bless you, and pray that your sovereignty and power may remain stedfast for ever."

The Maharaja of Kashmir said that in the shadow of Her Majesty's gracious Empire would be his chief protection.

The speech of the Viceroy at the State banquet contained a great undertaking:

"There is one thing above all others that this British Empire in India does mean. It means this. It means that all its subjects shall live at peace with one another; that every one of them shall be free to grow rich in his own way, provided his way be not a criminal way; that every one of them shall be free to hold and follow his own religious belief without assailing the religious beliefs of other people, and to live unmolested by his neighbour. At first sight, that may seem a very plain and simple polity, and very easy to be applied. But, when you come to apply it to an empire multitudinous in its traditions, as well as in its inhabitants, almost infinite in the variety of races which populate it and of creeds which have shaped their character, you find that it involves administrative problems unsolved by Cæsar, unsolved by Charlemagne, unsolved by Akbar. It seems a very simple thing to say that we shall keep the peace of the empire; but if we are to keep the peace of it, we must have laws to

[1] See Appendix VIII.

settle quarrels which would otherwise disturb its peace; and if we are to have such laws, we must frame them into a system at once comprehensive and intelligible. Again, if we are to enforce any such system of law, we must have judges to administer it, and police to carry out the orders of the judges, and then we must have troops to protect the judges, the police, the people and all concerned. Well then, when you come to introduce this elaborate system of administration into a vast continent . . . you find that the work in which you are engaged is nothing less than this, that you are modifying, unavoidably modifying—not harshly, not suddenly, but slowly, gently and with sympathy, but still modifying—the whole collective social life and character of the population of the Empire. . . . But our proclamation of the Imperial title implies something more. It implies that henceforth the honour of the British Crown, and consequently the power of the British Empire, are committed to the continued maintenance and defence of this Empire. . . . For my own part, I hope and believe that the impressive demonstration of an Imperial power, conscious of its duties, but also confident in its rights which it was our privilege to witness this morning, will be a significant and sufficient intimation that Her Majesty . . . will not relinquish under any difficulty the task in which she is engaged as regards this Empire; that she will not abandon to any enemy the great inheritance she holds in trust for her descendants."

I return to a less cheerful page in Indian politics. The question at issue in the Ilbert Bill controversy was originally raised by a note forwarded to the Bengal Provincial Government by a Bengali Hindu civilian serving in his own province. He represented the anomalous position in which the Indian members of the Civil Service were placed under the provisions of the Code of Criminal Procedure, which limited the jurisdiction to be exercised over European British subjects outside Calcutta to judicial officers who were themselves European British subjects.

The note was forwarded to the Government of India with the views of the Government of Bengal; and the Government of India published proposals the effect of which would have been "to settle the question of jurisdiction over European British subjects in such a way as to remove from the Code at once and immediately every judicial qualification which is based merely on race distinctions." The proposals met with fierce European opposition. They were considered to imperil the liberties of British non-officials. After being under consideration for over a year, they were finally largely withdrawn. "Nothing could be more lamentable," it has truly been said, "than the animosities of race that the whole controversy aroused." There can be no doubt that it was a serious catastrophe, especially in Bengal, exciting keen racial feeling on both sides, and impressing many educated Indians with the idea that in British India they must, unless a reorganisation of relations could be contrived, for ever occupy a hopelessly subject position. Lord Ripon, then Viceroy, was, they knew, on their side in these contentions, and he further gratified their aspirations by exerting himself to extend and advance local self-government through increasing the powers and functions of the municipal boards and local cess committees instituted in the sixties. His aim was by such methods to forward general political education.

He left India at the end of 1884 amid such acclamations from the educated classes as had been accorded to no preceding Governor-General, and has ever since been regarded by those classes as their great champion and patron.

And before closing this introductory chapter, I must

mention another movement, hardly noticed in those days, which was, later on, to take no small part in moulding the aspirations of the English-educated classes.

"India," it has been said, "is not only a land of romance, art, and beauty. It is, in religion, earth's central shrine." The face of the country is covered with places of worship.[1] India, as Sir Alfred Lyall has said, contains three great historic religions and has given birth to a fourth. Yet Western rationalism was turning the minds of some Indians away from religion, when a Hindu ascetic, Swami Dayanand, began to preach return from idols to the faith of the early Aryans, of a reputed golden age when the land prospered and was blessed, before the foreigner came. He founded the now large and growing sect of the *Arya Samaj*, and familiarised many Hindus with the conception of a far-away great and independent Hindu India, since degraded, by corrupt religious teaching and foreign intrusion. His efforts were assisted by the Theosophists, Colonel Olcott, an American, Madame Blavatsky, a Russian, and their followers, who, in 1878, called themselves the Theosophical Society of the *Arya Samaj*, but subsequently separated from the disciples of Dayanand as too sectarian for their taste. Nevertheless Madame Blavatsky, a lady who believed herself to have been Hindu in a previous incarnation, and those with her, continued to proclaim the greatness of the Hindu religion and the present degeneration of India from the era of ancient Aryan grandeur.

The idea of an ancient unified independent Hindu

[1] "Buildings devoted to religious worship are extremely numerous in India. There are few villages or hamlets which have not at least one. It is even a generally received opinion that no place should be inhabited where there is no temple, for otherwise the inhabitants would run grave risks of misfortune."—ABBÉ DUBOIS.

Empire owed its origin to the fact that once in the third century B.C., and again in the fourth century A.D., the greater part of India had been governed by Hindu emperors. Each period produced a great ruler; but information regarding these empires is scanty. They were strong and prosperous, but neither lasted long. They were fugitive intervals in ages of disintegration.[1]

In Europe, at this time, Professor Max Müller's edition of the *Rig Veda*, the knowledge of the law, had introduced a new period in Sanskrit scholarship, and had preached to all the beauties of Indo-Aryan literature, the flights of India's native philosophy, the devotion of its ancient faith.

And so, about the time when English-educated Hindus were impelled by particular circumstances to impatience of British domination, and Hindu youths were reading in schools and colleges of British love of Britain, of British struggles to be free, certain Hindus and Europeans were assuring all who listened that India too had a glorious past and a religion supreme and elevating. It was not surprising that in some minds the conception of an India famous and prosperous long ago, before the foreigner came, began to obliterate thoughts of the subsequent centuries of inglorious discord before the first Muhammadan invasion from Central Asia and of the India much later still, rescued, as the greatest of Hindu politicians has admitted, from chaos and oppression by British rule.[2] Later on we shall see how among certain classes of Hindus peculiar circumstances developed this concep-

[1] See Appendix I.

[2] "The blessings of peace, the establishment of law and order, the introduction of Western education, and the freedom of speech and the appreciation of liberal institutions that have followed in its wake—all these are things that stand to the credit of your rule."—*Speech by Mr. Gokhale on November 5th*, 1905.

tion into a genuine enthusiasm; but, Colonel Olcott asserts that even in the early 'eighties the new idea was able to awake no ordinary sympathy among emotional English-educated audiences. Of a lecture on the past, present, and future of India, delivered at Amritsar in October 1881, his diaries, published long afterwards, record:

"People who imagine the Hindus to be devoid of patriotic feeling should have seen the effect on my huge audience as I depicted the greatness of ancient and the fallen state of modern India. Murmurs of pleasure or sighs of pain broke from them; at one moment they would be cheering and vehemently applauding, the next keeping silent while the tears were streaming from their eyes."

Behind feelings of this kind was the racial resentment which had already manifested itself in the press, and had been intensified by the Ilbert Bill controversy. Altogether it is clear that when Lord Ripon was succeeded in the Viceroyalty by Lord Dufferin, various influences were working to produce some kind of upheaval among certain Hindus who, with English education, were learning to feel after English political ideals. They were few in number. They were coldly regarded by the aristocracy, by the territorial and martial classes, by the Muhammadans. They stood apart from the masses. They were peaceable people, and their ambitions were peaceable. In the path of these ambitions stood a social system opposed to democratic ideals, and buttressed by the influence of a powerful hierarchy on rigid caste organisations.

"We have been subject," said a learned Hindu professor,[1] in a lecture delivered before the close of the

[1] Sir R. G. Bhandarkar.

last century, "to a three-fold tyranny; political tyranny, priestly tyranny, and a social tyranny or the tyranny of caste. Crushed down by this, no man has dared to stand and assert himself. Even religious reformers have shunned the legitimate consequences of their doctrines to avoid coming into conflict with the established order of things. . . . At present, however, though we live under a foreign government, we enjoy a freedom of thought and action, such as we never enjoyed before under our own Hindu princes. But have we shown a capacity to shake ourselves free from priestly and social tyranny[1]? I am afraid, not much."

The path to wider political freedom was to prove by no means difficult to tread. The path to religious and social emancipation was far steeper and less attractive. It has not yet been trodden with determined purpose by the great majority of Hindus.

[1] The President of the 1917 Indian National Social Conference emphasised the necessity of "extending the right hand of fellowship to the backward classes," promoting the education of women, and raising the age of Hindu marriage. These he considered the main social objectives.

CHAPTER II

POLITICAL MOVEMENTS—FIRST STAGE

THE year 1885 saw the formal inauguration of modern Indian politics. Lord Dufferin had just succeeded Lord Ripon, and it will be useful to summarise general conditions.

I have already shown how the country was administered. In every district were some beginnings of popular control in the shape of Lord Ripon's municipal and district Boards, but higher up nothing of this nature existed. No Indian was member of any Imperial or Provincial Executive Council, and the few Indians who sat on Legislative Councils were nominated or selected by Government. A very few Indians, for the most part Hindus, were Judges of High Courts. The number of Indians in the Covenanted Civil Service was infinitesimal. It was open to those who could afford the effort to compete for the Service in England, but few availed themselves of this opportunity and fewer obtained admission. Indians were hardly, if at all, represented on the higher grades of the Indian Medical Service, and almost all the leaders of the Bar were Europeans. The dominant influence too in Anglo-Vernacular schools and colleges was English, although a change was impending in Bengal in consequence of the recommendations of the Education Commission of 1882–3.

British exclusiveness was far stronger than it has

since become; but the subordinate services were chiefly manned by Indians; and it must be remembered that the English-educated were far less numerous than they are now. Since the Viceroyalty of Lord Dufferin, "schools have more than doubled; higher education has increased threefold; printing presses and newspapers have multiplied; and the production of books in English has increased by 200 per cent."[1] The English-educated, too, were then, as now, mainly Hindus of the peaceful castes. Among them the fighting races—the Sikhs, the Gurkhas, the Rajputs, the Pathans—were hardly represented at all. The Brahmans indeed have contributed valuable soldiers to the Indian Army, and had, in considerable measure, availed themselves of English education; but the English-educated Brahmans did not, as a rule, belong to the martial families. Nor did advanced Indians count among their ranks many members of the territorial aristocracy. Their recruits were almost entirely drawn from castes clerical, professional, or mercantile by tradition. Thus it is easy to understand why, in spite of the liberal wording of Queen Victoria's Proclamation of 1858, the Government of a highly conservative country, inhabited by various intermingled races hitherto ruled by the strongest, hesitated to call to its highest places Indians who owed their status solely to their literary accomplishments. For centuries before British rule the history of India had been a history of conquests from Central Asia, each conquest enduring until the invaders from the hills and uplands had largely merged in the industrious and less vigorous people of the plains. From the day of Plassey, the British had been constantly opposed by armed States or levies, and within the twelve years before the Proclamation had been engaged in desperate

[1] Montagu-Chelmsford Report, paragraph 141.

wars with the Sikhs and with their own Indian Army. The strongest had always prevailed.

The English-educated section of Indians did not represent any of these late adversaries. That it would one day become a power in the land, a power of an altogether new kind, was vaguely recognised; but that day was relegated by general opinion to a far-distant future. Inadequate count was taken of the trend of politics in Great Britain herself, and of the slowly growing interest of a small section of the British democracy in Indian affairs; and no one foresaw the extraordinary progress and triumphs of Japan or the stimulus which these were to impart to Indian aspirations.

By one observer, indeed, the significance of the enthusiastic demonstrations which had accompanied Lord Ripon's departure was noted. In a leading English newspaper appeared an article "If it be real, what does it mean?" The author was the late Sir Auckland Colvin, a Civil Servant of wide practical experience. In eloquent language, he warned his countrymen to "search for the spirit of the time to which the present days are bringing us, to recognise that the rapid development of railways was facilitating the interchange of ideas among Indians, the beat of the engine was breaking down barriers which the voices of many missionaries had failed to remove; that the Indian mind was marching on, eager to do what it, for its own part, had to do." But, just as now, even the most ambitious section of Indian Progressives has been compelled to recognise the perils from Central Asia to which India, unsheltered by British protection, would certainly be exposed, so in 1885 disputes with Russia about the Afghan frontier caused all classes in India to realise their dependence on the stability of British rule. "The danger," wrote the late Sir Alfred Lyall, then Lieutenant-Governor of the North-West Provinces, "has made the Indian people very loyal; they are in great dread of some widespread political revolution if we get an upset, and they are all afraid of each other. In short, we represent peace and a firm government, whereas anything else leads to unfathomable confusion."

In March, 1885, some Indians of the new school of thought, seeking for a remedy for the then existing state of things, decided to hold a Congress of delegates of their own persuasion from all parts of British India. This resolution appears to have been largely inspired by the late Mr. Allan Octavian Hume, whom his followers have always called "the Father of the Congress." Mr. Hume was the son of Joseph Hume, a well-known Liberal. From 1849 to 1882 he had been a member of the Covenanted Civil Service. He had been decorated for good work in the Mutiny, and had retired from a Secretaryship to the Government of India. Since retirement he had lived at Simla, largely devoting his energies to propagating among educated Indians the precepts of English Radicalism. In a published correspondence of a later date, which once attracted considerable attention, but has long been generally forgotten, he justified his propaganda by alleging that the *Pax Britannica* had failed to solve the economic problem; that the peasantry were ravaged by famine and despair; that Government was out of touch with the people; that there was no safety for the masses till the administration was gradually leavened by a representative Indian element. He considered it "of paramount importance to find an overt and constitutional channel for discharge of the increasing ferment which had resulted from Western ideas and education."

The prospectus of the new movement stated that

the direct objects of the Conference would be—(*a*) to enable the most earnest labourers in the cause of national progress to become personally known to each other; (*b*) to discuss and decide upon the political operations to be undertaken during the ensuing year. The prospectus further announced: "Indirectly this Conference will form the germ of a Native Parliament, and if properly conducted will constitute in a few years an unanswerable reply to the assertion that India is still wholly unfit for any form of representative institution." In pursuance of these instructions the first Congress met in Bombay on December 28th, 29th, and 30th, 1885. It was attended by seventy-two delegates, mostly lawyers, schoolmasters, or newspaper editors, collected, sometimes after considerable effort, from various cities or large towns, and by a few Indian Government servants as friendly lookers-on. Only two of the delegates present were Muhammadans, and these were Bombay attorneys. Mr. W. Bonerjee, then Standing Counsel to Government in Calcutta, was elected president. He proclaimed that one of the objects of the Association was "the eradication, by direct friendly personal intercourse, of all possible race, creed, or provincial prejudices amongst all lovers of our country, and the fuller development and consolidation of those sentiments of national unity that had their origin in our beloved Lord Ripon's memorable reign." Britain had given them order, railways, "above all, the inestimable benefit of Western education. But the more progress a people made in education and material prosperity, the greater would be their insight into political matters and the keener their desire for political advancement." He thought that their desire to be governed according to the ideas of government prevalent in Europe was in no way incompatible with their thorough loyalty to the British Government. All that they desired was that the basis of government should be widened, and that the people should have their natural and legitimate share therein.

The first speaker to the first resolution, Mr. Subramania Aiyar,[1] of Madras, said:

"By a merciful dispensation of Providence, India, which was for centuries the victim of external aggression and plunder, of internal civil wars and general confusion, has been brought under the dominion of the great British Power. I need not tell you how that event introduced a great change in the destiny of her people, how the inestimable good that has flowed from it has been appreciated by them. The rule of Great Britain has, on the whole, been better in its results and direction than any former rule. Without descanting at length upon the benefits of that rule, I can summarise them in one remarkable fact that for the first time in the history of the Indian populations there is to be beheld the phenomenon of national unity among them, of a sense of national existence."

Various resolutions were passed, one demanding the expansion of the supreme and Provincial Legislative Councils by the admission of a considerable number of members elected by such organised bodies as municipal and district boards. Thus enlarged, these Councils were to have a voice to interpellate the Executive on all points of administration.

[1] Lately famous as the author of a letter to President Wilson, which contained the following passage:

"Permit me to add that you and the other leaders have been kept in ignorance of the full measure of misrule and oppression in India. Officials of an alien nation, speaking a foreign tongue, force their will upon us; they grant themselves exorbitant salaries and large allowances; they refuse us education; they sap us of our wealth; they impose crushing taxes without our consent; they cast thousands of our people into prisons for uttering patriotic sentiments—prisons so filthy that often the inmates die from loathsome diseases."

It was also recommended that a Standing Committee of the House of Commons should be constituted to receive and consider any formal protests that might be recorded by majorities of the new Legislative Councils against the exercise by the Executive Government of the power, which would be vested in it, of overruling the decisions of any such majorities.

Another resolution recommended simultaneous examinations in India and England for admission into the Indian Civil Service. There had been some idea of discussing social reform, but only two addresses were delivered on the subject, the main objective being political.

The next Congress met at Calcutta on December 27th, 28th, 29th, and 30th, 1886. It was claimed for this Congress that it marked " a total change of character. Everybody wanted to come of his own accord." It was admitted that in 1885 " people had to be pressed and entreated to come."

The Conference was attended by 440 delegates, elected either at public meetings or by societies and associations. Two hundred and thirty of these came from Bengal. The old aristocracy were entirely absent. The shopkeeping classes were represented by one member. This deficiency was ascribed by the author of the introductory article to the record of proceedings, to the fact that these classes, ignorant and immersed in their own concerns, cared for no change in a form of government which both prevented others from robbing them and " by its system of civil jurisprudence " afforded them ample opportunities for enriching themselves. The cultivating classes were " inadequately represented." This was because " though a great number realise that the times are out of joint, they have not learnt to rise from particular instances to generalisations, and they neither understand clearly what is wrong, nor have they as a class any clear or definite ideas as to what could or ought to be done to lighten somewhat their lot in life." There were thirty-three Muhammadan delegates. This was ascribed partly to the "present lack of higher education among our Muhammadan brethren," and partly to the fact that three prominent Calcutta Muhammadans had publicly declared against the Congress, preferring "a policy of confidence in the Government." By far the greater majority of the delegates came from Bengal. The Punjab sent only seventeen and the Central Provinces eight. Mr. Dadabhai Naoroji, a Parsi, and well known as the first Indian who has sat in the British Parliament, was elected President. The resolutions closely resembled those of the previous year. One asked for the authorisation of a system of volunteering for Indians which would enable them to support Government in any crisis. Another related to "the increasing poverty of vast numbers of the population of India."

The president remarked on the blessings of British rule, in the stable foundation of which the Congress was another stone.

"Let us speak out," he said, "like men, and proclaim that we are loyal to the backbone; that we understand the benefits English rule has conferred on us; the education that has been given to us; the new light which has been poured on us, turning us from darkness into light, and teaching us the new lesson that kings are made for the people, not peoples for their kings; and this lesson we have learned amid the darkness of Asiatic despotism only by the light of free English civilisation."[1]

[1] These words may be compared with some sentences from a recent speech by Mr. B. G. Tilak, reported in the *Leader* issue of October 10th, 1917.

"They knew on what principle the bureaucracy governed India for

The virtual abstention of Muhammadans from the Congress movement was largely due to the influence of Sir Saiyid Ahmad, and it is worth while to turn aside from the main course of my narrative in order to give some account of this great man.

Sir Saiyid Ahmad was born at Delhi in the year 1817, and belonged to a family of considerable note at the court of the Moghal Emperors. In the year 1837 he obtained a clerical post in the British service. Twenty years later he had risen to the position of a Subordinate Judge, and when the Mutiny broke out at Bijnor in these provinces, he gave noble proofs of loyalty. "No language that I could use," said a Lieutenant-Governor in subsequently referring to Saiyid Ahmad's Mutiny services, "would be worthy of the devotion which he showed."

In 1858 Saiyid Ahmad wrote in his own vernacular an account of the causes of the revolt which was long afterwards translated and published in English. His appreciation of British rule in India was by no means wholesale, and his criticisms deserve our careful consideration even now. It is remarkable that he attributed the outbreak largely to the absence of all Indians from the Supreme Legislative Council.

"The evils," he wrote, "which resulted from the non-admission of natives into the Legislative Council were various. Government could never know the inadvisability of the laws and regulations which it passed. It could never hear the voice of the people on such a subject. The people had no means of protesting against what they might feel to be a foolish measure, or of

the last 100 years. They were a self-governing nation before. They knew how to organise an army, they knew how to dispense justice, they had laws, regulations, etc. All those had been swept away, and now the bureaucracy said that they knew nothing about them. Who was responsible for that? Not the Indians."

giving public expression to their wishes. But the greatest mischief lay in this, that the people misunderstood the views and intentions of Government. They misapprehended every act, and whatever law was passed was misconstrued by men who had no share in the framing of it and hence no means of judging of its spirit. . . . I wish to say that the views of Government were misconstrued by the people, and that this misconstruction hurried on the rebellion. Had there been a native of Hindustan in the Legislative Council, the people would never have fallen into such errors. . . . There was no real communication between the governors and the governed, no living together or near one another as has always been the custom of the Muhammadans in countries which they subjected to their rule. Government and its officials have never adopted this course, without which no real knowledge of the people can be gained." Further on he asserted: "Now, in the first years of the British rule in India, the people were heartily in favour of it. This good feeling the Government has now forfeited, and the natives very generally say that they are treated with contempt. A native gentleman is, in the eyes of any petty official, as much lower than that official as that same official esteems himself lower than a duke. The opinion of many of these officials is that no native can be a gentleman. . . . There are many English officials who are well-known for their kindness and friendly feeling toward the natives, and these are in consequence much beloved by them, are, to use a native expression, as the sun and moon to them, and are pointed out as types of the old race of officials."

After the Mutiny Saiyid Ahmad exerted himself strenuously to make peace between the Government and his co-religionists and to reform the Muhammadan educational system. Although his boyhood had known no other, he was convinced that the ordinary Muhammadan education was inadequate and out of date.

"Cure the root," he said, "and the tree will flourish." He did all he could to "cure the root," and, at the age of fifty-two, travelled to England to enter his son at Cambridge University, and to see what measures were desirable for the establishment of a Muhammadan Anglo-Oriental College in Upper India. This he finally accomplished, and the famous College at Aligarh is his abiding monument. While affording religious instruction to Muhammadans alone, it admits scholars of all faiths; and the whole attitude of its great founder, who frequently and strongly championed the tenets of Islam, was invariably tolerant and liberal. He rejoiced in the spread and growth of English education in India, believing that enlightenment meant loyalty to Britain. His spirit is reflected in the address presented to Lord Ripon in 1884 by the Aligarh College Committee, which contains the following passage:

"The time has happily passed when the Muhammadans of India looked upon their condition as hopeless, when they regarded the past with feelings of mournful sorrow. Their hopes are now inclined to the promise of the future; their hearts, full of loyalty to the rule of the Queen-Empress, aspire to finding distinction and prominence among the various races of the vast Empire over which Her Majesty holds sway. It is to help the realisation of these aspirations that this College has been founded; and we fervently hope that among the results which may flow from our system of education, not the least important will be the promotion of friendly feelings of social intercourse and interchange of amenities of life between the English community in India and the Muhammadan population."

In spite of his strong liberal sympathies, Sir Saiyid Ahmad would have nothing to do with the Congress, and advised his co-religionists to follow his example.

Although he had his enemies and detractors, his influence was enormous, and it determined the attitude of the great majority of his people. Some years ago one of his co-religionists attributed this attitude to three causes:

(*a*) the violence of many publications distributed broadcast before the launching of the Congress;

(*b*) the excessive blandishments of the Congress leaders;

(*c*) the advocacy by the Congress of elective principles, and open competition, with no regard for minorities.

I now return to the Congress movement. In December 1888, Lord Dufferin was succeeded in the Viceroyalty by Lord Lansdowne. At a farewell dinner in Calcutta he had referred to the Congress party as a "microscopic minority," but he was far too astute a statesman not to be impressed by the movement, and confidentially sent home proposals for liberalising the Legislative Councils, "which," he wrote to the Secretary of State, "is all that the reasonable leaders even of the most advanced section of Young India dream of."

He was, however, dealing with wider ambitions. There was a strong demand for more general and higher employment in the Public Services, a belief that in this respect the educated classes were dwarfed and stunted. He had indeed appointed a Commission of inquiry into this matter, but its recommendations were received some time after his departure, and by no means pleased the advanced party.

The Congress of 1888 was attended by 1,248 delegates. Great efforts had been made by the leaders to stultify Lord Dufferin's estimate of their importance. Six Europeans attended, and the president was Mr. George Yule, a prominent Calcutta merchant, who complained that the British non-official class was disfranchised in India, and had no more voice than Indians in the government of the country. Complaint was made by various speakers of the official attitude as needlessly unfriendly. The resolutions passed were on lines already described. Among other things, they recommended abolition of the distinctions created by the Arms Act, military colleges for natives of India, and an inquiry into the industrial condition of the country.

At the sixth Congress, held at Calcutta in 1890, and attended by 702 delegates, including 156 Muhammadans, the Chairman of the Reception Committee welcomed the delegates in the following words:

"It is perfectly correct that the ignorant classes whom we seek to represent are still unable in many provinces to take an active interest in the many social and administrative problems which are now engaging the attention of the educated classes; but history teaches us that in all countries and in all ages it is the thinking who lead the unthinking, and we are bound to think for ourselves and others who are still too ignorant to exercise that important function."

A speaker relied on some words of Mr. Gladstone to the effect that a man would be deemed mad who denounced the system of popular representation. Two other speakers alleged the existence of a political faith common to Hindus and Muhammadans. A note in the introduction to the printed account of the Congress proceedings observed, in regard to the alleged antagonism between the two communities: "We would like very much to know whether Great Britain herself is not divided into two sections, one of which is bitterly hostile to the other and desirous of opposing it on all occasions." The tone of the concluding passages of the same introduction was more antagonistic to British rule than any previous official Congress utterance. Acknowledgment was made during the meetings of the kind reception in England of certain delegates. The Congress was supplemented by a Social Conference.

National Social Conferences had begun in 1887, but languished later. At the social conference of 1895 the following message from the Congress President-elect was read to the meeting. "The *raison d'être* for excluding social questions from our deliberations is that if we were to take up such questions, it might lead to serious differences, ultimately culminating in a schism, and it is a matter of the first importance to prevent a split." Mr. Justice Ranade, an ardent social reformer, held different views. At the Bombay social conference held at Satara in 1900, he said, in his inaugural address:

"I know that there are those among us who see no advantage in holding local or national gatherings of this sort for the consideration of social topics. There are others who think that though such gatherings have their uses, they should not be joined together in place and time with the political meeting, as they only serve to detract the attention of the workers and lead to no practical results. It may be of use to attempt a brief reply to both objections. As regards the first difficulty, it seems to me to arise from a confusion of ideas which is prejudicial to the right appreciation of our duties, both in the political and in the social sphere. . . . As I understand it, this distinction between the two spheres of our activities is based on a radical mistake. . . . Politics are not merely petitioning and memorialising for gifts and favours. Gifts and favours are of no value unless we have deserved the concessions by our own elevation and our own struggles. "You shall live by the sweat of your brow" is not the curse pronounced on man, but the very conditions of his existence and growth. Whether in the political, or social or religious or commercial, or manufacturing or æsthetical spheres, in literature, in science, in art, in war, in peace, it is the individual and collective man who has to develop his powers by his own exertions in conquering the difficulties in his way. If he is down for the time, he has to get up with the whole of his strength, physical, moral, and intellectual; and you may as well suppose that he can develop one of those elements of strength and neglect the others, as try to separate the light from the heat of the sun or the beauty and fragrance from the rose. You cannot have a good social system when you find yourself low in the scale of political rights, nor can you be fit to exercise political rights and privileges unless your social system is based on reason and justice."

These were wise words; but the obstacles to social reform were partly religious, and Indian social reformers have seldom been able to carry their cause far beyond conferences and resolutions. It suffered severely from the death of Ranade, who was a man of genuine courage and character.

A question which arose in connection with the 1890 Congress elicited the following reply from the Viceroy's Private Secretary:

"The Government of India recognise that the Congress movement is regarded as representing what would in Europe be called the advanced Liberal party, as distinguished from the great body of Conservative opinion which exists side by side with it. They desire themselves to maintain an attitude of neutrality in their relations with both parties, so long as these act strictly within their constitutional functions."

In 1892 a new Councils Act was passed. Its provisions had been outlined by Lord Dufferin before his departure.[1] It enlarged the Legislative Councils,

[1] See paragraphs 60–69 of the Montagu-Chelmsford Report.

conferring on local boards and corporations the right of recommending persons for appointment thereto, subject to the approval of the recommendations by Government. It safeguarded the authority of Government by leaving it a majority on each Council and by restricting the right of debate and of asking questions; but it decidedly extended the application of the principle, first admitted in 1858, of associating prominent non-officials in legislation. The Congress of 1892 was dissatisfied, and further expressed disappointment with the orders passed on the report of the Public Services Commission appointed by Lord Dufferin. About this time, the Congress Committee, which had been established in London, and consisted mainly of English Radicals, started the periodical *India* for the promotion of Congress propaganda.

I have now traced in some detail the early history of the Congress movement, allowing its leaders to speak for themselves. I now propose to review briefly the period from 1892 to 1897.

The proceedings of the annual meetings during this period were similar in character to those which I have already described. As English-educated Indians multiplied, adherents of the Congress increased not only in the big cities, but also in the smaller centres, the great majority coming from the classes which had initiated the movement. The tone of the Indian press toward the British Government and British officials did not improve; and although the politicians did not seriously attempt to advance their main position, largely, no doubt, because the period in Britain was one of decided conservative ascendency, they developed a practice of sending delegates to allege before British audiences the poverty of India, the exclusive and selfish character of the Administraton, the need of popular government.

It would, however, be a mistake to suppose that all the party really meant as much as this. Many were prosperous under the existing order of things, were on friendly terms with European officials, and were perfectly well aware that strong and effective British control was essential for the welfare of the country. And many were capable of bringing Western political ideas into practical relation with the peculiar conditions of India, but were perhaps inclined to keep their least popular opinions to themselves.

Muhammadans continued to hold aloof from the movement; but in 1894 appeared more vigorous manifestations of Hindu impatience with existing conditions.

In 1893, riots had occurred in the city of Bombay, between Hindus and Muhammadans; and, subsequently, in order to stimulate Hindu enthusiasm, persons who wished to widen the breach between the two communities started public festivals in honour of Ganpati, the elephant-headed god of wisdom and success. It was arranged that images of Ganpati should be attended by melas, or groups of young men trained in fencing with sticks and physical exercises, that verses should be sung and leaflets distributed in the streets of Poona, the capital of the Deccan and the second city in the Bombay Presidency. These were to stimulate hatred of Muhammadans and of the British Government, of foreigners generally.

A movement, too, was inaugurated for the repair of the tomb of the famous Maratha Hindu hero, Sivaji, who, more than two centuries before, had successfully revolted against Muhammadan domination. Sivaji had killed Afzal Khan, a Muslim general, at a conference between two armies. Festivals were held in his honour, and the memory of his exploits was revived by enthusiasts in such verses as these:

"Merely reciting Sivaji's story like a lord does not secure independence; it is necessary to be prompt in engaging in desperate enterprises like Sivaji and Baji; knowing, you good people should take up swords and shields at all events now; we shall cut off countless heads of enemies. Listen! We shall risk our lives on the battle-field in a national war; we shall shed upon the earth the life-blood of the enemies who destroy our religion; we shall die only, while you will hear the story like women."

Sivaji had established a Maratha kingdom, but his dynasty had been supplanted by a dynasty of Chitpavan Brahmans (Brahmans purified by the funeral pyre) who had reigned at Poona with the title of Peishwa. The last Peishwa had quarrelled with and had been overthrown by the British. Chitpavans had prospered under British rule. They had shown remarkable ability, and were prominent at the Bar, in education, and in the public services; but some had never ceased to regret the fallen glories of the Peishwas. Ranade's *Rise of the Maratha Empire* recalled the history of the Maratha country in which their ancestors had played a prominent part. In a book entitled *Sources of Marathi History*, it was confidently alleged that the state of the Deccan under the Chitpavan Peishwas was far superior to its condition under British rule.

In the year 1880, a Chitpavan Brahman named Bal Gangadhar Tilak, who had, a few years before, graduated with honours in the Bombay University, started two papers, one of which was destined to attain a very wide circulation. This was the *Kesari* (the "Lion"). It was in Marathi, and was supplemented by an English weekly *The Maratha*. Later, Mr. Tilak distinguished himself in educational work, joined the Congress, and became secretary of the Standing Committee for the

Deccan. He was a vigorous critic of government measures, and strongly opposed the Age of Consent Bill, which had been devised in order to mitigate the crying evils of Hindu child-marriage. His political attitude, his learning in the Hindu scriptures, his ability as a journalist, his readiness to assist his poorer countrymen in trouble, all contributed to win for him remarkable influence.

Famine had resulted from shortage of rain in 1896, and the plague had arrived at Bombay and spread to Poona. Famine and plague caused widespread distress; and, according to invariable custom in times of calamity, the masses were inclined to blame their rulers. In order to arrest the spread of plague, the Bombay Government adopted measures which seemed to promise success, but were repugnant to the customs of the people and interfered with their home-life. Persons suffering from the disease were separated from persons not attacked; house-to-house visitations were resorted to; and in Poona it was for some time considered necessary to employ British soldiers on search parties. Popular feeling was keenly stirred, and on [1] May 4th, 1897, Mr. Tilak, who had at first to some extent co-operated with Mr. Rand, the Plague Commissioner, published an article charging the British soldiers employed on plague duty with every sort of excess, and imputing not merely to subordinate officials, but to the whole Government itself deliberate direction to oppress the people. He described Mr. Rand as tyrannical, and stated that the Government was practising oppression. It was useless to petition the Supreme Government, as from it the orders for oppression had emanated. On the 15th of

[1] The statements in this and the following pages are founded on the judge's charge to the jury in the case Queen-Empress *versus* B. G. Tilak, 1897.

the following month he published two further articles in his paper. The first was a poem—"Sivaji's Utterances"—and represented Sivaji waking from a long dream and deploring the present-day state of affairs in what had once been his kingdom. By annihilating the wicked he had lightened the great weight of the globe. He had delivered the country by establishing *Swarajya* (one's own kingdom). Now foreigners were taking away the wealth of the country; plenty and health had fled; famine and epidemic disease stalked through the land. Brahmans were imprisoned. The cow was daily slaughtered. White men escaped justice by urging meaningless pleas. Women were dragged out of railway carriages. Sivaji had protected the English when they were traders, and it was for them to show their gratitude by making his subjects happy.

The second article gave an account of lectures delivered by two professors on the murder of Afzal Khan by Sivaji. They argued that Sivaji was above the moral code. "Every Hindu, every Maratha," said one of the lecturers, "must rejoice at this Sivaji celebration. We are all striving to regain our lost independence." The other professor observed: "The people who took part in the French Revolution denied that they had committed murders, and maintained that they were only removing thorns from their path. Why should not the same principle (argument) be applied to Maharashtra?" Finally came a discourse from Mr. Tilak, who said, after remarking that great men are above the common principles of morality, "Did Sivaji commit a sin in killing Afzal Khan or not?" The answer to this question can be found in the *Mahabharat*[1]

[1] The *Mahabharat* is the famous Hindu epic. It contains the *Bhagwat-Gita*, or Lord's Song, recited by Krishna, an incarnation of the Preserver of the world, before the great battle of Kurukshetra.

itself. Shrimat Krishna's advice in the *gita* is to kill even our own teachers and our kinsmen. No blame attaches to any person if he is doing deeds without being actuated by a desire to reap the fruits of his deeds. Shri Sivaji did nothing with a view to fill the small void of his own stomach. With benevolent intentions he murdered Afzal Khan for the good of others. If thieves enter our house and we have not sufficient strength to drive them out, we should, without hesitation, shut them up and burn them alive. God has not conferred on *Mlenchas* (foreigners or barbarians) the grant inscribed on copper-plate of the kingdom of Hindustan.

. . . . . .

"Do not circumscribe your vision like a frog in a well. Get out of the Penal Code, enter into the extremely high atmosphere of the *Bhagwat-Gita*, and then consider the actions of great men."

A week after these articles appeared, and on the day of the celebration of the Diamond Jubilee of Queen Victoria, Mr. Rand and another British officer were assassinated at Poona by two Chitpavan Brahman brothers, Damodar and Balkrishna Chapekar, who were subsequently tried and executed. The former said in a confession, subsequently retracted, but believed by the court that tried him to be genuine, that "as the operations for the suppression of the plague were beginning to cause annoyance to the people and great oppression was caused by the soldiers, they had determined to avenge these acts and to kill the chief man in charge of the plague operations." The Chapekars had founded an association for physical and military training which they called the "Society for the removal of obstacles to the Hindu religion." Two of the associates murdered two brothers who had been rewarded by Govern-

5

ment for information which led to the arrest and conviction of Damodar Chapekar. They were themselves arrested, convicted, and executed.

Mr. Tilak was prosecuted for exciting disaffection to Government by means of the *Kesari* articles of June 15th, was convicted, and was sentenced to eighteen months' rigorous imprisonment, but six months of his sentence were subsequently remitted. For a space he disappeared from the ranks of the Congress politicians; but the *Kesari* continued to issue during his imprisonment, and on his release attained a very wide circulation. Its financial success attracted keen emulation. Its tone was caught by journalists in other provinces.

The criticisms of the Congress probably counted both in the appointment of a Commission which was to advise police reforms, and in the improvements in the revenue system initiated and carried through by Lord Curzon. On the other hand, although the Plague afforded the leaders of the movement an unique opportunity of standing forward and assisting Government to counteract the prejudiced hostility of their more ignorant countrymen to remediary measures, they took small advantage of this opportunity. And throughout the whole of this period the tone of the majority of Indian-owned newspapers became more and more hostile to the form of British rule established by law. With monotonous regularity their readers were regaled with diatribes against the constitution and policy of the British Government. India was being drained of her resources; India was being plundered and oppressed by aliens. This was the constant burden of a constantly repeated song, varied now and then, when the occasion demanded caution, by conventional phrases about the blessings of British rule. Grave stress was laid on the unfortunate fact that in 1894 the Government of India had been compelled by the Secretary of State to reduce the duty on Lancashire woven cotton goods from 5 to 3½ per cent., and to impose a countervailing excise duty of 3½ per cent. on woven cotton fabrics manufactured in Indian mills. And over and over again were the doctrines preached that the peasantry[1] were crushed by the land revenue demand, and that the country was exploited by foreign capital. ~~I shall refer more fully to the latter accusation later on.~~

The death of Queen Victoria profoundly affected public sentiment, for her messages to India on great occasions had taught Indians to regard her as their own Sovereign. At the time of the 1903 Durbar, which celebrated the accession of King Edward, the political barometer seemed steady

The ceremonies were splendid; the speech of the Viceroy, Lord Curzon, disclosed no presentiment of the difficulties and trials which were to come with an early morrow.

"Princes and people," he said, "if we turn our eyes for a moment to the future, a great development appears with little doubt to lie before this country. There is no Indian problem, be it of population, or education, or labour, or subsistence, which it is not within the power of statesmanship to solve. The solution of many is even now proceeding before our eyes. If the combined Armies of Great Britain and India can secure combined peace upon our borders; if unity prevails within them, between princes and people, between European and Indian, and between rulers and ruled, and if the seasons fail not in their bounty, then nothing can arrest the march of progress, the India of the future will, under Providence, not be an India of diminishing plenty, of empty prospect, or of justifiable discontent; but one of expanding industry, of

[1] The end of the last century was marked by bad agricultural seasons and the rapid spread of plague with disastrous economic consequences.

awakened faculties, of increasing prosperity, and of more widely distributed comfort and wealth. I have faith in the conscience and the purpose of my own country, and I believe in the almost illimitable capacities of this. But under no conditions can this future be realised than the unchallenged supremacy of the paramount power, and under no controlling authority is this capable of being maintained than that of the British Crown."

Yet, in fact, this Durbar marked the end of the comparatively restful and untroubled era which had lasted for forty years. It was an era of successful and unchallenged government, of increasing and widening education, of growing commerce, of an improving land revenue system, of all-round progress. Yet, among the still scanty Western educated classes, discontent slumbered lightly under a surface that was usually smooth. Peculiar economic conditions were producing an increasing number of youths for whom life seemed hard and difficult, in spite of English education; the ideas and customs of ages had been shaken; political gatherings were beginning to surpass fairs and caste-meetings in social interest. There was a desire for change, an impatience of the present, a growing doctrine that the old times were better than the new. In one part of India this doctrine had been openly preached; and there and elsewhere advantage was taken of famines, of plague, of poverty, of lack of occupation, of the chequered incidents of the Boer War, to depreciate British efficiency and British rule. Already, in Bombay, the circulation of such ideas had received a special stimulus from peculiar circumstances, and murder had resulted. Coming years were to prove that if an edge could be given to such latent discontent, the Poona incidents would not stand alone. But the ruling princes, the territorial and rural classes, the military castes, the masses, were tranquil and unchanged; the outside of affairs was calm; and Lord Curzon proceeded with characteristic determination and enthusiasm to grapple with the great problem of Indian education.

The results of the orders passed on the reports of the Indian Education and Public Services Commissions appointed by Lords Ripon and Dufferin had been in some measure disastrous to secondary education, especially in Bengal, where an excessive devolution of control to non-official agency had resulted in a serious lowering of standards. The Calcutta University Syndicate, which presided over English education in that province, and regulated the standards of the examinations which lay before the thronging candidates for Government service, had exercised little control over secondary schools, leaving them largely to local committees. These committees consisted mainly of men of small ideas, who thought only of providing sufficient teaching to meet examination requirements. Moral influences and training of character they comparatively disregarded; and, cutting down the cost of buildings, and salaries of schoolmasters, to the lowest possible levels, they provided the cheapest instruction that they could contrive.[1] Vainly did the Government empha-

[1] The following passages from a speech by the Hindu head master of a high school in a prominent city of the United Provinces show clearly the pitfalls which beset popular education in India:

"This school owes its expansion more to the Government and the Government officials than to the general public, unless fees are regarded as a public contribution.

"I make these remarks not because we fail to acknowledge the help received from the public, but to emphasise the fact that the cause of the education of our nation's children occupies only a secondary place in the minds of the rich men and other people. We have yet to realise the full responsibility of educating our children. Many parents seem to feel absolved from all responsibility after sending their children to school,

sise its view that it was "of little use to spend money on schools where the teachers were either inefficient or unable to maintain discipline or a healthy moral tone." No serious attempt was made to alter things, and grave abuses became increasingly apparent throughout the whole Indian school and university system. Lord Curzon determined to insist on thorough reforms. He threw all his energies into the task, appealing earnestly for non-official co-operation, and emphasising the importance of the interests at stake. The education which is the necessary preliminary to all professional and industrial work was obviously a great national

without inquiring whether the school concerned is a recognised institution or not. In this place there have sprung up a number of schools from which the sanctity that should be attached to an educational institution is entirely absent, and of which money-making seems to be the primary aim. The gullible parents are ready to pay exorbitant fees, and those also in advance for many months, when they are promised that their boys would be put up three or four classes above the one for which they were really fit. It must be acknowledged that this state of affairs calls for the necessity of opening more schools of an approved type. But I have to complain even against the parent whose sons read in a recognised school, for he, too, is alive to his responsibility only when a seat has to be secured for them—not an easy endeavour in these days—or perhaps when they fail to obtain promotion. Only lately I had an occasion to address a circular letter to the guardians of such students as failed in two subjects at the first periodical examination, with a view to conferring with them regarding the progress of their wards, but not more than two per cent. cared to respond.

"When such is the apathy of the parents, the indifference at home must be great indeed. Far be it from me to attribute want of affection to the parents for their children, but this affection is more in evidence when you see the little one at school patronising the sweetmeat vendor than in properly regulating their life at home. The teacher hopes that his work would be supplemented with adequate supervision at home, but the parents expect that a few hours at school should make their sons paragons of all virtues. To my mind one of the problems of education in India is to make the home of the child in proper unison with his school. If this were done, many social, educational, and, I dare say, even political difficulties could be solved, and our boys would not be exposed to dangers, as unfortunately they are now."

concern; it was "the key to employment, the condition of all national advance and prosperity, and the sole stepping-stone for every class of the community to higher things." It was a social and political, even more than an intellectual demand.

The Congress leaders, however, mainly because they suspected that Lord Curzon's secret intention was to check the growing numbers of the restless English-educated classes, strenuously opposed the Viceroy, and succeeded in impressing their ideas on the minds of many persons incapable of appreciating the realities of the situation. In spite of their opposition, Lord Curzon passed a Universities Act of considerable importance; but he left India suddenly, his work came to an abrupt termination, and drastic improvement in secondary education has hung fire in Bengal from that day to this. The Viceroy's efforts had, however, produced restlessness and resentment among the literate classes, and these feelings were widened and deepened by the Partition agitation.

No one has ever seriously denied that the old province of Bengal, Bihar and Orissa was, by reason of its magnitude, an impossible and, because impossible, a sadly neglected charge.

The Supreme Government had been slow to realise that times had altered since 1785, when Warren Hastings, reviewing his eventful administration, wrote that the submissive character of the people of this province, the fewness of their wants, "the abundant sources of subsistence and of trafficable wealth which may be drawn from the natural productions, and from the manufactures, both of established usage and of new institutions, left little to the duty of the magistrate; in effect nothing but attention, protection, and forbearance." No soldiers of the Indian Army had been drawn from Bengal, and Bengalis had taken no share in the rebellion of 1857. But as prosperity and population increased, as English education spread, administration became more complex, and the character of the educated classes stiffened and altered. The charge of 78,000,000 of people, including the inhabitants of the largest and most Europeanised city in the East, was far too onerous for one provincial administration; and, after considerable deliberation and consultation, Lord Curzon decided to divide the old province and Assam into the new provinces of Western Bengal, Bihar and Orissa, and Eastern Bengal and Assam.

Administratively, this was the best arrangement. It afforded most promise of opening up and developing the rich, difficult, and populous water districts of Eastern Bengal. But it split Bengal proper into two, and gave Muhammadans a decided majority in the Eastern Province. It was, therefore, strongly opposed by the Congress leaders at Calcutta, the centre of Hindu legal, educational, and political activities. They proclaimed that a foreign government wished to insult and efface Bengali nationality. When the partition was carried out, they enlisted ardent support from sympathisers all over India, proclaimed a boycott of European goods, to be effected by the aid of students and schoolboys, and organised a violent agitation on a widespread and elaborate scale. Many of them were moved by a new kind of sentiment. The achievements of Japan had profoundly affected Indian political thought. Their plans took time to develop, and were largely suspended during the visit of the Prince and Princess of Wales, which passed off successfully in the cold season of 1905–6. Before the Congress of 1905 met at Benares, Lord Curzon had left India, and the Unionist Ministry in England had been followed by the representatives of a mammoth Liberal majority. Lord Minto had succeeded to the Viceroyalty, and Mr. John Morley had been appointed Secretary of State for India.

The events which closed the administration of the departing Viceroy were destined to influence profoundly the subsequent course of affairs. No viceroy has ever played a part larger than the part played by Lord Curzon. His influence on all branches of administration was vigorous and beneficial; he placed the arrangements for the security of the North-West frontier on a stable footing; he set an example of industry and devotion which was finely expressed in his memorable parting words.[1]

But we can see now that his bold and confident nature led him to underrate the combination between the opposition to the Partition of Bengal and the new spirit which had arisen in India. The loosening of control which was certain to follow on his departure; the number and bitterness of his enemies; their eagerness and the anxiety of those who resented British rule to seize any opportunity of misinterpreting all government measures; the plastic material which lay ready

[1] "Oh that to every Englishman in this country, as he ends his work, might truthfully be applied the phrase: 'Thou hast loved righteousness and hated iniquity.' No man has, I believe, ever served India faithfully of whom that could not be said. Perhaps there are few of us who make anything but a poor approximation to that ideal; but let it be our ideal all the same. To fight for the right, to abhor the imperfect, the unjust, to swerve neither to the right hand nor to the left. . . . Never to let your enthusiasm be soured, or your courage grow dim, but to remember that the Almighty has placed His hand on the greatest of His ploughs in whose furrow the nations of the future are germinating and taking shape, to drive the blade a little forward in your time—that is enough, that is the Englishman's justification in India. It is good enough for his justification while he is here, for his epitaph when he is gone."

to their hands; all these were factors of so far undiscovered potency. But, when accounts are balanced, posterity will say, with Lord Morley:

> "You never will send to India a Viceroy his superior, if, indeed, his equal, in force of mind, in passionate and devoted interest in all that concerns the well-being of India, with an imagination fired by the grandeur of the political problem that India presents. You never sent a man with more of all these attributes than when you sent Lord Curzon."

CHAPTER III

POLITICAL MOVEMENTS—SECOND STAGE

THE Twenty-first Congress, held at Benares in December 1905, was attended by 756 delegates, of whom 718 were Hindus, 17 were Muhammadans, and 14 were Sikhs. The tone of the introductory note to the printed record of proceedings is notably aggressive. India was declared to be "distracted, discontented, despondent, the victim of many misfortunes, political and others"; the "cup of national indignation had been filled to overflowing by the Partition designed to break down the political power and influence of the educated opinion of Bengal." The rise of Japan had, however, it was said, produced a great moral impression, and a new epoch had begun in the work of political regeneration and emancipation not only for Bengal, but for all India. The service of the motherland would become "as great and overmastering a passion as in Japan."

The late Mr. Gokhale, a Chitpavan[1] Brahman of great intellectual power, was elected President. He justified the boycott of European goods which had been proclaimed by the leaders of the anti-Partition agitation in Bengal, and declared that the time was sensibly nearer when the bureaucratic monopoly of power could be successfully assailed. He asked for a proportion of one-half elected members in all the Councils, for an extension of Council privileges, and for the

[1] Chitpavan Brahmans. (See page 48.)

appointment of three Indians to the Council of the Secretary of State. He considered that the time was auspicious for these demands. Mr. John Morley was at the India Office, and "our heart hopes and yet tremble as it has never yet hoped and trembled before."

Bitter complaint was made of the treatment of Indians in the British colonies—a grievance of some standing even then—and of the recent educational policy of Lord Curzon's Government. The "pluck and heroism" of the young Bengali anti-Partitionists were commended. They were termed "pillars of the popular movement." Reference was made to the rising sun of Japan.

In the new province of Eastern Bengal things grew worse during 1906. As purely sentimental appeals were ineffectual to excite sufficient popular sympathy, the leaders of the anti-Partition movement, searching for a national hero, endeavoured to import from Bombay the cult of Sivaji, and appealed to the religion of the multitude by placing their efforts under the patronage of Kali, the goddess of strength and destruction. Another device to which they resorted was borrowed from Europe. Years before a Bengali named Bankim Chandra had written a novel [1] based on incursions by some bands of *Sanyasis*,[2] fanatical Hindu banditti, who in the year 1772, after a severe famine, had descended on Bengal, their ranks swollen by a crowd of starving peasants, and had obtained temporary successes against some Government levies under British officers. The novel contained a song which was adopted as a Marseillaise by the anti-Partitionists, and has since become famous as "Bande Mataram"—Hail, Motherland! Its sentiment is expressed in the following lines:

[1] *The Ananda Math.* See Appendix II.

[2] Sanyasi means renouncer, i.e. renouncer of the world and even of caste. The ordinary Sanyasi is simply an ascetic.

"We have no mother," sings the leader of the Sanyasis.
"We have no father, no brother, no wife, no child, no hearth, no home. We acknowledge nothing save the motherland.
My Motherland I sing; Thou art my head,
Thou art my heart.
My life and soul art Thou, my soul, my worship, and my art.
Before Thy feet I bow."

From the context in the novel it seems that the Sanyasi's appeal was rather to his mother's land, the land of Mother Kali, than to his motherland.

"Bande Mataram" and other effusions of a more militant character were eagerly taken up by the masses of Hindu youths who thronged the numerous schools and colleges in Bengal under needy discontented teachers. Indeed it was to enlist these facile recruits that the Calcutta leaders addressed their main efforts. "Swadeshi," or indigenous, industrial enterprises were hastily started; a boycott of foreign goods was proclaimed as the best and most effective weapon of retaliation for the Partition, and arrangements were made to carry out this boycott by persuasion, forcible if necessary, through the agency of schoolboys and students. The whole agitation was Hindu, and was strongly resented by the Muhammadans, who form the majority in Eastern Bengal, and had derived substantial and obvious advantages from the new arrangements. But the latter controlled no newspapers of importance, and had few orators to voice their wishes. Their leaders were few, their press was insignificant, and they lacked the previous stimulus which had prepared the Hindu youth of educated Bengal for a passionate agitation.

In 1902 had died the Bengali enthusiast, Swami

Vivekananda, whose words inculcating nationalism and religion had sunk deep into the minds of many of the educated classes, and not long ago might be seen printed as texts on the walls of the rooms of students in Bengal. His real name was Norendro Nath Datta, and he had graduated in the Calcutta University, but, subsequently, became an ascetic. He had visited the Chicago Congress of religions as a missionary of Hinduism. Returning, he preached and lectured in various parts of India, acquiring a number of eager followers. The nature of his teaching may best be illustrated by quotations from a lecture on "The Work before us," delivered in Madras:

"With all my love for India, and with all my patriotism and veneration for the ancients, I cannot but think that we have to learn many things from the world. We must be always ready to sit at the feet of all to learn great lessons; for, mark you, every one can teach us great lessons. . . . At the same time we must not forget that we have also to teach a great lesson to the world. We cannot do without the world outside India; it was our foolishness that we thought we could, and we have paid the penalty by about a thousand years of slavery. That we did not go out to compare things with other nations, did not mark the workings that have been all around us, has been the one great cause of this degradation of the Indian mind. All such foolish ideas that Indians must not go out of India are childish; they must be knocked on the head; the more you go out and travel among the nations of the world, the better for you and for your country. If you had done that for hundreds of years past, you would not be here to-day at the feet of every country that wants to rule India. The first manifest effect of life is expansion. You must expand if you want to live. The moment you have ceased to expand, death is upon you, danger is ahead. I went to America and

Europe, to which you so kindly allude; I had to go because that is the first sign of the revival of national life—expansion. . . . Those of you who think that the Hindus have been always confined within the four walls of their country through all ages are entirely mistaken; they have not studied the whole books; they have not studied the history of the race aright. . . . I am an imaginative man, and my idea is the conquest of the whole world by the Hindu race. There have been great conquering races in the world. We also have been great conquerors. The story of our conquest has been described by the great Emperor of India, Asoka, as the conquest of religion and spirituality. Once more the world must be conquered by India. . . . Let foreigners come and flood the land with their armies, never mind. Up, India, and conquer the world with your spirituality! Aye, as has been declared on this soil, first love must conquer hatred; hatred cannot conquer itself. Materialism and all its miseries can never be conquered by materialism. Armies, when they attempt to conquer armies, only multiply and make brutes of humanity. Spirituality must conquer the West. Slowly they are finding it out that what they want is spirituality to preserve them as nations."

Force and bitterness were added to ideas inspired by such teaching, when it was possible to represent an administrative measure as designed to thwart national expansion, when numbers of publications were alleging that the British were cunning oppressors.

As in Bengal the Hindu political leaders wanted the boycott, while the Muhammadans did not, relations between the two communities rapidly deteriorated, and attempts to enforce disuse or destruction of European goods led to blows and riots. Hindu agitation steadily intensified in bitterness. The first Lieutenant-Governor of the new eastern province, Sir Bamfylde Fuller, endeavoured to stem the current, but was not supported by the Supreme Government in certain action which he considered essential, and resigned office. His resignation increased an impression, already current, that the Government feared to use effective preventives. The Indian army then took no recruits from Bengal, and the villages contain no sobering element of pensioned soldiers who are acquainted with the realities of British power. Few of the village people outside Calcutta had seen British troops, and some in the remote water-logged under-administered districts of the eastern province were encouraged by the lawlessness of the agitators and the forbearance of Government to believe that the days of British rule were drawing to an end. Boycott and picketing frequently ended in disturbances in which schoolboys and teachers were prominent.

The Congress of 1906 again justified the boycott, and requested annulment of the Partition. It also formulated a new demand which was intended to, and did, unite for a time those Indian politicians who aspired to a far larger share in the Government and other more violent spirits who were beginning to visualise an end of British rule. The demand was that the system of government obtaining in the self-governing British colonies should be extended to India. As preliminaries, such reforms as simultaneous examinations for the Civil Service and considerably enlarged Legislative Councils should be immediately instituted. In the presidential address of Mr. Dadabhai Naoroji, after an appeal to the Muhammadans for co-operation, occurred the following words: "Once self-government is attained, there will be prosperity enough for all, but not till then." He thought that union therefore of all the people for their emancipation was an absolute necessity.

"Agitation," he considered, "is the life and soul of the whole political, social, and industrial history of England. The life of England is all agitation. . . . Agitation is the civilised peaceful weapon of moral force, and infinitely preferable to brute physical force, when possible. Agitate, agitate over the whole length and breadth of India, peacefully of course, if we mean really to get justice from John Bull. Satisfy him that we are in earnest. The Bengalis, I am glad, have learnt the lesson and led the march. . . . Agitate means inform. Inform the Indian people what their rights are, and why and how they should obtain them."

Mr. Naoroji ignored the important fact that agitation in homogeneous England does not mean the exacerbation of colour-feeling, of racial jealousy and hatred. In India it is generally carried on by methods which mean this.

As a matter of fact, however, those leaders of the Congress movement who had not become intoxicated with excitement and racial animosity, had before this meeting begun to see that things were going too far. It is probable too that some at least were becoming aware that behind all the whirlwind of passion in Bengal, behind the schools and colleges which were developing into seed-beds of sedition, behind the pamphlets and newspapers which were disseminating hatred and bitterness far and wide, the ground was being prepared for even more serious doings by fanatics inflamed with the purpose of gradually organising a bloody revolt. This the Government was slow to realise. The movement was persistently misunderstood by its friends in England. It had not touched the fighting races or the fighting castes, and the main grievance was sentimental. Few anticipated that it would lead to actual bloodshed.[1] Fewer dreamt that it would bring

[1] A loyal Bengali gentleman once told the author that he was so amazed by the first outrages that he refused to credit them.

forth an unending series of violent crimes, or that, in a country where sons closely adhere to the occupations of their fathers, the sons of clerks, lawyers, and schoolmasters would, under the influence of racial sentiment and vague idealism, abjure the ambitions of their class and drill with daggers and pistols; and indeed it is certain that had more of these young men and boys ever known firm discipline and intelligent supervision, in and out of study hours, they would not have fallen so easy a prey to the plots of unscrupulous revolutionaries.

The mixture of ideas which appealed to such victims is illustrated by a confession which the author has read. It stated that the promptings to which the young revolutionary had succumbed were derived from histories of India and the rise of other nations, newspaper tales of ill-treatment of Indians by Europeans, stories of secret societies in magazines like the *Strand*, "accounts of the present better condition of other countries." He had later begun to doubt the veracity of these accounts. Finally, he joined because the boycott agitation afforded a "grand opportunity."

But although the reasonable members of the Congress of 1906, who had acquired the title of "Moderates," wished to call a halt, they did not as yet separate from their more intemperate and thorough-going colleagues who, pushing recklessly on, were becoming known as Extremists. In March 1907 the Viceroy (Lord Minto) publicly announced that he had sent home a despatch to the Secretary of State proposing administrative reforms on a liberal basis. About the same time serious disturbances occurred in the Punjab. In that province [1] Arya Samajists are numerous, and the large cities contain many Bengali immigrants. Disturbances took place; attempts were made to tamper with

[1] See page 27.

Sikh and Jat regiments, and two leading Arya Samajists were deported. In the two Bengals things were growing worse. The provinces at large were peaceful, but Revolutionaries were increasing and were preparing to improve on Extremist doctrines. Societies composed mainly of youths belonging to respectable and educated families were studying the use of pistols and explosives. Publications were industriously circulated which, as there is conclusive evidence to show, enormously excited Hindu opinion. The most famous of these was the *Yugantar* (*New Era*) newspaper, which from 1906 to July 1907, when its first editor went to prison, poured forth passages exhibiting, as a judge afterwards said, "a burning hatred of the British race." This paper was not finally suppressed till 1908. The mischief caused by it and its kind is incalculable.

In December the Congress met at Surat. Nagpur in the Central Provinces, midway between Bengal and Bombay, had been selected as the meeting-place, but arrangements were altered, as the reception committee was broken up by a gang of Extremists. The pen was seized from the hands of the chairman, and the Moderates were pushed out of a hall and assailed with stones and mud. At Surat again the Extremists tried to impose their will by force on those who differed from them, and the Congress ended in riotous scenes. The chief Moderates on this memorable occasion were Mr. Gokhale and Mr. Surendra Nath Banerjee. The Extremist leaders were Mr. Tilak and Mr. Arabindo Ghose. Bombay and Bengal led on each side. The Extremists were either "academic" or "physical force," argumentative or practical. The latter identified themselves with the revolutionary societies which were forming in Bengal and Bombay, and in the former Presidency had already committed several outrages.

On May 3rd, 1908, two English ladies were assassinated at Muzaffarpur in Bihar by a Bengali bomb-thrower, who intended his missile for a British magistrate; and after this horrible event the arrest of a number of young men in a garden in Maniktollah, a suburb of Calcutta, and their subsequent trial ended in the conviction of nineteen out of thirty-six accused, and in the disclosure of an elaborate conspiracy for securing the liberation of India through the "easily aroused and misdirected ardour of youth." It was proved that the convicts had, for over two years, launched on the public a highly inflammatory propaganda; they had collected arms and ammunition; they had studied bombs. The following words of the Sessions Judge show how the licence of the Press had assisted their purpose:

"There can be no doubt that the majority of the witnesses . . . are in sympathy with the accused. I do not say with their motives, but with their objects; and it is only natural that they should be. Their natural desire for independence was not likely to be weakened by the constant vilification in season and out of season of Government measures, not only by the Yellow Press, but by papers which claim to be respectable."

The Maniktollah conspirators were for the most part men of good education. Their leader, Barindra, was born in England. His faith was apparently this. He considered that Hindu manhood was stunted, and Hindu religion and mysticism were losing vitality under foreign rule. To strive without scruple or intermission for the expulsion of the foreigners was therefore a duty which sanctified any means whereby the object might be achieved. It could be achieved eventually by sedulous diffusion of revolutionary propaganda,[1] by winning over the Indian troops, by sapping the confidence of the people in their foreign rulers, and by a widespread concentration of determined effort. The struggle might be long, but was worth undertaking.

Such were the original leaders and organisers of the Bengal revolutionary movement; but many of their followers were more ordinary men, and some were students and schoolboys, whose initiation had come through the picketing which accompanied the boycott movement. Aided by inflammatory newspapers, the conspirators enormously impressed the youth of Bengal and some sections of the people of Calcutta. The cruel and inhuman nature of successive crimes was ignored in admiration for criminals who had shown that Bengalis could follow plots into action, could risk their lives for a cause. A single instance of this perverted hero-worship may be quoted. One of the conspirators, a graduate of the Dupleix College, Chandernagore, named Kanai Lal Datt, was executed for the murder of an associate who had turned informer. His body was handed over to his relatives and was cremated. The obsequies were accompanied by such fervid and sensational scenes that not long afterwards a Bengali youth falsely confessed to the murder of a police sub-inspector because he desired to have a funeral like Kanai's.

While in Bengal the Maniktollah conspirators were being brought to account, in Bombay Mr. Tilak published articles in the *Kesari* to the effect that the Muzaffarpur murders were the result of oppression and of the refusal of *swaraj* (self-government). The language and spirit of these articles resulted in his prosecution for attempting to bring the British Government

[1] The literature of the movement is fully described in the published report of the Sedition Committee.

into hatred and contempt, and for endeavouring to provoke enmity and hatred between different classes of His Majesty's subjects. He was convicted and sentenced to six years' imprisonment.[1] His admirers instigated rioting for several days in Bombay, and attempted to hold a separate congress in Nagpur, but were prohibited from doing so by the Central Provinces Government. They showed their displeasure by assaulting solitary Europeans, and breaking the windows of a flourishing Indian factory because the factory hands would not join their disorderly demonstrations.

The newspaper, *India*, the organ of the British committee of the Congress, thus commented on the split of 1907 :

> "If the young men are throwing in their lot with Mr. Tilak, and have ceased to believe in the promises of Englishmen, Englishmen have only themselves to thank for it. When Mr. Morley came into office two years ago, he had the ball at his feet. The party of Extremists existed, it is true, but it had neither numbers nor influence. A policy of concession and conciliation was needed to disarm them. It was deliberately ignored."

These words, however, do not truly describe the situation. Lord Morley's policy *was* a policy of concession and conciliation. Reforms had been incubating for some time, and the attitude of the Indian and Home Governments toward the Partition agitation and its accompaniments had been remarkably forbearing under exceptional provocation. It is possible that preventive and remedial measures would have been less tardy had not the depth and violence of the movement been only gradually and imperfectly appreciated by the

[1] See paragraph 8, Chapter I—Report of the (Rowlatt) Sedition Committee.

highest authorities. The agitators and their disciples belonged to the peaceable castes; and even persons who were well acquainted with Bengal failed to realise the strength of three influences: the triumph of Japan over Russia; the new nationalism and the carefully instilled racial hatred, as well as the effect of all these factors on the uncritical and altruistic spirit of youth. Such currents were favoured by a growing economic pressure to which I will later recur. They were driven on by calumnies sown broadcast of the most subtle and unscrupulous kind.

The history of revolutionary conspiracy in Bengal and India has recently been investigated by a special Committee, whose report will be noticed fully in a later chapter. It shows that from 1907 until now political crimes, murders, bomb-outrages, robberies, have been committed in Bengal, and that secret revolutionary societies have attracted an unfailing flow of recruits. The poisonous contagion has now and then spread to other provinces and gathered force from other currents, but has borne most fruit in Bengal. Its genesis and progress are detailed in the Sedition Committee's Report.

Before proceeding further with the history of Hindu political movements, it is necessary to give some account of the origin of the Muslim League.

Sir Saiyid Ahmad had died in 1898, shortly after rendering a last valuable service to the British Government. In order to combat pan-Islamic sentiment excited by the Greco-Turkish War, he contributed articles to the *Aligarh Institute Gazette*, denying the pretensions of Sultan Abdul Hamid to the Khalifat (*i.e.* the temporal and spiritual succession to the Prophet Muhammad),[1] and preaching loyalty to the British

[1] See Appendix III.

rulers of India even if they were "compelled to pursue an unfriendly policy toward Turkey." A great leader had passed from Muhammadan India and left no successor. Times, too, were changed, and new problems had arisen. The Muhammadans had become uneasy as to the place which they would occupy in the reforms which were under discussion in 1906; and on October 1st of that year their principal leaders, headed by His Highness the Agha Khan, presented an address to the Viceroy gratefully acknowledging the peace, security, and liberty of person and worship conferred by the British Government, and emphasising the fact that one of the most important characteristics of British rule was the deference paid to the views and wishes of all races and religions. The object of the deputation was to present the claims of 62,000,000 of Muhammadans to a fair share in any modified system of representation that might be contemplated, the share to be commensurate with their numbers *and political importance.* Representative institutions of the European type were new to Indians, and, in the absence of the greatest caution, dangerous to their national interests. The deputation deprecated a system of individual enfranchisement, and complained of the monopoly of official influence by one class, pointing out that no Muhammadan Judge sat in any Supreme Court. Continuing, the address urged the need of a Muhammadan university, and insisted on the importance of local boards and municipalities as the basis of all local self-government.

The Viceroy replied that:

"although British ideas must prevail, they must not carry with them an impracticable insistence on the acceptance of political methods. . . . You justly claim that your position should be estimated not merely on your numerical strength, but in respect of the political importance of your community and the service it has rendered to the Empire. I am in accordance with you."

Thus originated the concession to minorities of communal representation. The Muslim League then came gradually into widespread existence. Meetings were held at Dacca in 1906 at the invitation of the late Nawab Salim-ullah Khan, who was making a strong stand for law and order in Eastern Bengal, and at Karachi in 1907 under Sir Adamjee Peerbhoy. The resolutions passed related to adequate Muslim representation in the new Councils, to Muslim places in the public service, and to Muslim loyalty. In March 1908 a meeting was held at Aligarh under the presidency of the Agha Khan. A branch had been started in London under the Honourable Mr. Amir Ali. The principles of the promoters of the League were thus expounded in a letter addressed by the Agha Khan to a meeting of the Deccan branch. He wrote that amid much that was good in India, they saw a growing indiscipline and contempt for authority, a striving after change without perceiving whither change would lead, and the setting up of false and impracticable constitutional ideas. No man who loved his country as the Indian Muslims did could stand idly by and see India drifting irrevocably to disaster. Prosperity and contentment could only be reached by processes of development and evolution working on natural lines. These processes required the existence of a strong, just, and stable Government, a Government securing justice and equal opportunity to all, minorities as well as majorities. It was the duty of all patriots to strengthen British control under which had been effected the amazing progress of a century.

The Muhammadan representations came none too

soon, for, on November 2nd, 1908, the fiftieth anniversary of Queen Victoria's Proclamation, King Edward VII issued a second Proclamation to the Princes and people of India. It claimed that "the incorporation of many strangely diversified communities and of some 300,000,000 of the human race, under British guidance and control, has proceeded steadfastly and without pause: that difficulties such as attend all human rule had been faced by servants of the British Crown with toil and courage and patience, with deep counsel and a resolution that has never faltered nor shaken." It undertook to repress anarchy and to take continuously steps towards obliterating distinctions of race as the test for access to posts of public authority. It announced that the time had come to "prudently extend the principle of representative institutions." It foreshadowed reforms in "politic satisfaction" of the claims of important classes "representing ideas that have been fostered and encouraged by British rule."

These reforms were announced by Lord Morley on the 17th of the following month. They had been under consideration for two years, and every effort had been made to gauge the trend of public opinion and to consult all interests concerned. The reforms were on a large and generous scale. The Legislative Councils were greatly enlarged. The Provincial Councils were given non-official majorities. So far the nearest approach to the election of non-official members had been nominations by Government upon the recommendations of majorities of the voters on certain public bodies. Now Parliament was asked, "in a very definite way, to introduce election working alongside of nomination with a view to the due representation of the different classes of the community." Any member was to be allowed to divide his Legislative Council on financial questions, and all such Councils were to be invested with power to discuss matters of public and general importance and to pass recommendations or resolutions to the Executive Government. The Government would deal with such resolutions as they thought fit; but the concession was one of great importance, and has materially influenced the course of political events. Further, the Executive Councils of the Supreme and Subordinate Governments were to receive Indian members. Lord Morley had already appointed two Indians, one Hindu and one Muhammadan, to the Council of the Secretary of State. His reforms were, with slight variations, accepted by both Houses. In explaining them, he took pains to disclaim all intention of inaugurating a system of parliamentary government in India. Such a system he apparently considered unsuited to Indian conditions, and for this reason, while conceding non-official majorities in the Provincial Legislative Councils, he retained the official majority in the Imperial Council. He explained this distinction in the following words:

"But in the Imperial Council we consider an official majority essential. It may be said that this is a most flagrant logical inconsistency. So it would be on one condition. If I were attempting to set up a parliamentary system in India, or if it could be said that this chapter of reforms led directly or indirectly to the establishment of a parliamentary system in India, I, for one, would have nothing at all to do with it. I do not believe—it is not of very great consequence what I believe, because the fulfilment of my vaticinations could not come off very soon—in spite of the attempts in Oriental countries at this moment, interesting attempts to which we all wish well, to set up some sort of parliamentary system—it is no ambition of mine at all events to have any share in beginning that operation in India. If my existence, either officially or corporeally, were to be prolonged twenty times longer than either of them is likely to be, a parliamentary system in India is not at all the goal to which I would for one moment aspire."[1]

It is, however, not surprising that the reforms were regarded by Indian politicians as a decided step toward parliamentary government, for it is difficult to reconcile Lord Morley's words with his establishment of non-official majorities in the provincial Legislative Councils, or with his policy of prudently extending "the principle of representative institutions." Lord Curzon, in the House of Lords on February 23rd, 1909, criticised the new measure in the following terms:

"I wonder how these changes will, in the last resort, affect the great mass of the people of India, the people who have no vote and have scarcely a voice. Remember that to these people, representative government and electoral institutions are nothing whatever. The good government that appeals to them is the government which protects them from the rapacious money-lender and landlord, from the local vakil, and all the other sharks in human disguise who prey upon these unfortunate people. I have a misgiving that this class will not fare much better under these changes than they do now. At any rate I see no place for them in these enlarged Councils which are to be created, and I am under the strong opinion that as government in India becomes more and more parliamentary—as will be the inevitable result—so it will become less paternal and less beneficent to the poorer classes of the population."

The reception accorded to these changes by the Congress, now void of Extremists, was enthusiastic.

[1] The difficulties of forming parliamentary electorates in India are clearly set forth in paragraph 203 of the Montagu-Chelmsford Report.

A Bengali deputation to the Viceroy presented an address containing the following passage: "It is a step worthy of the noble traditions of the Government which has given us liberty of thought and of speech, high education, and local self-government." The late Mr. Gokhale, the leader of the Moderates, whose outlook had altered since December 1906, spoke of "the generous and fair nature" of the reforms, and urged that they should be gratefully accepted. Co-operation with Government must take the place of mere criticism of Government. *The attitude of constant antagonism must be abandoned.* Hindus, Muhammadans, and Parsis were mostly a dreamy race, and the Hindus were especially so.

"I admit," he said, "the importance of dreams in shaping our aspirations; but in practical matters we have to be practical men and remember two things. Life is not like writing on a clean slate. We have to take the words existing on the slate and add other words so as to make complete sentences and produce a harmonious meaning. Secondly, whatever you may ask for is not the same thing as that which you will get, or will be qualified to, in practice, maintain if you get."

The Muhammadans, however, asked for representation in excess of their numerical strength, and arrangements were made to meet their wishes in accordance with the undertaking given by Lord Minto, and subsequently endorsed by Lord Morley in the House of Lords on February 23rd, 1909.

For this and other reasons the regulations which were framed in India to carry into effect the intentions of the British Parliament failed in some measure to give complete satisfaction to advanced Hindus. Still, on the whole, reasonable Progressives were satisfied; and the Conservative classes, whose interests had been carefully considered in the regulations, were pleased with the stir and novelty of the new order of things.

The partition of Bengal, however, was still denounced by the Bengali Moderate leaders: and on the stream of anarchic crime the reforms produced no effect. The police had been strengthened in Bengal, and remediary measures had been adopted; but it was plain to all that the seeds so long and widely sown among the youth of the country by deliberate propaganda and poisonous newspapers was still bearing abundant fruit. At Poona, on July 8th, 1909, Mr. Gokhale again urged loyal acquiescence in British rule for two reasons:

"One that, considering the difficulties of the position, Britain had done very well in India, the other that there was no alternative to British rule and could be none for a long time. . . . They could proceed in two directions: first toward an obliteration of distinctions, on the grounds of race, between individual Indians and individual Englishmen, and second by way of advance toward the form of government enjoyed in other parts of the Empire. *The latter was an ideal for which the Indian people had to qualify themselves, for the whole question turned on character and capacity, and they must realise that their main difficulties lay with themselves.*"

Again at Bombay, on October 9th of the same year, in addressing the Students' Brotherhood, he strongly denounced the active participation of students in politics, and the tactics and objects of the Extremists, in the following memorable terms:

"The active participation of students in political agitation really tends to lower the dignity and the responsible character of public life and impair its true effectiveness. It also fills the students themselves with unhealthy excitement, often evoking in them a bitter partisan spirit which cannot fail to interfere with their studies and prove injurious to their intellectual and moral growth. . . . I venture to think that a stage has been reached in our affairs when it is necessary for us to face resolutely our responsibilities in this matter. Every one knows that during the past few years a new school of political thought has arisen in the country, and that it has exercised a powerful fascination over the minds of young men more or less in all parts of India. A considerable part of what it has preached could not but find ready acceptance on every hand, that love of country should be a ruling principle of our lives; that we should rejoice in making sacrifices for her sake; that we should rely, wherever we could, on our own exertions . . . side by side with this undoubtedly valuable work, the new party gave to the country a great deal of what could only be regarded as unsound political teaching. That teaching was in the first instance directed to the destruction of the very foundations of the old public life of the country. But, once started, it could not be confined to that object, and in course of time it came to be applied generally. Its chief error lies in ignoring all historical considerations and tracing our political troubles to the existence of a foreign Government in the country. Our old public life was based on frank and loyal acceptance of British rule, due to a recognition of the fact that it alone could secure to the country the peace and order which were necessary for slowly evolving a nation out of the heterogeneous elements of which India was composed, and for ensuring to it a steady advance in different directions. The new teaching condemns all faith in the British Government as childish and all hope of real progress under it as vain. . . . Our general lack of political judgment is also responsible for the large measure of acceptance which it ('the new teaching') received. Not many of us care to think for ourselves in political matters, or, for the matter of that, in any public matters. Ready-made opinions are as convenient as ready-made clothes and not so noticeable. . . . I think those of our public men who realise the harm which the new teaching has done, have not so far done their duty by the student community of this country. . . . I feel that it is now incumbent on us to speak out freely. As I have said, the self-reliance which is part of the new propaganda cannot but be acceptable to all. It is in regard to the attitude toward the Government which the programme advocates that the need for a protest and a warning arises. . . . When one talks to young men of independence in a country like this, only two ideas are likely to present themselves clearly before their minds. One is how to get rid of the foreigner, and the other is how soon to get rid of him. All else must appear to them as comparatively of minor importance. . . . We have to recognise that British rule, in spite of its inevitable drawbacks as a foreign rule, has been on the whole a great instrument of progress for our people. *Its continuance means the continuance of that peace and order which it alone can maintain in our country, and with which our best interests, among them, those of our growing nationality, are bound up.* . . . Our rulers stand pledged to extend to us equality of treatment with themselves. This equality is to be sought in two fields : equality for individual Indians with individual Englishmen, and equality in regard to the form of government which Englishmen enjoy in other parts of the Empire. The attainment of full equality with Englishmen, if ever it is accomplished, is bound to be a slow and weary affair. But one thing is clear. It is both our right and our duty to press along this road, and further, good faith requires that we should not think of taking any other. Of the twofold equality we have to seek with Englishmen, the first, though difficult of attainment, is not so difficult as the second. For it is possible to find in this country a fair number of Indians who in character and capacity could hold their own against individual Englishmen. But the attainment of a democratic form of self-government such as obtains in other parts of the Empire must depend upon the average strength in character and capacity of our people taken as a whole, for it is on our average strength that the weight of the edifice of self-government will have to rest. And here it must be regretfully admitted that our average strength to-day is far below the British average. The most important work before us, therefore, is to endeavour to raise this average. There is work enough for the most enthusiastic lover of his country. In fact on every side, whichever way we turn, only one sight meets the eye—that of work to be done—and only one cry is heard—that there are but few faithful workers. The elevation of the depressed classes, who have to be brought up to the level of the rest of our people, universal elementary education, co-operation, improvement of the economic condition of the peasantry, higher education of women, spread of industrial and technical education and building up the industrial strength of the country, promotion of closer relations between the different communities—these are some of the tasks which lie in front of us, and each needs a whole army of devoted missionaries."

Unfortunately, however, revolutionary teaching and revolutionary crime had passed beyond the stage at which any words of Mr. Gokhale's could avail to arrest them. The masses were unaffected; but violent crime, frequently unpunished, and racial hatred, widely preached, were producing their natural influence on many members of the rising generation of the better educated. As a counterpoise, Mr. Gokhale had founded the "Servants of India" society, the objects of which were "to train national missionaries for the Service of India and to promote by all constitutional means the true interest of the Indian people." The members of the society were bound to accept the British connection, and to recognise that self-government within the Empire and a higher life for their countrymen constituted an end which could not be attained without years of patient effort and building up in the country a higher type of character and capacity than was then generally available.

So ominous was the outlook at this time, that the Viceroy took the unusual step of communicating direct with the Ruling Chiefs on the subject of the active unrest prevalent in various parts of India, and invited an exchange of opinions "with a view to mutual co-operation against a common danger." The replies which he received were both sympathetic and suggestive, the majority strongly recommending the necessity of checking the licence of the Indian press, to which they attributed the responsibility for the widening of the gulf between the rulers and the ruled. The Revolutionaries had themselves addressed a menacing pamphlet to the Chiefs. The letters of the latter contributed toward the passing of that long-needed and long-deferred measure, the Indian Press Act, by the newly constituted Imperial Legislative Council in February 1910. The Act imposes no censorship; it practically substitutes forfeiture of security for criminal prosecution, and while conceding a certain amount to executive discretion, it tempers that discretion by making orders of forfeiture appealable to a High Court.

The loyal attitude of the Chiefs was subsequently intensified by the impressions left by the royal visit, and has been of great assistance to the British Government. Lord Morley had commented in Parliament on the importance of "these powerful princes" as standing forces in India, but had not accepted a proposal of Lord Minto's Government for the institution of an advisory Council of Ruling Chiefs and territorial magnates. It is of course arguable that Ruling Chiefs can have nothing to do with affairs in British India, yet these affairs may most seriously affect their position in their States.

The firm loyalty of the Princes, the personal popularity of the Viceroy, the Reforms and the altered attitude of the purified Congress party, the long-needed Press Act, the breaking up and bringing to trial of two notorious gangs of revolutionary conspirators in Calcutta and Dacca—all combined to make the last year of Lord Minto's rule comparatively peaceful. Soon after his departure Lord Morley left the India Office. They had passed through critical times. They were jointly responsible for measures which temporarily satisfied sober political opinion, and, but for the war, would probably have worked sufficiently well for a considerable period. But in coping with the revolutionary movement, they were slow to realise the virulence of the propaganda and the rapidity with which it was spreading among the schools and colleges of Bengal, fostered by bad conditions and ill-paid seditious teachers, "proclaiming to beguiled youth that outrage was the evidence of patriotism and its reward a martyr's crown."[1] The wide extent of the mischief was at first discredited, and the whole conspiracy obtained a long start.

No Secretary of State ever devoted more anxious or thorough attention to India than did Lord Morley. The distinction of his speeches and writings did much to invest Indian affairs with interest for the ordinary British citizen. But it is evident from them and from his Recollections that he was frequently perplexed by conflict between measures advised from India and his own predilections combined with the ideas of many of his political supporters. It may be said roughly that throughout the period of calm that followed the Mutiny

[1] Speech by Lord Minto in 1908.

up to the last year of Lord Curzon's régime the British principle of governing India had been "Trust the man on the spot." Lord Curzon, during his visit to England at the end of his first term of office, in a public speech laid stress on the importance of this principle. Until then he had no cause to complain of its non-observance. But the reason and manner of his resignation, and the troubles which followed on the partition of Bengal, damaged it severely. It is plain from Lord Morley's writings that he thought that these troubles were largely due to mismanagement by the men on the spot, and that the Viceroy was liable to be too greatly impressed by the atmosphere in which he worked. As a matter of fact, however, both the men on the spot and the Secretary of State were confronted by a novel and complex state of things. The effect of the Russo-Japanese War on Indian political thought, the sudden gathering in of the harvest of years of Western education and increasing contact with an increasingly democratic England, combined with narrowing employment, ill-managed schools, and virulent racial propaganda, to produce in Bengal an unprecedented ferment which affected the rest of India. The bad schools and starved schoolmasters of Bengal were the fruits of official and non-official miscalculations. They resulted from the adoption of recommendations made by an Educational Commission appointed in the early 'eighties. The whole movement, which developed so rapidly, was handled by those in daily contact with it in a spirit of patient courage. The British officials in India were in the trenches. They had to bear the brunt of the attack. They dealt with it as best they could, and reported what they saw. No doubt, being near, they saw through a glass darkly. It was no part of their duty to join in depreciation of or yield to attacks on the Government which they endeavoured faithfully to serve, nor were they responsible for the strategy that directed their efforts. On the other hand they were not concerned with considerations other than those which were suggested by the difficult conditions which confronted them. In the course of my narrative I am endeavouring to make some of these conditions apparent.

Lord Minto was a gallant, chivalrous gentleman, of the stamp which his own countrymen and Indians alike admire. He was succeeded by Lord Hardinge of Penshurst, who held office for five and a half eventful years. Shortly after his arrival came the Congress of December 1910, presided over by Sir William Wedderburn. This meeting demanded that certain salutary repressive Acts be removed from the Statute book, and protested strongly against the treatment of Indians in British colonies, but concluded without excitement. Three leading Muhammadans of a new school, which was to become prominent later, attended. For the first time an address of welcome was presented to a Viceroy. He was asked to show clemency to all purely political offenders. The academic Extremists were entreated to return to the Congress fold. The partition of Bengal was denounced by a Bengali. The President proposed a conference of Hindus and Muhammadans, in order to effect a *rapprochement* on the burning question of special or communal representation on religious grounds, combined with the corollary question of weighting for Muslim minorities. But the conference never met, though delegates were appointed, because a prominent Hindu politician moved a resolution in the Imperial Legislative Council requesting the abolition of all separate representation of Muhammadans or councils and local boards. He was opposed by Mr. Gokhale and by the Home Member of the Government of India, who said that the fullest and clearest pledges had been given to the Muhammadans "that they should have separate representation."

The year 1911 was marked by some degree of trouble in Bengal; but everywhere else things were quiet, and people generally waited expectantly for the royal visit, which achieved brilliant success, bringing the gracious and sympathetic personalities of Their Majesties as Sovereigns of India closely home to all classes, striking a keynote of chivalry and loyalty that has reverberated in many hearts throughout the troubles of the past four years. No one who witnessed the enthusiasm displayed by that great gathering could doubt that Great Britain has no reason to be ashamed of her record in India.

The partition of Bengal was altered in a manner that gratified Congress sentiment, but annoyed the Muhammadans, especially those of the six-year-old Eastern Bengal and Assam province, and seriously disturbed Indian belief in the ability of the British Government to adhere to a declared resolution.[1] The Capital was removed from Calcutta to Delhi. In the despatch from the Government of India to the Secretary of State proposing these changes for sanction, occurred a passage which advocated a policy of provincial decentralisation and widening self-government, "until India would at last consist of a number of administrations autonomous in all provincial matters, with the Government of India above them all, possessing power to interfere in cases of misgovernment, but ordinarily restricting their functions to matters of Imperial concern."

When the papers were published, this passage was interpreted by advanced Indians as clearly foreshadowing self-government on colonial lines. This idea, how-

[1] Lord Morley, while disapproving of the partition, regarded it as a "settled fact."

ever, was expressly disclaimed in Parliament by Lord Crewe, then Secretary of State, on June 24th, 1912, in the following words:

"There is a certain section in India which looks forward to a measure of self-government approaching that which has been granted in the Dominions. I see no future for India on these lines. The experiment of extending a measure of self-government practically free from parliamentary control to a race which is not our own, even though that race enjoys the services of the best men belonging to our race, is one which cannot be tried. It is my duty as Secretary of State to repudiate the idea that the despatch implies anything of the kind as the hope or goal of the policy of Government.

"At the same time I think it is the duty of the nation, and of the Government for the time being of the nation, to encourage in every possible way the desire of the inhabitants of India to take a further share in the management of their country."

Again, he said, on June 29th, 1912:

"There is nothing whatever in the teachings of history, so far as I know them, or in the present condition of the world which makes such a dream" (as complete self-government within the British Empire) "even remotely probable. . . . Is it conceivable that at any time an Indian Empire could exist, on the lines, say, of Australia and New Zealand, with no British officials, and no tie of creed and blood which takes the place of these material bonds? . . . To me that is a world as imaginary as any Atlantis or any that was ever thought of by the ingenious brain of any imaginative writer. . . . I venture to think that it is only those who think less of service and more of distinction who would lose heart if they braced themselves to set aside this vision altogether and to settle down to closer co-operation with the Western race, to which they can teach much, and from which they can learn much, in co-operation for the moral and material bettering of the country to which they are so deeply attached and of which we are so proud to be governors."

In spite of this advice the Congress leaders preferred to adhere to their original interpretation of the meaning of the disputed passage, and continued to profess self-government on colonial lines as their goal, striving to accelerate advance by unremitting pressure, sometimes employing analogies which are apt to deceive if applied to cases which are not really parallel.

The year 1912 was further marked by the appointment of a Royal Commission to report on the constitution and conditions of the Public Services, with the main object of investigating the possibilities of admitting Indians in larger numbers to the higher grades. The report of this body was only published in January 1917. Publication had been delayed by the war. Political expectations had greatly risen, and proposals which were, in fact, liberal, were denounced as grossly inadequate.

In the meantime a change had been gradually coming over the spirit and aims of the Muslim League. The war between Italy and Turkey, events in Persia, and, above all, the Balkan war, created considerable sympathy with Turkey and resentment at the apparently passive attitude of the British Government. The sympathy of Indian Muhammadans, especially the Sunnis, with Turkey was prominent as long ago as the time of the Crimean war, and is referred to in the private correspondence of Lord Dalhousie, recently published. It had strengthened with time and improved communications. Above all, it had grown with a pan-Islamic propaganda, which, originally inculcating religious and political reform, and preached in Turkey and Egypt by Shaikh Jamal-ud-din el Afghani, an

Afghan educated in Bokhara, had been subsequently converted, first by Sultan Abd-ul-Hamid and afterwards by the Young Turks, into an appeal to the Faithful to rally round the Ottoman Khalifat.[1]

Many Muhammadan politicians disliked our agreement with Russia, and contrasted British inaction during the Balkan war with her championship of Turkey in former days. They saw that while Japan was proving the ability of an Asiatic power to make herself respected, the few remaining Muslim powers, Morocco, Persia, and Turkey, were sinking lower into depths of submission or calamity. And, turning their eyes on their own country, they beheld in Lord Morley's Reforms and the alteration of the partition of Bengal what they regarded as conclusive triumphs for the policy of agitation pursued by the Congress. While these impressions were working on their minds, Congress newspapers were profuse in expressions of sympathy over the misfortunes of Turkey. All these things, working together, produced a remarkable effect. In 1908 the President of the All-India Muhammadan Conference, Mr., now Sir, Saiyid Ali Imam, had declared that the Muslim League and the Congress differed fundamentally.

"Has not," he said, "this ideal of self-government created impatience, because of its impracticability, carrying idealism off its feet and creating extremism? Let the Congress announce that in practical politics loyalty to the British administration is loyalty to India, and that reform in the existing administration is possible only with the maintenance of British control. . . . As long as the leaders of the Indian National Congress will not give us a workable policy like the one indicated above, so long the All-India Muslim League has a sacred duty to perform. That duty is to save the

[1] See Appendix III.

community it represents from the political error of joining in an organisation that in the main, as Lord Morley says, cries for the moon."

Even in January 1910 the Muslim League, under the presidency of the Agha Khan, had expressed gratitude for the consideration showed to the Muhammadans in the Reform arrangements; but a remarkable change was imminent. In August 1912 the majority of leading Muhammadans were unable to come to terms with Government in regard to the conditions under which a Muhammadan university should be established at Aligarh. Later on in the year Indian Muslims despatched a medical Red Crescent Mission to Turkey. In January 1913 the council of the Muslim League decided to recommend a new constitution to their association. The objects were henceforth to be—"the promotion among Indians of loyalty to the British Crown, the protection of the rights of Muhammadans *and, without detriment to the foregoing objects, the attainment of the system of self-government suitable to India.*" These recommendations were accepted by the association at Lucknow on March 22nd, 1913. There it was said that if Sir Edward Grey remained arbiter of Britain's foreign policy, the Muslim status in Asia would be swallowed up by Russia. The adoption of suitable self-government as an ideal was adopted, after a heated discussion, by a large majority. Influential Mussulmans present regarded the proposal as a departure from the fixed policy of the Muhammadans and destructive to their interests as a minority in India. Others thought the aim proposed not high enough, and desired identity with that expressed by the Congress. The Agha Khan was not present at the meetings. But afterwards he commented to the London branch of the League on the resolutions passed. If, he said, self-government for India meant, as he took it to mean, an ideal involving many decades of effort toward self-improvement, social reform, educational diffusion, and complete amity between the various communities, the ideal must commend itself to thoughtful approval. But if it meant a mere hasty impulse to jump at the apple when only the blossoming stage was over, then the day that witnessed the formulation of the ideal would be a very unfortunate one in the annals of their country.

Not long afterwards he resigned the presidency of the League. The change in the ideals of that body was confirmed at the sessions of December 1913, and was eulogised by the Congress meeting of the same month.

The qualification " self-government of a kind suited to India " appears to mean self-government in which Muhammadans will have a share proportioned to what they consider to be their political rather than their numerical importance. As we shall see later, an attempt has recently been made to define this share.

In the year 1912, revolutionary stores, arms, and documents were discovered in Eastern Bengal; a bomb outrage was attempted in Western Bengal; and, in December, as Lord Hardinge was making his state entry into the new capital, a bomb was thrown which wounded him very seriously and killed one of his attendants. The perpetrator of the outrage was not discovered, although there is little doubt that he was one of an association of Hindu revolutionaries who were brought to justice for a subsequent murder.

Revolutionary effort intensified in Bengal during 1913, and afterwards up to the outbreak of the war. It established a terrorism which largely prevented witnesses from coming forward to testify to the crimes that were committed. In other provinces things went smoothly, and the business of the new Legislative Councils progressed with satisfactory harmony. The Viceroy had earned remarkable popularity by his firm and courageous bearing under the outrage which so nearly killed him, as well as by his outspoken sympathy with the cause of Indians in South Africa. Thus the outbreak of the Great War found India generally tranquil. Advanced politicians—Hindus and Mussulmans—mainly lawyers and journalists, were drawing near a common platform, and seeking vaguely for representative government on colonial lines. With some this goal was merely a nominal article of faith, but with others it was a genuine objective. On the whole, however, they were satisfied with the recent reforms. But behind them was a small section of revolutionaries, who, sometimes encouraged from abroad, were asserting their presence by intermittent manifestations of subterranean activities of the most sinister kind. Apart entirely from political contentions stood the great majority, the masses of conservative and indifferent opinion, the main body of the territorial aristocracy, the landlords, the military castes, the cultivators, the ordinary trading population. Apart also, though not inattentive, was the European mercantile and non-official community. The ranks of the Nationalists, though slender, were drawn from the better educated and more systematically organised intelligence of the country. They dominated the Indian Press. They had started and spread the idea of a united self-governing India. In the process their views and policy had become increasingly biased by racial feeling, by a lessening faith in British efficiency, and by a growing belief that India, unfettered by foreign ascendancy, could rival the success of Japan. The notable differences between conditions in India and those in Japan they seldom regarded. For some years their extreme wing had been discredited. Its leaders had temporarily vanished. Its most ardent followers had been absorbed by revolutionary associations.

CHAPTER IV

POLITICS FROM THE OUTBREAK OF THE WAR TO THE END OF 1916

IN August 1914, Lord Hardinge of Penshurst had been Viceroy for three years and nine months. He had achieved remarkable popularity. The country was exceedingly quiet, the sole disturbing features being the frequency of revolutionary crimes in Bengal. The Legislative Councils were working well; the Ruling Chiefs, the commercial, military, and territorial classes, were loyal and contented; relations with Afghanistan and the frontier tribes were good. India was ready to meet the storm which burst so suddenly, and she met it well. The circumstances of the beginning of the great struggle, the cause in which Britain was to fight, touched the warm Indian imagination. Conservative and advanced classes alike rejoiced in the despatch of Indian troops to the Front. The energetic loyalty of the Ruling Chiefs set a splendid example to the whole country. Politicians followed the initiative of one of their leaders, who moved in the Imperial Council that India should be allowed to share in the financial burdens which the war must entail. They responded to the Viceroy's appeal for suspension of domestic controversy.

The position of the Muhammadans soon became exceedingly difficult. To appreciate it properly we must remember what religion is to ordinary Indian Muslims, the depth of their innate fanaticism, and the regard in which, at times encouraged by us, they have been accustomed to hold the Sultan of Turkey. It is certain, moreover, that pro-Turkish influences were actively at work. When we consider all these things, we must heartily appreciate the general loyalty which Muslims showed to the British Crown. That pan-Islamism should be silent in such circumstances, that it should not cause trouble here and there, was hardly to be anticipated. But, on the whole, Indian Muhammadans have deserved well of the British Government. Their path was smoothed by the declaration, which immediately followed the entry of Turkey into the war, that the Holy Places of Arabia and sacred shrines of Mesopotamia would be immune from attack by Britain and her allies, so long as Indian pilgrims remained unmolested. And the loyal manifesto simultaneously published by the premier Ruling Chief, himself a Sunni Muhammadan,[1] exercised a calming influence.

In the early days of the war there were signs of a willingness on the part of the Press to abandon the time-honoured practice of incessant carping at the Indian Civil Service, but these signs were evanescent. A zealous desire was shown by some Moderates for accommodation with the academic Extremists, and was necessarily accompanied by reluctance to recognise the reality and dangers of the revolutionary movement. As regards, however, the main issue—the war—the heart of the Congress remained sound, both for sentimental and for selfish reasons. The eyes of intelligent Indians were sufficiently open to see that the enemies of England were their enemies.

Revolutionary activity, however, continued in palpable evidence in spite of repressive measures. Conspiracies at Delhi, Lahore, and elsewhere came to light,

[1] Sunni Muhammadans. See Appendix IV.

and efforts were made by plotters to undermine the loyalty of Indian troops. The theft of a large quantity of Mauser pistols and ammunition through the treachery of the clerk of a Calcutta firm of gun makers, the return from America and Canada of large bodies of Sikh emigrants, the combination between some of the more dangerous of these and Bengali plotters, and the danger of a bloody outbreak which was only narrowly averted in February 1915, are all set forth in the recently published report of the Sedition Committee. The same report traces the malignant efforts of Germany to stir up trouble in India. The Government was compelled to have recourse to a special Defence Act for the better security of the country, and Sir Michael O'Dwyer, Lieutenant-Governor of the Punjab, controlled a most difficult situation with remarkable energy and success. Fortunate indeed it was for all that the administration of this province was fully equal to a most serious emergency, for to this circumstance, to the general loyalty of the people, and to the unwearying labours of the much-abused Criminal Investigation Department, it was due that nowhere in India were the revolutionaries able to effect anything beyond occasional murders or robberies. In Calcutta and Bengal they committed a number of outrages; but their plots to bring about paralysis of authority, widespread terrorism and murder, and finally general rebellion, completely failed.

The Defence Act was, in the words of the Montagu-Chelmsford Report:

"inevitably a drastic measure; it gave to the Governor-General in Council wide rule-making powers with a view to securing the public safety and defence of the country, and also provided for the creation of special tribunals for the quicker trial of certain classes of cases in specially disturbed tracts. It was comparable to a similar Act passed in the United Kingdom also as a war measure. The Bill was naturally rather a severe trial to the Indian elected members; as loyal citizens they supported its principle; but they made no secret of their aversion to particular provisions, and moved many amendments, against which Government used its official majority without hesitation, as they would have destroyed the efficacy of the Bill. The Act was immediately applied in the Punjab, and later elsewhere as circumstances demanded."

Early in the year 1915 Mr. Gokhale died: and there can be no doubt that his death was a serious loss to Indian politics. He had shown himself able to adjust idealism to circumstances, and bold enough to preach common sense. At the same time, up to the day of his death, he maintained his widespread influence. His place remained empty.

1915 was a difficult year; but, as far as India generally was concerned, the victory of law and order in its earlier months was decisive. The Congress and Muslim League met in December at Bombay. The Honourable Mr. Sinha,[1] President of the Congress Sessions, spoke with "a feeling of profound pride" that India had not fallen behind other portions of the British Empire, but had stood shoulder to shoulder with them in the hour of her sorest trial. . . . Princes and people alike had vied with one another to prove to the great British nation their gratitude for peace and blessings of civilisation secured to them under its ægis for the last hundred and fifty years and more. He said that a reasoned ideal of the future was required; an ideal which would satisfy the ambitions of the rising generation and arrest anarchism; an ideal which would at the same

[1] Now Lord Sinha, K.C.

time meet with British approval. This ideal was the establishment of democracy pure and simple—"government of the people by the people." The British Government was the best government India had had for ages. But good government could not be a substitute for self-government. Every British official in India must consider himself a trustee "bound to make over his charges to the rightful owners the moment the latter attain to years of discretion." At present India was not fit for self-government. Free from England, and without a real power of resistance, she would be immediately in the thick of another struggle of nations. But when Indians had advanced under the guidance and protection of England so far as to be able not only to manage their own domestic affairs, but to secure internal peace and to prevent external aggression, it would be the interest and duty of England to concede the "fullest autonomy" to India. What this expression, "fullest autonomy," means, it was unnecessary to say. He found it difficult to believe that Indian patriotism would not be reconciled to the ideal of Englishmen and Indians united as fellow-citizens of a common empire. For the attainment of this ideal patience was requisite. Indians must continue to press for admission in larger and larger numbers to the public service and for the progressive nationalisation of the government of the country. Their labours must continue till "really free" institutions are established for the whole of India by gradual evolution and cautious progress.

He concluded with the following exhortation:

"I believe in the doctrine of self-help as much as, probably more than, any of you here. I ask, therefore, that, not content with these oratorical feasts for three days in the year, we should have a continuous programme of work—work not political in the sense of public meetings, but work in the sense of trying to uplift the low and weak . . . remedying the evils that there are in our daily lives—ignorance, poverty, and disease. It is the people whom we want to be capable of self-government, not merely Indians like ourselves, but the people in the villages, who toil with the sweat of their brow. . . . You have got to work day and night, patiently and strenuously, if you desire to achieve the object which you profess—government of the people, for the people, and by the people."

A committee was appointed to consider a Home Rule scheme propounded by Mrs. Annie Besant, the chief of the Theosophists, and before the meetings broke up some modifications were made in the rules which were designed to facilitate the return of Mr. Tilak and his party to the Congress fold. Mr. Tilak had been released from prison in 1914, had disclaimed all hostility to the British Government, and had repudiated the acts of violence that had been committed by the revolutionaries.

The speech of the president of the Muslim League emphasised the need for "self-government suitable to the needs and requirements of the country under the ægis of the British Crown," and concluded with the following sentences:

"It is a sore point with us that the Government of our Caliph should be at war with the Government of our King-Emperor. We should all have been pleased to see our brethren in the Faith fighting side by side with the soldiers of the British Empire. Whatever view one may take of the policy adopted by Islamic countries in the present war, Indian Muslims never desired, nor ever can desire, hostility between the British and Islamic Governments. That hostility should have come about is the greatest misfortune that could possibly have befallen Muslims. I have no desire to enter into details, but a vast majority of my co-religionists, and, for the matter of that, numerous Englishmen too, attribute it to the past foreign policy of Great Britain, and to the failure of British diplomacy. However that may be, it is the cherished desire of the followers of Islam that when peace comes—and pray God that it may come soon—Muslim countries should be dealt with in such a way that their dignity will not be compromised in the future."

The League decided to consider Mrs. Besant's Home Rule project; and as during the following year this lady assumed a remarkable lead in Indian politics, it is necessary to review briefly her antecedents.

Mrs. Besant's story up to the year 1890 is related in a published autobiography. Wife of an English clergyman, when quite young, she started independently as a keen radical and atheist pamphleteer and speaker. For years she worked with the late Charles Bradlaugh, and gradually gravitated to socialism. From this cause she was diverted by theosophy, which she learnt from Madame Blavatsky, a Russian, with whom she lived for some time. After that lady's death she went to India, in 1893, in order to work for the Theosophical Society. Mr. Hume, the "Father of the Congress," had been one of the pioneers of theosophy in India, and all Mrs. Besant's antecedents impelled her to sympathise with revivalist Hindu religion and politics. Her eloquence, energy, and ability made her a valuable adherent, but at first she devoted herself to education. It was due to her that the Central Hindu College was opened in July 1898, in a small house in Benares City, with only a few boys; it was she who induced the Maharaja of Benares to give this struggling institution a fine piece of land and spacious buildings; it was her energy and capacity for organisation that, surmounting one difficulty after another, brought the College to a position which enabled it to become the nucleus of a new university. But, before this final success, Mrs. Besant had become involved in a strange controversy which occupied considerable public attention. She resigned the presidency of the College, but retained the headship of the Theosophical Society. She turned to active participation in politics, started two newspapers, and proposed to both the Congress and the Muslim League the initiation of a Home Rule League. The project did not at first find favour with many members of either association; and all that she could obtain was undertakings that it should be taken into consideration.

Things had gone well during the period from August 1914 to December 1915. Revolutionary effort had been checked and largely suppressed. General politics had maintained a high level. Relations between the various communities had been good. The seasons had been kind and the harvests bountiful. Indian soldiers belonging to the martial castes had done good service at the various fronts. But in Europe the prospect was gloomy, and in Asia the Mesopotamian Expeditionary Force, after winning considerable success, had been compelled to retreat, and was besieged at Kut-el-Amara by a superior Turkish force. It is noteworthy that neither the siege nor its disastrous termination produced any visible effect in India.

Early in the year 1916 Lord Hardinge left India after an eventful and arduous Viceroyalty. His farewell advice to Indian Nationalists was to remember that the development of self-governing institutions had been achieved not by sudden strokes of statesmanship, but by a process of steady and patient evolution which had gradually united and raised all classes of the community.

The year, however, was marked by the inception and rapid growth of a political agitation which was inspired by a call for more precipitate progress. Before, however, describing it, I will glance at a minor matter which disturbed Muhammadan sentiment.

In June it became known in India that the Grand Sharif of Mecca had revolted from the authority of the Sultan of Turkey. The Grand Sharif is chief of the Arabs of the Hedjaz, and belongs to the tribe of the Koreish from which the Prophet himself sprang. For a considerable period the Sultans and Sharifs had acted in harmony, the Sharifs acknowledging the Khalifat of the Sultans in return for general protection and heavy subsidies. In times more remote, however, the Turkish Sultans had not claimed to be Khalifas, and the Hedjaz had not owned their sway. The title of the original Arab Khalifs, who had disappeared, was first assumed by the Sultan of Turkey in 1575.

The reasons for the Sharif's rebellion were stated in a proclamation which he subsequently issued, to have been the proceedings of the Turkish Committee of Union and Progress, their departure from the principles of the *Koran*, their contumelious treatment of the Sultan, their bloody and inhuman outrages on Muslims.[1]

It was natural that the British Government should sympathise with the Sharif. It had become known that the Turks and Germans proposed to make the Hedjaz and Yamen coasts the basis of attacks on British vessels and commerce. The Allies had of course undertaken to respect the safety and sanctity of the Holy Places of Islam in Arabia; but these were now in

[1] See Appendix III.

jeopardy from other sources, and the Hedjaz was in peril of Turco-German military occupation.

The revolt of the Sharif, however, was keenly regretted by some prominent members of the Muslim Indian League. It seemed likely to lead to the desecration of the Holy Places of the Hedjaz, and they resented a telegram which had appeared in a newspaper to the effect that the Calcutta Mussulmans approved of the rebellion. They believed that the Sharif had acted with British encouragement and were unaware of the grave underlying military considerations. They considered the Sharif totally incapable of maintaining independent sovereignty over the ark and shrine of Islam. They convened a public meeting which, on June 27th, passed a resolution condemning the "Arab rebels headed by the Sharif of Mecca *and their sympathisers* as enemies of Islam." Another resolution repudiated "the suggestion conveyed in a Calcutta telegram that any class of Indian Mussulmans could be delighted with the reported Arab rebellion or could view with any feeling other than alarm and disgust the consequences likely to follow therefrom."

All possible publicity was given to these resolutions; but it was explained to the persons aggrieved that agitation of this kind in such circumstances was working on behalf of the King's enemies and must cease. They readily acquiesced. The movement was mainly confined to the educated and politically advanced Muhammadans. It was not taken up by the religious leaders, and therefore did not spread among the masses of the people. It is probable, however, that these would have been impressed had not preventive action been prompt.

In this year in Bengal increasing murders and robberies, committed for the purpose of extracting money to be used in financing revolutionary effort, compelled the Government to order a considerable number of internments under the Defence of India Act, with the result that at last anarchical crime received a decisive check.

We now come to important political events connected with the Home Rule movement which had originated in two assumptions (*a*) that there is already such a bond between the politicians and the peoples of India as that which unites the Irish Home Rule leaders with the majority of their fellow-countrymen; (*b*) that the scales between creeds and castes in India will adjust themselves peacefully if the British Government will only leave them alone. The agitation cannot be clearly understood unless it be described not as an isolated movement, but in connection with certain other events of the year. It is possible that its promoters were influenced by the course of events in Ireland.

On April 22nd, 23rd, and 24th the All-India Congress Committee met at Allahabad, and at private meetings passed certain resolutions which were tentative and were to be discussed in consultation with the committee of the Muslim League. These meetings were presided over by a Congress ex-President, and were attended by an ex-President of the Muslim League, by Mrs. Besant, and by other less prominent persons. After the meetings Mrs. Besant, working from the headquarters of the Theosophical Society at Adyar in Madras, with the openly professed object of awakening the country, busily pushed Home Rule propaganda on the platform by orations, and in the Press by two newspapers and many pamphlets. The spirit of her harangues is apparent from the following quotations:

"I quite realise that when people are asleep, and

especially if they are rather heavy, they do not like the tomtom that goes on all the night through, beating and beating and never stopping. I am an Indian tomtom, waking up all the sleepers so that they may wake and work for their Motherland. That is my task. And they are waking on every side, and the young ones, even more than the old ones, are waking to the possibilities that lie before them. You must remember what India was: you must realise that three thousand years before the time of Christ, India was great in her commerce, great in her trade.

. . . . . .

"Is India different from any other country, that she also may not be proud of her wars, her invasions, her conquests, and her defeats, for India has assimilated every conqueror and has made them contribute to the greatness of herself. I know that the English have not been assimilated, but 2,000 or 3,000 years hence they may be. They have been here but a day or two, only for a poor 150 years. What is that in the 5,000 years recognised by European history of Indian greatness, Indian wealth, and Indian culture? You have no need to be ashamed of India's past, no need to be ashamed of being born an Indian. There is no living country in the world with such a past, no country that can look forward to such a future. For the value of the past is that it shows you how to build for the future; the value of the past for you to-day when you are breathing what Mr. Gokhale called an atmosphere of inferiority; the value of the past is to remind you of what you were; the value of the past is to awaken self-respect; the value of the past is to make that feeling of national pride, without which no nation can be, and no national greatness can accrue. So I point to your past, and that is what makes our antagonists more angry."

Other of her newspaper utterances were considered by the Madras Government to be provocative of racial feeling, and finally she was called on to give pecuniary security under the Press Act for the better conduct of her publications. She soon forfeited the security and, depositing the larger sum required of her for renewed journalism, appealed to the High Court against the order of forfeiture. Her appeal was dismissed, but in the meantime Mr. Tilak had raised his standard.

In May and June he delivered speeches at Belgaum and Ahmednagar in favour of Home Rule which were considered by the Bombay Government to be likely to bring British rule into hatred and contempt. Substantial security for good behaviour for a period of one year was demanded from him by a District Magistrate, but the order was subsequently cancelled by the Bombay High Court, on the ground that the general tenor of the speeches, which were delivered in vernacular, was not such as to justify the prosecution. The following passages from one speech are illustrative of Mr. Tilak's style :

"When the people in the nation become educated and begin to know how they should manage their affairs, it is quite natural for them that they themselves should manage the affairs which are managed for them by others. But the amusing thing in this history of politics is that the above law about twenty-one years has no existence in politics. Though we may perhaps somehow imagine a law enjoining that when you have educated a nation for a hundred years you should give its administration into its hands, it is not possible to enforce it. The people themselves must get this effected. They have a right (to do so). Hence there must be some such arrangement here. Formerly there was some such arrangement to a little extent. Such an arrangement does not exist now. And herein lies the root of all these our demands, the grievances which we have, the want which we feel (and) the inconvenience which we notice in the administration. And the remedy which is proposed after making inquiries about that root in the above manner is called Home Rule. Its name is '*Swarajya.*' To put it briefly, the demand that the management of our (affairs) should be in our hands is the demand for *Swarajya*.

. . . .

"Formerly there were our kingdoms in this country. There were administrators. The proof of this is that before the advent of the English Government in this country there was at least some order; there was no disorder everywhere. One man did not kill another. Since there existed such order, how are we to say that the people are not fit (for powers)? At the present time, science has made progress; knowledge has increased; (and) experience has accumulated in one place. Hence we must have more liberty than before, and we must have become fitter. (But) on the contrary (it is said) we are not fit. Whatever might have been the case in former times, this allegation is utterly false. Better say, (it) is not to be given. (*Cheers.*) What I say is, don't apply the words 'not fit' (to us). At least we shall know that this is not really to be given. We shall get it. But why do we not get it? It is indirectly said that we are not fit. It is to teach you that we have come here. This is admitted. But how long will you teach us? (*Laughter.*) For one generation, two generations, or three generations? Is there any end to this? Or must we, just like this, work under you like slaves till the end? (*Cheers.*) Set some limit. You come to teach us. When we appoint a teacher at home for a boy, we ask him within how many days he would teach him, whether in ten, twenty, or twenty-five years."

. . . .

Mr. Tilak went on to say that the object of saying that Indians were not fit to carry on the administration was to keep them always in slavery. It must be noted that such harangues are generally delivered to town audiences largely composed of lawyers, educationists, and students. A notable feature of this campaign was to attract and enlist the young. The bitter lessons taught by action in Bengal on these lines some years before were disregarded.

The Home Rule propaganda appealed in a marked manner to students and schoolboys. Mrs. Besant formally established her League on September 3rd, 1916. The issue of her paper, *New India*, dated October 11th, gave her prospectus. It asserted that fifty branches had been established in the principal provinces of India (excepting the Punjab); that her papers and pamphlets were being translated into the vernaculars; that the membership was between 2,000 and 3,000; that "Home Rule Day"—September 14th—was enthusiastically celebrated by a number of branches, as well as by a great meeting held at Madras in the Gokhale Hall of the Young Men's Indian Association—an organisation founded by Mrs. Besant. It stated that the members of the League mostly belonged to Madras and Bombay.

Political excitement intensified among the English-educated classes; and under the Defence of India Act Mrs. Besant was formally forbidden to enter the Bombay Presidency. Later on she was also prohibited from visiting the Central Provinces. She did not, however, relax her activities. Their general object was to spread the doctrine that British rule in India, as then established, was injurious to liberty, and that a strong and effective demand for Home Rule must be organised without delay.[1]

[1] On behalf of the Secretary of State for India it was asserted in the House of Commons, on July 25th, 1917, that "the action taken against Mrs. Besant was due to her activities, such as misrepresenting the acts and intentions of Government, and was not due to the ideals professed in their justification."

Before proceeding further with the history of the Home Rule League, I must state that, in October 1916, nineteen elected Indian members of the Imperial Legislative Council submitted a memorandum of proposed reforms to the Supreme Government. The memorandum noted that "the people of India have good reason to be grateful to England for the great progress in her material resources and the widening of her intellectual and political outlook and for the steady, if slow, advances in her national life commencing with the Charter Act of India of 1833." It affirmed the "very limited character" of the Indian element introduced into the administration by the Reforms of 1909. It stated that the Legislative Councils were mere advisory bodies "without any power of effective control over the Government Imperial or Provincial." It stated that the people of India were placed "under great and galling disabilities from which the other members of the British Empire were exempt." These disabilities had reduced them to a state of "utter helplessness." It referred to such grievances as the Arms Act and the system of indentured emigration [1] into certain British Colonies. It asserted that the loyalty of the country during the war entitled India to a position of comradeship, not subordination, to "Government that is acceptable to the people because responsible to them." It suggested specific reforms on Congress lines, and practically declared for parliamentary government in India.

It is useful to note one argument which was at this time advanced by the more enthusiastic Indian politicians with considerable effect on their countrymen. They pointed to the prospect of federation of the British Empire after the war, and deduced the consequent pro-

[1] Indentured emigration has now been abolished.

bability that unless India strongly asserted herself, she would become the subject not only of Great, but of Greater Britain, of the Colonies "with their declared superiority of white races and their unblushing policies of Government against all coloured races." But the inclusion of representatives of India in the Imperial War Conference largely exploded this alarm.

Except in the case of the Muhammadan aberration already described, the attitude of Indian politicians toward the enemies of Britain remained solid throughout 1916. But their attitude toward the system of British government established in India became increasingly restless under the strenuous and persistent influence of the Home Rule propaganda. Mrs. Besant stood for the president's chair at the December Congress which was to take place in Lucknow and received a considerable number of votes, but was defeated by Mr. Ambika Charan Mazumdar, an ex-schoolmaster from Eastern Bengal, a pleader, and a veteran Congressman. So electric became the political atmosphere, that the Government of the United Provinces addressed a letter to the president and secretary of the Congress Reception Committee calling their attention to the undesirable nature of speeches which had recently been made in other parts of India, and calling on them to do their best to prevent anything of the kind occurring in Lucknow. They were plainly warned that if the law were transgressed, necessary action would be taken. The letter was of course resented, but probably it strengthened the hands of the soberer politicians and contributed toward the peace and quietness which characterised the subsequent Congress proceedings.

In November representatives of the Congress and the Muslim League had met in Calcutta and had decided to accept the Home Rule programme. As to special

Muhammadan electorates they could not then agree, and the question was postponed for further consideration at Lucknow.

An important political event of the year was the announcement, on August 7th, of the intended experiment of raising a double-company of Bengalis for military service. The announcement was received with enthusiasm by all loyal gentlemen in Bengal. The double-company afterwards developed into a regiment.

The last week of December will be for ever memorable in the history of Indian politics, for then it was that the Congress Moderates and academic Extremists proclaimed their reunion, and the principal leaders of the Congress and the Muslim League, finally composing their principal differences, alike declared for Home Rule. The proceedings of both bodies were orderly, and the resolutions and speeches had been carefully considered.

The Chairman of the Congress Reception Committee, a Lucknow pleader, announced that leaders of both bodies had formulated a scheme of reforms to be pressed upon the attention of the British Parliament and people after the conclusion of the war, in the name of United India, " in order that we may have a controlling voice in the direction of our internal affairs." Indian patriotism was the greatest guarantee of India's loyalty, for the realisation of her most cherished hopes depended upon the continuance of British rule.

The President, Mr. Mazumdar, in a very long address stigmatised the Morley reforms, for which so much gratitude had been expressed in 1909, as " mere moonshine," and, in a brief historical review, stated that the East India Company, " after a hundred years of misrule," had been at last overthrown by a military rising which transferred the government of the country from the Company to the Crown.

"It was this Government," he said, "which, actuated by its benevolent intentions, introduced by slow degrees various reforms and changes which gradually broadened and liberalised the administration, and restored peace and order throughout the country. In its gradual development it introduced, though in a limited form, self-government in the local concerns of the people, admitted the children of the soil to a limited extent into the administration of the country, and reformed the Councils by introducing an appreciable element of representation in them. It has annihilated time and space by the construction of railways and the establishment of telegraphic communication. It has established a form of administration which in its integrity and purity could well vie with that of any other civilised country in the world, while the security of life and property which it conferred was, until lately, a boon of which any people may be justly proud."

In his qualification Mr. Mazumdar evidently referred to measures adopted under the Defence of India Act,[1] and especially to internments of persons considered by Government, on carefully tested evidence, to belong to revolutionary criminal gangs. In fact, however, had he and his friends ever organised a serious and concentrated non-official campaign against the propaganda which breeds revolutionary crime, no internments would have been required.

He went on to complain that now the Administration had resolved itself into a barren and sterile bureaucracy which was "despotism condensed and crystallised."[2] But, he argued, this despotism had, in fact, worked up to its own subversion for "from the Queen's

[1] See page 98.

[2] This is a curiously misleading statement. The administration is subject not only to vigilant criticism and supervision, but to elaborate systems of laws and regulations.

Proclamation of 1858 down to Lord Morley's Reforms of 1909, the British Parliament had not taken a single step which was not calculated finally to overthrow this despotic form of government. The education given to the people, the system of local self-government introduced, and the elective principle recognised in the higher Councils of the Empire, had all tended to undermine the old system of government." He animadverted on the educational policy initiated by Lord Curzon's Universities Act, and condemned the working of the Defence Act. The sovereign remedy for all evils was Representative Government alias Home Rule alias *Swaraj*. Self-government should come after the war because it must pass through a preparatory process. It is through failure that success is achieved in practical politics. As regards the masses, the Congress had always pleaded for their amelioration, *and would there not always be the paramount authority of Government to correct abuses and remedy injustice wherever committed?* The recommendations of the Indian Public Services Commission would be of no consequence, for a bureaucratic administration could in no circumstances be liberalised. Anarchism had its roots deep in economic and political conditions. It was due to misrule, and could only be removed by conciliation. Repression was useless.[1]

[1] It is instructive to consider Mr. Mazumdar's words in the light of the state of affairs revealed by the Governor of Bengal in a speech at Dacca on July 25th, 1917:

"Last year Lord Carmichael spoke to you very frankly upon the question of revolutionary crimes committed by men whose object is the overthrowing of the existing Government in this country. He gave you figures of outrages which had, he believed, been committed with revolutionary ends in view from 1907 up to that time. He told you that no less than 39 murders and over 100 dacoities had been committed—a sufficiently melancholy tale for any Governor to have to tell, and I regret to say that this gruesome catalogue has been added to even during the

India must have a place in the coming Federal Council of the Empire. Their demands would be—(I enumerate the most important):

"(1) India must cease to be a dependency and be raised to the status of a self-governing State as an equal partner with equal rights and responsibilities as an independent unit of the Empire.

"(2) In any scheme of readjustment after the war, India should have a fair representation in the Federal Council like the Colonies of the Empire.

"(3) India must be governed from Delhi and Simla, and not from Whitehall or Downing Street. The Council of the Secretary of State should be either abolished or its constitution so modified as to admit of substantial Indian representation on it. Of the two Under-Secretaries of State for India, one should be an Indian, and the salary of the Secretary of State should be placed on the British estimates, as in the case of the Secretary for the Colonies. The Secretary of State for India should, however, have no more powers over the Government of India than those exercised by the Secretary for the Colonies in the case of the Dominions. India must have complete autonomy, financial, legislative, as well as administrative.

"(4) The Government of India is the most vital point in the proposed reforms. It is the fountain-head of all the local administrations, and unless we can ensure

short period of my own rule. . . . Widespread and carefully organised though the conspiracy was there shown to be, the experience of its ramifications and the knowledge of its methods which have been gained during the year that has elapsed have shown that it is even more widespread and carefully organised than was known at that time. The second thing that I would commend to your thoughtful consideration is that without the powers conferred upon Government by the Defence of India Act of 1915, it would have been impossible for Government to have obtained control of the movement and to have given to the people of Bengal the comparative immunity from serious revolutionary outrages which they have recently enjoyed."

The Report of the Sedition Committee amply confirms these words.

its progressive character, any effective reform of the Local Governments would be impossible. Thus the Services must be completely separated from the State, and no member of any Service should be a member of the Government. The knowledge and experience of competent members of a Service may be utilised in the departments, but they should not be allowed to be members of the Executive Council or the Cabinet of the Government itself.

"(5) The Executive Government must vest in a Governor-General and ministers, half of whom should be Indians elected by the Imperial Legislative Council and members of that body.

"(6) The annual budget should be introduced into the Legislative Council as a money bill, and, except the military estimates, the entire budget should be subject to the vote of the Council.

"(7) The Provincial Governments should be perfectly autonomous, each province developing and enjoying its own resources, subject only to a contribution toward the maintenance of the supreme Government.

"(8) A Provincial Administration should be vested, as in the case of the supreme Government, in a Governor with a cabinet not less than one-half of whom should be Indians elected by the non-official elected Indian members of its Legislative Council.

"(9) India should have a national militia to which all the races should be eligible under proper safeguards; all should be allowed to volunteer for service under such conditions as may be found necessary for the maintenance of efficiency and discipline. The commissioned ranks of the army should be thrown open to His Majesty's Indian subjects.

"(10) All local bodies should have elected chairmen of their own."

Mr. Mazundar would agree to no indefinite postponement of satisfaction of his demands. He concluded with a special appeal to the young among his audience. They were to take their place in the bloodless revolution which was going on. "Widespread unrest would inevitably follow light-hearted treatment of the solemn pledges and assurances on which the people had built their hopes."

There is a discussion of the main principles of this scheme in Chapter VII of the Montagu-Chelmsford Report.

In the course of his address the President had alluded to the "sufferings" of Mr. Tilak and Mrs. Besant, and these two persons supported a resolution moved by Mr. Surendra Nath Banerjee requesting that His Majesty the King-Emperor might be pleased soon "to issue a proclamation announcing that it is the aim and intention of British policy to confer self-government on India at an early date." The Congress should also demand that a definite step should be taken toward self-government by granting the reforms enumerated by Mr. Mazumdar.

Mr. Banerjee had been the leader of the Moderates in the Surat Congress. His speech was remarkable in striking an entirely separate note. The ancestors of the Hindus, he said, had been the spiritual teachers of mankind. Their mission had been arrested. Its retardation must be removed so that they might be able to rescue mankind from the gross materialism and perverse moral culture which had heaped the battle-fields of Europe with hecatombs of dead. But they must be fully equipped before they could fulfil their high commission. The indispensable equipment was self-government. Their work was not political, but moral and religious. Therefore they were invincible. They were now within measurable distance of victory. The promised land was in sight.

Mr. Tilak, who had met with a rapturous reception, both at the railway station and on arrival in the Congress *pandal*, said that the ovation which he had received was obviously intended for the principles for which he had been fighting. They were embodied in the resolution moved by Mr. Banerjee. Mrs. Besant spoke of the intolerable condition of things under which Indians were living. Parliament would pass an Act granting freedom. India's belief rested on England and not on the bureaucracy.

The resolution was carried, and the President announced that a copy thereof would be sent to His Majesty the King-Emperor.

I have summarised the prominent proceedings at this most important Congress. It will be seen that they constituted a remarkable leap forward from the position taken up by Mr. Sinha in the previous year, and a remarkable triumph for Mr. Tilak and Mrs. Besant. They did more. They showed that absolute political independence had become the professed ideal of Moderate and Extreme politicians alike, and that Government was confronted with a more definite situation than any that had hitherto presented itself in this connection. There was a note in the proceedings which implied that if the Extremists had adopted the ideal of the Moderates, they were leading the latter, so far as the Congress was concerned, into the very paths against which Mr. Gokhale warned his countrymen in 1909—the paths trodden by the new school of political thought to which he alluded. On December 20th, 1907, Lord Morley had written to Lord Minto—"The news has just come in that the Congress so far from being flat, has gone to pieces, which is the exact opposite of flat no doubt. For it means, I suppose, the victory of Extremist over Moderate, going no further at this stage than the breaking up of the Congress, but pointing to a future stage in which the Congress will have become an Extremist organisation." This future stage had arrived, but later it led, and was bound to lead, to a renewed split.

The Congress agreed to call on Mrs. Besant's Home Rule League for co-operation; and after long private discussion Congress and Muslim Leaguers reached an agreement as to proportions of political representation on the Legislative Councils of the future. The agreement was supplemented by the condition that if in any province two-thirds of either community did not want a Bill or a measure, that Bill or measure should be dropped by both communities. They could not agree as to proportions on local bodies. The Hindu Sabha, or general assembly, which met in the same week, for the purpose of dealing with religious, communal, and social questions, and was largely attended, protested strongly against any Hindu weakening on this subject.

The chairman of the Reception Committee of the Muslim League, a Lucknow barrister, enlarged on the determination of Indians to devote themselves to and support the British Imperial cause until it should be triumphantly vindicated on the field of battle. The Muslim League must co-operate with other communities for the attainment of self-government or Home Rule, and the minority must and would be safeguarded. The speaker need not undertake a detailed review of the administrative sins and shortcomings "which, like the poor, have always been with us." He referred to the Press Act, the Defence Act, and certain internments.

The address of the president, Mr. Muhammad Ali Jinnah, a Bombay barrister, was, in spite of some rapid skating over thin ice, one of the ablest speeches delivered during these days of oratory. He said that the Muhammadan gaze was, like the Hindu gaze, fixed upon the future. The decisions which they then arrived at would go forth with all the force and weight that could legitimately be claimed by the chosen leaders of 70,000,000 of Indian Muhammadans. He commented in moving terms on the war and on the issues at stake therein. He remarked on the necessity for reconstruction after the war and on the difficulties of the Indian problem.

"There is," he said, "first the great fact of the British rule in India with its Western character and standards of administration, which, while retaining absolute power of initiative, direction, and decision, has maintained for many decades unbroken peace and order in the land, administered even-handed justice, brought the Indian mind, through a widespread system of Western education, into contact with the thoughts and ideals of the West, and thus led to the birth of a great and living movement for the intellectual and moral regeneration of the people. . . . Secondly, there is the fact of the existence of a powerful, unifying process—the most vital and interesting result of Western education in the country—which is creating, out of the diverse mass of race and creed, a new India fast growing to unity of thought, purpose, and outlook, responsive to new appeals of territorial patriotism and nationality, stirring with new energy and aspiration, and becoming daily more purposeful and eager to recover its birthright to direct its own affairs and govern itself. To put it briefly, we have a powerful and efficient bureaucracy of British officers responsible only to the British Parliament, governing, with methods known as benevolent despotism, a people that have grown fully conscious of their destiny and are peacefully struggling for political freedom. This is the Indian problem in a nutshell. The task of British statesmanship is to find a prompt, peaceful, and enduring solution of this problem."

He described the internal situation in the following terms:

"We have a vast continent inhabited by 315 millions of people sprung from various racial stocks, inheriting various cultures, and professing a variety of religious creeds. This stupendous human group, thrown together under one physical and political environment, is still in various stages of intellectual and moral growth. All this means a great diversity of outlook, purpose, and endeavour." Indian Nationalists were not afraid of frankly admitting that difficulties beset their path, but these difficulties were "already vanishing before the forces which are developing in the new spirit."

Indians, he concluded, were determined to prove their fitness for self-government. The Hindu-Muslim *rapprochement* was the sign of the birth of an United India. The scheme of reforms promulgated by the Congress must be adopted, and a Bill must be introduced into the British Parliament to give effect to it. He entirely identified the Muhammadan political objectives with those of the Hindus, and he urged that no decisions should be arrived at by supreme authority without the publication of proposals in India for public criticism and opinions. He briefly asked that Muhammadans might be allowed to choose their own Caliph. He thanked Government for the assurance that the Holy Places of Islam would receive special consideration. He concluded by applying the recent utterances of the Prime Minister regarding Ireland to the Indian situation. Muhammadans must work and trust in God, so that they might leave to their children the heritage of freedom.

The resolutions adopted by the League closely corresponded to those passed by the Congress. It is remarkable that Mr. Bipin Chandra Pal, a well-known Bengali Hindu agitator, was asked to speak on the subject of the Defence Act, and was received with enthusiasm. He remarked that there were no anarchists in

Bengal. There were revolutionary patriots. Revolutionary patriotism would never have been born if there had been no attempt to stifle evolutionary patriotism.

It is important to notice that in spite of the ambitious character of some of the resolutions passed at the Congress and Muslim League meetings, the behaviour of the audiences was generally unexceptionable. The Lieutenant-Governor was present for a brief period on one day of each session and was well received. The proceedings were characterised by orderliness, good humour, and absence of unpleasant demonstrations. The League audiences were far smaller than those of the Congress, and consisted partly of persons who seemed hardly to comprehend all the speeches or subjects referred to by the various speakers. In fact, Mr. Jinnah's representation of himself and his friends as the chosen leaders of 70,000,000 of Mussulmans was decidedly misleading. They had been elected by a small fraction of the 70,000,000. The sessions had been preceded by a regular split among the Muhammadans of the Punjab, and by signs of a split among those of the United Provinces. But the Lucknow Leaguers worked the machine and the finances. They were solid for union with the Congress and carried the meetings, but their action was disapproved by many of their co-religionists, who consider that, whatever politicians may agree upon, the Hindu and Muhammadan masses will, for years to come, need an unbiased arbiter; for in the ordinary life of the ordinary Hindu or Muhammadan, religion and religious susceptibility still play as vigorous a part as they played years ago.[1]

Special efforts had been previously made by the

[1] The great bone of contention is cow-sacrifice by Muhammadans on the occasion of the Bakr-Id festival. This is abhorrent to Hindus, who are taught by their religion to hold the cow sacred.

politicians to enlist the sympathy and help of the students. These efforts naturally obtained a wide success, and the behaviour of all the "volunteers" enlisted was excellent. Many Indian ladies attended the Congress meetings. A noteworthy outcome of the week was the declared determination of Indian Nationalists to push their demands for self-government by introducing a Bill into the Imperial Parliament. There can be no doubt that favoured by the sense of self-esteem produced by the loyal and gallant conduct of Indian soldiers in the war, the general effect of these meetings was to extend the influence of nationalism in the country.

On his return journey to Bombay Mr. Tilak lectured at Cawnpore to a large mass meeting on Home Rule, and met with a remarkably enthusiastic reception ascribed by one of his principal hearers to "the sacrifices that he had made."

CHAPTER V

THE DECLARATION OF AUGUST 20TH, 1917

WHILE the politicians had been concentrating their energies on the attainment of constitutional changes, and Mrs. Besant had been declaiming against the "intolerable condition of things in which Indians lived," the country had been profoundly calm. Although for more than two years the Great War had distracted the world; although in other countries bloodshed and misery, oppression and civil dissension had reigned supreme; India, the ancient battle-ground of Asia, had, in spite of the intermittent and malignant efforts of desperate revolutionaries, throughout remained free from any sort of serious disturbance. The masses had followed their customary callings with their customary placid contentment; the aristocracy had lived their usual sheltered lives; the lawyers had pocketed their fees; journalism had thriven; trade, commerce and business had suffered only from such disturbance as was inevitable during a great world-strain. Markets had at first been affected, but had improved; industrial activities were expanding. The seasons had been good, and the rural population was prosperous.

Only from the martial classes, and especially from the martial classes of the Punjab, was the war exacting sacrifices of severity. The provision of recruits, labour, supplies, railway material, munitions, was adding to the ordinarily heavy tasks of the Government of India, but had not prevented it from taking thought for the removal of Indian grievances and the promotion of Indian prosperity. And among grave preoccupations, it had been seeking means for the practical solution of the difficult problems presented by the much-desired furtherance of Indian industrial enterprise.

Since the beginning of this century a popular demand had grown up and increased in India for the development of industries and for vigorous action by the State to produce this development. The demand is an expression of political, social, and economic needs. For many reasons greater industrial activity is desirable. Young men of the English-educated classes are increasingly crowding into the traditional professions of their order, government service, law, medicine, and teaching. Commercial openings are comparatively few, for commercial enterprise on a considerable scale has hitherto been rare among Indians. Economically greater national wealth is desirable, not only for itself, but as a condition necessary for the development of national life.

India was and is mainly an agricultural country. Only 9·5 per cent. of her population are found in towns as against the 78·1 per cent. of England and Wales in pre-war days. Agriculture is her great industry, though it is yielding a far smaller return than it should and, with more skill and applied knowledge, would yield. But India had once, and has still to a shrunken extent, her own minor industries. In rural India, before the days of the steamship and the railway, the village was more or less self-sufficing. It grew its own food and supplied its own simple wants, its agricultural implements and household utensils; and beyond the village in a few larger centres of trade, situated on important land routes, navigable rivers or the coast, a market existed for rarer and costlier articles which largely found their way to foreign countries. Traders and artisans clustered round the courts of Indian princes; rich silks, jewellery, articles of wood, ivory and metal, were manufactured, sometimes of exquisite workmanship. Communications were difficult, however, and industries of this nature were mainly confined to the manufacture of commodities the costliness of which was sufficient to counterbalance the expense and risk of carriage to a distance. The invention of steam power wrought a complete revolution in this simple economy. The opening of the Suez Canal and the extension of communications by rail and sea encouraged the import of foreign machine-made goods, while it stimulated the cultivation of raw materials for export. The market for the products of the Indian artisan declined. The nature of his calling was modified.

In the application of machinery to industrial development, India has begun to follow Europe, but tardily. Europeans introduced and have practically monopolised the jute manufacturing industry of Calcutta. The first cotton mill in India was set up by a Parsi; and in the cotton spinning and weaving industry in the Bombay Presidency Indians have always occupied a prominent place. There was no systematic investigation, however, of the problems peculiar to India, and there was no attempt on the part of Government or the people to make India economically self-supporting. The general policy was to procure from abroad what could be obtained thence more cheaply and to accept the situation.

As already remarked, however, Indians have been prominent as mill-owners in Bombay, and there it was that the late Mr. Justice Ranade, the social reformer, in a paper read in 1893 before an Industrial Conference at Poona, observed that some of his countrymen were recognising the importance of adopting modern methods of manufacture and the necessity of reviving and encouraging indigenous industries. His expectations of progress were over-sanguine. Early in the present century, however, the demand for "Swadeshi" or indigenous industries, which started in Bengal in association with Bengali politics, was considerably intensified by observation of the economic progress of Japan. A number of factory enterprises were undertaken, especially in Bengal, mostly on a small scale, but being devoid of business knowledge or direction, as well as of substantial pecuniary support, these generally failed. For some time the Government stood aside from the effort, content to trust to technical education and the example of British industries, but rapidly it grew obvious that India possessed materials for a large and varied industrial output, and that to call forth these materials would be a great and beneficent work for which far more capital and enterprise were urgently needed. Money, competent managers of labour, expert guidance, were all essential. It became equally plain that unless a strong lead were taken by Government, these would not be found, even though the possibility of the large-scale enterprise in India had been established by some jute and cotton mills as well as by the Tata Iron Works, "a veritable steel city with trans-Atlantic completeness of equipment," which has sprung up within the present century.[1] Progressive Indians frankly expected material State assistance toward commercial and industrial progress.

With the outbreak of the war the political and economic importance of raising India from the position of a mere exporter of raw produce was soon emphasised.

[1] "The really great and typical advance of industry in India has been the Tata Iron and Steel Company." Evidence of Sir John Hewett before the Parliamentary Committee.

The success of practical demonstration following on investigation had been previously evidenced in the case of agriculture. It was obvious that this process might be extended to industries. The question of industrial improvement was raised in the Imperial Legislative Council Sessions of 1915, and it was decided that a Commission should be appointed to consider how it could be effected. Some Indian members were anxious for measures of tariff protection, but these were specifically excluded from the terms of reference, although tariff protection is one of the main objectives of Indian Nationalists. A strong British and Indian Commission was constituted under the presidency of Sir Thomas Holland, K.C.I.E., who had been Director of the Indian Geological Survey, and after retirement from office had taken up work as Professor in the University of Manchester and as a consulting geologist.

The proceedings of the Commission were followed with considerable interest. Recognising their lack of technical knowledge and of instruction in the business side of industry, as well as the difficulty of raising funds, the advocates of indigenous enterprise asked for an extreme measure of Government help in regard to both technical education and the grant of special facilities to particular industries. They also requested financial assistance by way of subscription of shares or guarantees. The leading business men made practical suggestions regarding individual difficulties, and a great deal of information of all kinds was obtained. There were, however, some complaints that the Commission was a device on the part of Government for postponing the grant of solid assistance to Indian industries, or for providing openings for British capital, and very strong exception was taken to the exclusion of tariff questions from the terms of reference.

One important result early accrued from the investigations of this Commission. A Munitions Board was constituted, under the presidency of Sir Thomas Holland, which worked toward co-ordinating Government demands for all war supplies, except food and forage, as well as assisting manufacturers to deal with these demands. Organisation had been needed both among Indian industrialists and among the consuming departments of Government with reference to war conditions. There had been considerable lack of knowledge among manufacturers as to the present and probable requirements of Government; and supplies had been purchased, both by public departments and by private firms, from the United Kingdom and elsewhere which could with more contrivance have been provided in the country. All these shortcomings were vigorously combated, and Government indents began to pass through the hands of the Munitions Board, who, with the help of local controllers in all provinces, obtained information as to the possibilities of manufacture, passed on to industrialists information regarding Government demands, and assisted them, so far as possible, in meeting requirements which could be dealt with by some modification of the existing machinery or process. It was hoped that by the conclusion of peace this Board would have created a Government Stores department, and have itself developed into an industrial department which would ensure the placing in India of the largest possible number of Government and private orders for manufactured articles while, by affording information and advice, it would assist manufacturers to meet those orders.

The Report of the Commission was published late in the year 1918, is now under the consideration of the Secretary of State, and should lay the foundation of an advance in Indian industries which may greatly extend the field of employment for the Indian professional classes.

The Government had also been examining another question much debated by politicians, the possibility of substituting a less objectionable scheme for the system of indentured emigration of Indian labourers to certain British Crown-Colonies. There had long been some confusion in the political mind between abuses arising from this system and the exclusion of free Indians from the self-governing Dominions. In fact no Crown-Colony has ever imported Indian indentured labour and simultaneously restricted free Indian immigration, and no self-governing Dominion except Natal has ever imported indentured Indian labour. Export of such labour to Natal was stopped some years ago by the Government of India; as they were dissatisfied with the treatment of free Indians by Natal colonists. In declaiming against the export of indentured labour to Crown-Colonies, Indian Nationalists have been influenced partly by the exclusion of free Indian immigrants from self-governing Dominions. Lord Hardinge had said that the then existing export arrangements must be maintained until the new conditions under which labour should be permitted to proceed to the Colonies had been worked out in conjunction with the Colonial Office and the Colonies concerned. But some politicians were pressing for early solution, and their representations were being considered by the Government of India in a sympathetic spirit. A temporary solution was found during the February sessions of the Imperial Legislative Council.

These sessions require careful notice, for they were of exceptional interest and importance. They commenced, in fact, a period which has not yet concluded,

10

a period of strenuous efforts by the Government of India to pacify political excitement. These attempts have met with considerable disappointment. The arbitrament now lies with the Imperial Parliament.

The sessions were opened by His Excellency Lord Chelmsford, who announced that the Report of the Royal Commission on Public Services, appointed in 1912, which had just been published, would be carefully considered. The major questions, among which the increased employment of Indians in the higher branches of the services was one of the most important, would not be prejudiced or delayed by lesser problems. He also announced that the expediency of broadening the basis of government and the demand of Indians to play a greater share in the conduct of public affairs were receiving attention. Progress must be on well-considered and circumspect lines. Subject to these considerations, sympathetic response would be made to the existing spirit of progress. The Government of India had addressed a despatch to the Secretary of State on this subject in the previous autumn. The Viceroy had noted that the reforms proposed in the Memorandum of the nineteen members had received endorsement by resolutions passed by the National Congress. His Majesty's Government were at present entirely occupied on matters connected with the war, and would not be able to give speedy attention to the despatch.

A further opportunity of service had been offered to India by the announcement of an Indian War Loan which would soon be launched. His Excellency referred to the devoted and loyal assistance given by the Ruling Chiefs towards the prosecution of the war, to the flow of contributions, and offers of service from their States. He concluded by announcing the impending organisation of an Indian Defence Force, which would include

Indians, and the representation of India by three selected members at the coming special War Conference in London. These announcements were received with enthusiasm.

On February 21st, the Commander-in-Chief introduced the Defence Force Bill. Its provisions included voluntary enrolment for Indians of the non-martial and political classes. They were welcomed by Indian members of the Council.

The Finance Member, Sir William Meyer, announced on March 1st that, in pursuance of two resolutions moved by Indian non-official members and carried in the Council on September 8th, 1914, and February 24th, 1915, the Government of India had informed the Home Government of their willingness to borrow the largest sum that could be raised as a War Loan, to make a special contribution of £100,000,000 to the war, and to put forward proposals for increasing Indian resources in order to meet the consequent recurring liabilities. Sir William Meyer pointed out that this contribution amounted to nearly double the total Imperial revenue as it stood before the war. He announced that one method of meeting the contribution would be the raising of the import on cotton fabrics from 3½ to 7½ per cent., the general Indian tariff rate. But the cotton excise duty would remain 3½ per cent. A grievance of twenty years' standing,[1] which had virtually meant protection in favour of Lancashire, was thus removed, and the removal was not effected without a strong and bitter protest from the Lancashire cotton trade. But the action of the Government of India was powerfully upheld by the then Secretary of State, Mr. Austen Chamberlain, both in replying to a deputation and in the House of Commons. It was finally agreed

[1] See page 53.

there that the arrangement should stand, but should be subject to the review of the fiscal system of the whole Empire which would follow the war. Some passages from Mr. Chamberlain's reply to the Lancashire deputation show how much depended and depends on a just settlement of this and similar questions. "Do not underrate the strength of Indian feeling on this question. You said: 'If indeed it was necessary to raise the Customs duty, why did not you also raise the excise'? Well, you have been satisfied for twenty years with the arrangements made by the late Lord Wolverhampton, and afterwards modified by Lord George Hamilton. For all those twenty years the settlement which you have found satisfactory has been an open sore in India. It is twenty years ago that Lord Lansdowne used words which were quoted in the debates of those times by Sir Henry Fowler, and I venture to read them to you to-day, for, if they were true twenty years ago, they are of tenfold greater force and truth to-day. He said: 'There has never been a moment when it was more necessary to counteract the impression that our financial policy in India is dictated by selfish considerations. It is a gross libel to say, and I hope this is true to-day, that either of the great political parties of this country will for the sake of passing advantage deny to the people of India the fair play which they expect.'"

Sir William Meyer's words regarding the raising of the cotton import duties were welcomed with warm enthusiasm, and his announcement of the £100,000,000 loan was received with a single questioning murmur.

In a speech which wound up the Sessions His Excellency the Viceroy invited non-official members to co-operate with the Government of India in organised efforts to stimulate industrial and agricultural development, reminding them of the unlimited possibilities of usefulness in these directions, and impressing on them the importance of securing a maximum response to the War Loan. He recommended the new Defence Force measures. He referred to the imposition of the extra duty on cotton goods, reminding them that the Home Government had decided that this would be considered afresh when the fiscal arrangements of the Empire were reviewed as a whole after the war, but stating that what had passed in England should inspire confidence that when that review took place, Indian interests would be stoutly defended.

His Excellency further reminded the Council that, as a consequence of a recent *communiqué*, indentured emigration to Fiji and the West Indies, the only colonies for which the system had survived up to the war, was now at an end, and would probably not recommence. Free labour emigration to Ceylon and Malaya must be restricted by war exigencies. He announced that a Commission which had been appointed to inquire into the educational problems presented by the Calcutta University would meet in the following November. He concluded by reading a message of gratitude from the Premier of the United Kingdom for India's financial contribution to the war. Thus closed a pleasant and harmonious session.

The policy of the Government had been markedly conciliatory and the barometer seemed set fair. But the proceedings of the Imperial Legislative Council generally reflect the least turbid political moods. There are always persons busy outside whose unceasing object is to prevent the confidence and co-operation for which His Excellency had so earnestly appealed. On March 5th he had received a deputation which asked for repeal of the Press Act, and his reply to this body exposes so clearly the slanders and misrepresentations with which his Government was wrestling, that I give its prominent passages in a separate appendix.[1] Unfortunately the appeal with which it concluded fell on ears slow to hear.

Dissatisfaction was expressed with the conditions for recruitment of Indians under the Defence Force Bill; and for some time very few took advantage of the new opportunities offered. It had been announced that 6,000 were required. Within the first two months after the passing of the Bill only 300 were enrolled. Then a further appeal was issued by Government acknowledging that the conditions were open in some respects to criticism, stating that the question of Commissions was under consideration, and promising sympathetic treatment to all who should come forward. The conditions were to some extent altered, and the period originally fixed for enrolment was extended. The later response to this call on the part of the educated community was disappointing.

In the meantime the Home Rule campaign, which had been approved by the Congress and Muslim League, continued under the leadership of Mrs. Besant. The arguments which she employed in pleading her cause were published in her paper *New India*. Their nature will be apparent further on. Their influence upon the political public and Press was assisted by various speeches and lectures.

In June a *communiqué* was issued by the Government of Madras stating that, in the exercise of the powers given him under the Defence of India rules, the Governor in Council directed the service of orders on this lady and her two principal lieutenants, prohibiting them from attending or taking part in any meeting, or

[1] See Appendix IV.

from delivering any lecture, from making any speech, and from publishing or procuring the publication of any writing or speech composed by them, placing their correspondence under censorship, and directing that after the expiry of a brief prescribed period, they should take up their residence in one of various specified healthy localities, ceasing to reside at and near the city of Madras.

Mrs. Besant took leave of her public in a letter to the Press, describing herself as having been "drafted into the modern equivalent for the Middle Ages *oubliette*." Her real crime was that she had awakened in India national self-respect.

"Indian labour is wanted for the foreign firms. Indian capital is being drained away by the War Loan, which is to bring no freedom to India, if the autocracy has its way. Indian taxation to pay the interest on the War Loan will be crushing. When that comes, India will realise why I have striven for Home Rule after the war. Only by that can she be saved from ruin, from becoming a nation of coolies for the enrichment of others."

It is possible—and I have heard it asserted—that the internment of Mrs. Besant would not have awakened the excitement which it did awaken among her friends and followers had it not followed on speeches by the provincial heads of the Punjab and Madras which had been directed towards allaying the excitement and moderating the expectations caused by the Home Rule propaganda. These speeches [1] were construed as heralding a course of repression, and it was represented that Mrs. Besant's internment was the first step on that road.

[1] See Appendix V for an extract from the speech by Sir Michael O'Dwyer.

A non-official member of the Imperial Legislative Council announced in a Press interview:—"I take it she (Mrs. Besant) will be allowed to go on with her work. If she is exposed to suffering in that cause, thousands of Indians who have not been able to see eye to eye with her in all things will think it their duty to stand by her and to follow her." The same note was struck by many newspaper articles. An appeal was made to the Government of India to procure a reversal of the Madras orders; and when this failed, a wide agitation followed among the political classes both in the Madras Presidency and elsewhere. "Passive resistance" even was proposed and discussed. And while the sentiment was sincere among those who genuinely shared Mrs. Besant's creed and were aware of her considerable gifts of money to Hindu interests, it is probable that numbers of persons attended meetings on the subject who knew and cared little or nothing about Mrs. Besant and her proceedings. The issue of the *Non-Brahman* newspaper of Madras, dated July 15th, thus described some methods employed:

> "We can also assure the Government that Home Rule emissaries go about convening meetings and sending telegrams and cablegrams all round. It is this false nature of the agitation that detracts from its value. . . . But the newspaper accounts exaggerate, and there is the inevitable leading article."

And yet what were the facts? To what work had Mrs. Besant devoted her energies at a time when the Government by law established had particularly appealed for loyal assistance from all classes?

What spirit had she expected to call forth from impressionable young India when she published the following passages referring to Indian revolutionaries?

"Desperate they broke away from all control of their elders, began to conspire, and numbers of them have conspired ever since. Some have been hanged; some were sent to the living death of the Andaman Islands; some were imprisoned here. Now the students watch with amazement the Premier of Great Britain rejoicing over the results of the similar action of young Russian men and women who conspired and blew up trains and assassinated a Tsar, and who are now applauded as martyrs, and the still living of whom are being brought back in triumph to the Russia whose freedom they have made possible. The names which were execrated are held sacred and sufferings are crowned with triumph." [1]

And again, when she published her article, "The Great Betrayal," [2] in the *New India* issue of May 2nd, 1917, was her action calculated to promote loyal

[1] Extract from the issue of *New India*, dated May 23rd, 1917.

[2] "That vote (at the Imperial War Conference) compels India to remain a plantation, that which the East India Company made her, destroying her indigenous manufactures to that end, the manufactures which had created her enormous wealth, the wealth which lured the Western nations to her shores. . . . The policy which reduced the Indian masses to poverty and brought about the Rebellion of 1857, consisted of keeping India as a reservoir of raw materials. . . . The Imperial Conference now proposes to continue the process, but to deprive India of the small advantage she possesses of selling her raw materials in the open European market, and thus obtaining a price fixed by the need of competing nations. She is to sell her cotton within the Empire at a price fixed to suit the colourless purchasers of England and the Dominions, fixed in a market controlled by them, fixed to give them the largest profit and reduce her to the lowest point. . . . She will be paid the lowest price which her necessities compel her to accept, and will become the wage-labourer, the wage-slave of the Empire. . . . Such is the great betrayal of India by the Government of India nominees, But they have made one thing clear. Unless the coming of Home Rule be hastened, so that India is freed before the great battle for Imperial preference is fought out, India will be ruined. The trio of Government delegates, in concert with the Secretary of State for India, have voted away all hope of India's industrial regeneration."

support of the State in an hour of great need ? What had been the limitations imposed on her ? She had been asked to take her choice of several healthy places of residence, to desist from political activities, and to submit to restrictions on her correspondence. It is difficult to see how she was wronged by the action of the Madras Government.

The internment of Mrs. Besant had been shortly preceded by the return from the Imperial War Conference in England of the delegates selected by the Government of India, His Highness the Maharaja of Bikaner, Sir James Meston, Lieutenant-Governor of the United Provinces, and Sir Satyendra Sinha, member of the Bengal Executive Council. For the first time a ruling prince and an Indian member of Council had "shared in the innermost deliberations of the Empire."

The meaning and results of the occasion were explained by Sir James Meston in an eloquent speech to his provincial legislative Council, which concluded with an appeal for political patience and an assurance that those who were directing the affairs of India were not hostile, but favourable to her advance toward greater freedom in her national life.

Agitation, however, continued among the Home Rule Leaguers, and meetings were held in various towns. On August 2nd, however, a new direction was given to political meditations by two memorable pronouncements made by the Secretary of State for India. The first was to the following effect:

"The policy of His Majesty's Government, with which the Government of India are in complete accord, is that of the increasing association of Indians in every branch of the administration and the gradual development of self-governing institutions with a view to the progressive realisation of responsible government in India as an integral part of the British Empire. They have decided that substantial steps in this direction should be taken as soon as possible, and that it is of the highest importance as a preliminary to considering what these steps should be that there should be a free and informal exchange of opinion between those in authority at home and in India. His Majesty's Government have accordingly decided, with His Majesty's approval, that I should accept the Viceroy's invitation to proceed to India to discuss these matters with the Viceroy and the Government of India, to consider with the Viceroy the views of local governments, and to receive with him the suggestions of representative bodies and others.

"I would add that progress in this policy can only be achieved by successive stages. The British Government and the Government of India, on whom the responsibility lies for the welfare and advancement of the Indian peoples, must be judges of the time and measure of each advance, and they must be guided by the co-operation received from those upon whom new opportunities of service will thus be conferred and by the extent to which it is found that confidence can be reposed in their sense of responsibility.

"Ample opportunity will be afforded for public discussion of the proposals which will be submitted in due course to Parliament."

The second ran as follows:

"The Secretary of State for India has announced in the House of Commons the decision of His Majesty's Government to remove the bar which has hitherto precluded the admission of Indians to commissioned rank in His Majesty's Army, and steps are accordingly being taken respecting the grant of commissions to nine Indian officers belonging to Native Indian Land Forces who have served in the field in the present war and whom the Government of India recommended for this honour in recognition of their services. Their names will be notified in the *London Gazette*, and in the same gazette they will be posted to the Indian Army.

"The Secretary of State and the Government of India are discussing the general conditions under which Indians should in future be eligible for commissions. In due course the Army Council will be consulted with a view to the introduction of a carefully considered scheme to provide for the selection of candidates and for training them in important duties which will devolve upon them." [1]

It is remarkable that these announcements had been shortly preceded by the death of Mr. Dadabhai Naoroji,[2] the veteran Indian politician, who had sat in the British Parliament and had done as much as any other man to achieve the result which had been at last obtained. The ideal so often put forward by the Congress had been accepted as practicable, and steps would be taken to secure its achievement.

The September Sessions of the Imperial Legislative Council opened with a speech by His Excellency Lord Chelmsford, which carefully reviewed the work accomplished by his Government, including a remarkable record of war activities and the efforts already made to meet political objectives. The Viceroy concluded with an earnest appeal to leading politicians for cooperation. The speech had been preceded by the announcement made by the Home Member of Council that the Government of India were prepared to recommend to the Madras Government the removal of restrictions placed on Mrs. Besant and her coadjutors, if the

[1] On June 21st, 1918, the results of this consultation were announced.

[2] See Appendix VI.

Government of India were satisfied that these persons would abstain from unconstitutional and violent methods of political agitation during the remainder of the war. In taking this course the Government of India were actuated by the confident hope that the recent announcement of His Majesty's Government and the approaching visit of Mr. Montagu would have such a tranquillising effect on the political situation as to ensure a calm and dispassionate consideration of the difficult problems which were to be investigated during his stay in this country. The Government of India were prepared, subject to the same conditions, to take the same course in regard to other persons upon whom restrictions had been placed under those rules merely by reason of their violent methods of political agitation.

Both speech and announcement were well received by the political public, but before Mr. Montagu's arrival notable events occurred which sharply impressed on all concerned that there is another and a far larger public always present in India. Its needs may be elemental, but can at times become loudly clamorous.

It is, after all, the India which pays by far the larger share of taxes. It is also an India with which we may hazard too much.

Persons who observe the generally docile and law-abiding habits of the masses in India, are slow to realise that these same people can be worked up to an extraordinary pitch of fanatical fury, and that if captured by insidious appeals, especially appeals made in the name of religion, they are prone to act with unreasoning and brutal violence. Intensely credulous, they are also, if astutely approached, when they have reason to believe that the Government dare no longer restrain them, extremely excitable. The close of the year 1917 was marked by a rude reminder of the possibilities which this circumstance involves. A situation arose, and was later to arise even more abruptly in another part of India, for which the only immediate remedy was force applied in time by strong and resolute authority unbiased by any sectional influence. The story of the Arrah riots should be clearly understood by those who wish to form an idea of the emergencies for which Government in India must always be prepared.

The area in which these disturbances occurred is the flat tract of the Patna division of Bihar which lies north of the Kaimur Hills, south of the Ganges and adjoining the eastern districts of the United Provinces. The western portion of this tract belongs to the Shahabad district, and the eastern portion belongs to the Patna and Gaya districts; Arrah is the headquarters town of the Shahabad district.

The tract is for the most part a stiff clay country covered with rice-fields and poorly endowed with means of communication. It is interspersed with a network of ditches, drains, and village channels. Rapid movement is impossible to persons unversed in local geography.

The inhabitants are mainly Hindus, but there is also a considerable Muhammadan population. The Hindu landed proprietors there are extremely conservative, jealous of any agrarian measures or legislation that seem likely to lessen their powers over their tenants, and deeply imbued with the old Hindu reverence for the cow and aversion to all who sacrifice or slaughter that useful animal. In Shahabad alone of Bihar districts was there any indigenous rising during the Mutiny. Long after 1857, Kuar Singh, a Rajput landlord of Jagdispur in Shahabad, waged war against the British Government in the very country which is the subject of the following narrative and in the eastern districts of the United

Provinces. His exploits are well-remembered in Shahabad, and his family is present there.

During the early nineties serious opposition was offered to cow-killing in the Patna division, and culminated in riots which spread into the Benares and Gorakhpur divisions of the United Provinces. The people of these parts in races and character largely resemble their Bihar neighbours. The Bakr-Id Muhammadan festival of 1893, which was as usual celebrated by sacrifices of goats and cows, was signalised by the collection of mobs of Hindus organised with the intention of forcibly putting an end to cow-killing. In some, but not in all, cases considerable provocation had been given by Muhammadans, and there can be no doubt that the riots which occurred resulted from a roughly organised Hindu movement. One of its manifestations was attacks on cattle which had been purchased in Bihar for Army Commissariat purposes. This violent agitation was repressed by the Government, and has since subsided in the United Provinces, but in Bihar it again became prominent in 1911, when various disturbances occurred in the Monghyr and Patna districts. In the latter disorderly mobs of low caste Hindus collected and prevented cow-sacrifices at various places. Similar disturbances occurred in 1912. Some of the riots were organised by Hindus of the higher castes. Strong police forces were quartered in the more disturbed areas, but in 1915 precautions were relaxed, with the result that on the Bakr-Id day a large armed Hindu mob appeared at a village named Kanchanpur, and declared their intention of forcibly preventing cow-sacrifice. The local authorities could only prevail on this force to disperse by persuading the Muhammadans of the village to sell their cows to the Hindus and to abandon their sacrifices. Emboldened by success, the mob on the following day plundered another village. Their successful defiance of law and order led to further outrages in the following year. Meetings were held at which riots were carefully organised, and although a large force of military police had been drafted into the Patna district before the Bakr-Id of 1916, an armed mob of about 5,000 Hindus, arrayed in rude formation, attacked the military police at Kanchanpur who were protecting the resident Muhammadans after the conclusion of the sacrifices. The police were compelled to open fire, and several rioters were killed or wounded.

A more serious riot occurred in another police circle. Eight thousand Hindus collected from forty villages and, besieging the village of Jadupur, which was held by police, seized cows intended for sacrifice and dispersed. In a few cases, too, Commissariat cattle were rescued. About 150 of the rioters were convicted and punished, but Hindu and Muhammadan feelings were deeply stirred throughout Bihar. Hindus had become familiar with organised attacks, which had achieved considerable success. They had seen reason to think that if they could terrorise Muhammadans and force them to desist from sacrificing cows, the Government would not intervene, provided that the public peace remained unbroken.

In 1917 careful precautions were taken, but no information was received which pointed to the likelihood of disturbances in Shahabad, where there had been no anti-cow-killing riot for nearly a quarter of a century. Yet this district was to witness an outbreak beside which all the previous disturbances which we have mentioned were insignificant trifles. Each of these consisted of a single riot at a single village, and on the conclusion of the trouble the rioters dispersed to their homes. But the Shahabad or Arrah riots of 1917, many of which were equal in magnitude to any of the Patna riots, broke out simultaneously over the greater part of the district, and "to find any parallel to the state of turmoil and disorder that ensued, it is necessary to go back over a period of sixty years to the days of the great Mutiny." [1]

The first outbreak was at Ibrahimpur, a village near Piru, a large bazar and a station on the light railway, twenty-five miles south of Arrah. Information had been received by the District officials at Arrah on September 22nd of a Bakr-Id dispute, but this seemed to terminate in a compromise arranged between the parties by the good offices of the Muhammadan sub-divisional officer and a local Hindu barrister land-owner, the Muhammadans agreeing to sacrifice goats as well as cows, and the Hindus undertaking to provide the goats and make certain other concessions. In defiance of this compromise, on the morning of the 28th, a large mob of Hindus attacked Ibrahimpur and two neighbouring villages where cow-sacrifice had till then been performed without dispute. They drove off cattle and goats belonging to Muhammadans and plundered houses. As the Hindus had thus grossly violated the terms of the compromise, the authorities allowed the Muhammadans of Ibrahimpur to perform the cow-sacrifices which they had originally consented to forgo, and the Hindus of the village acquiesced in the justice of this decision. The sacrifices were thus performed on the 29th, but in private, and with precautions to avoid wanton offence to Hindu feeling.

On the morning of the 30th Ibrahimpur was attacked by a large Hindu mob, and houses were plundered before this mob was driven off by armed police,

[1] Resolution of the Government of Bihar and Orissa, dated June 13th, 1918.

who were on several occasions compelled to fire. On the same day extra police arrived under the Commissioner and the Deputy Inspector-General. Quiet was obtained for the time, but the air was full of alarming rumours, and the Muhammadans were in a state of terror. Two days later rioting began throughout a large tract of about forty miles square which passed into the hands of Hindu mobs. These attacked and plundered every Muhammadan house or village which they could reach. It was necessary to seek aid from the military, and British and Indian cavalry, in conjunction with British infantry, were pushed out in bodies to protect the affected villages. For some time riots continued, and Arrah itself was threatened with attack. In most cases the Muhammadans fled as the mobs approached, but in two villages, though hopelessly outnumbered, they offered a fierce resistance, beating off repeated attacks before they were finally overpowered. By October 7th 129 villages had been plundered in Shahabad, and it was only when troops had arrived in sufficient strength, and had established thirteen posts throughout the disturbed area which were connected by cavalry and motor-car patrols along the main roads, that the rioting ceased. Even then the country remained for some time in a state of ferment. The disturbances, too, spread to Gaya, where between October 8th and 13th over thirty villages were plundered.

During the days of mob-ascendancy, those Muhammadans who could not reach secure shelter were exposed to sufferings which it is unnecessary to detail here. They are set forth in the judgments of the Commissioners who tried the cases arising from the attacks on various villages.

Six days elapsed before the local officers were able

to get complete control of the situation. The police forces at their disposal were entirely inadequate, and the military forces within easy reach consisted only of one weak garrison. Troops from more distant places were only obtained with delay and in detachments. The wide area and indifferent communications of the tract concerned made it difficult to move the soldiers. But the rioters, on the other hand, moved freely about over narrow embankments between the waterlogged fields, and generally melted away on the approach of the troops, only to collect again at a safe distance and loot fresh villages. They took good care to disperse at once whenever the military appeared, and thus avoided being fired at.

All the time the Muhammadans of Patna and Gaya were in a condition little short of panic; and there can be no doubt that further continuance of the riots would have set the whole of Bihar ablaze and seriously affected the eastern districts of the United Provinces.

The disturbances had been organised with great care and skill. The religious dispute in Ibrahimpur, which was subsequently adduced as their cause, had been amicably settled, and nowhere had the Muhammadans offered any provocation. Numerous snowball letters inciting Hindus to loot certain villages on fixed dates came to light, and in many cases there was evidence that bands of rioters were operating on a definite plan. They had evidently been instructed as to the lengths to which they were to go. Murder was not committed except in overcoming resistance. Damage to Government property was avoided except in a few cases where the telegraph wires were cut so as to hamper the transmission of intelligence. Although the area concerned contains many post offices, canal headquarters, and other places where Government money was kept, these were left untouched. The object of the organisers appears to have been to convince the authorities that the movement was purely religious and anti-Muhammadan. According to a statement made by a convicted rioter, their plans were carefully elaborated. Their following was assured by the welding potency of the call to protect the cows, which appeals most strongly to all Hindus, and especially to those of the higher castes. The rioters apparently believed that they could deal such a blow at the Muhammadans as to finally end cow-sacrifice. They had been captured by war-unrest, and had imbibed the idea that the moment was opportune because British rule had sunk into weakness and decline. A perusal of some of the snow-ball leaflets shows that assurance was given therein of German and Bengali succour. The rioters of Piru attacked with cries of "British rule is gone," and at first believed that no troops were available to suppress them. When the troops arrived, it was rumoured that they had no ammunition or had been forbidden to fire.

The brutalities practised on the unfortunate victims of these riots were the theme of indignation meetings in many mosques in northern India, and collections were made in aid of the sufferers wherever there were Muhammadans. The organisers of many meetings came from classes which from indifference and fear of controversy had hitherto remained silent in politics. They expressed a deep and widespread sentiment. Relations between the two great communities were tense and uneasy throughout the concurrent Ram Lila and Muharram festivals in many districts of the neighbouring United Provinces. Serious disturbances occurred at three well-known places.

CHAPTER VI

THE REFORMS REPORT

THE object of Mr. Montagu's visit was to determine, on the spot and in consultation with the Viceroy, what steps should be taken in the direction of establishing in India government responsible to the peoples of the various provinces. The London Cabinet recognised that such establishment must be gradual, that progress towards it could be satisfactorily effected only by stages; but they considered that no time should be lost in making substantial steps toward the goal. What these substantial steps should be was the problem; but it was desired that a considerable advance should be made on the Minto-Morley Reforms which had been in operation for eight years only.

Mr. Montagu and his party arrived in India late in the year 1917, and after preliminary conferences with the Government of India and heads of provinces at Delhi, they toured to Calcutta, Madras, and Bombay. They were accompanied by the Viceroy and the Home Member of His Excellency's Executive Council, and everywhere consulted leading non-officials and officials. On the conclusion of the tour, further consultations were held, and it was not until near the end of April that the Secretary of State and his party returned to England.

The tour attracted universal attention. The European non-officials and other communities had appointed representative councils to draw up petitions for the protection of their interests. Addresses were presented by numerous associations; the landlords, the depressed classes, the Deccan Ryots, the Indian Christians, and many other sections of an enormous population claimed earnestly that in the new era that was dawning their peculiar interests might be duly safeguarded and not left to the unfettered arbitration of any numerical majority.

The Congress and the Muslim League urged the adoption of a constitution which would embody the provisions framed at their meetings of 1916. In December both bodies assembled at Calcutta. Mrs. Besant presided over the Congress, which was described by a leading Indian paper as "the Congress of Mrs. Besant and Mr. Tilak, of Mrs. Besant more than Mr. Tilak."

The attendance was large; but the Moderates were becoming surfeited with the dominant political powers, and the Muhammadans were establishing dissenting Muslim associations.

The British reverses in France arrested the attention of the country; and in April the Viceroy, at the instance of the Prime Minister of the United Kingdom, summoned the ruling chiefs and the leading non-official representatives of British India to a conference at Delhi. The object was to arrange that all possible assistance, in the shape of men, money, and supplies, should be given to the cause of the Allies at an hour of supreme need.

Sub-committees were appointed to devise ways and means, and speeches were delivered which breathed a spirit of energetic loyalty to the British Crown. Opportunity, however, was taken by the Honourable Mr. Khaparde, a member of the Imperial Legislative Council and of the Home Rule League, to bring forward a resolution recommending to the British Government immediate introduction into Parliament of a Bill "meeting the demands of the people to establish responsible government in India within a reasonable and specified period." The Conference was also to advise the immediate removal of all racial distinctions.

This resolution was disallowed by the Viceroy as foreign to the purpose of the Conference.

Among various eloquent utterances on a great occasion, those of His Highness the Maharaja of Ulwar and of the late Mr. Ironside, the representative of the Calcutta Chamber of Commerce, were particularly memorable.[1]

Conferences were also held at provincial centres. A great impulse was given to war-efforts of all kinds, especially to recruiting, which made remarkable progress in the United Provinces and the Punjab; but simultaneously it became increasingly clear that some elements of Indian society were bent on turning the difficulties of the hour to political advantage. On June 10th, at the Bombay Provincial War Conference, the Governor, H.E. Lord Willingdon declared that certain gentlemen, many of whom were connected with the Home Rule League, had not only not given the help to Government which it was fairly entitled to expect from them in such critical times, but had even endeavoured to increase its difficulties and embarrassment wherever and whenever they could.

His Excellency refused to allow Mr. B. G. Tilak and another Home Rule leader to offer observations which he characterised as political, although these gentlemen asserted that they and their League were loyal to the King-Emperor. Three of their sympathisers left the hall. The Conference, however, passed, with acclama-

[1] See Appendix VIII (*a*) and (*b*).

tion, a resolution authorising the Governor to convey to His Majésty an assurance of the determination of the Bombay Presidency to continue to do her duty to her utmost capacity in the great crisis through which the Empire was passing.

On June 16th Home Rule day was celebrated at Madras. That date was selected as it was the anniversary of the internment of Mrs. Besant and her lieutenants. The meeting was presided over by Sir Subramania Aiyar, who had once been a judge of the Madras High Court, but had later earned fame as the author of a letter to President Wilson which described India as a subject-nation held in chains, forbidden by alien rulers to express publicly her desire for the ideals proclaimed in the President's famous war message.[1] The meeting was addressed by the chairman, who advocated "passive resistance" as a constitutional method of enforcing the claim for Home Rule. Agitation, he said, was not enough. What was required was a promise of Home Rule at a definite period. Mrs. Besant, who was present, protested against the "insult" levelled against members of the Home Rule League by the Governor of Bombay, and stated that the share of India in the Empire was the giving of men and money. How could Indians be asked to fight for a liberty in which they would not share? Life without liberty was a poor and contemptible thing.

All these proceedings were repugnant to reasonable politicians who were disposed to do their best as loyal citizens, but found themselves frequently pushed aside. Passages in newspapers from time to time expressed their sentiments. These are best illustrated by a quotation:

"In nearly all parts of India where political life is

[1] See page 36.

earnest, certain persons have of late been preaching a crusade against the older leaders. The younger Congressmen have been made to believe that, if only they crippled these and laid them on the shelf, the principal obstacle in the way of India's progress would be removed. We do not grudge the new leaders their success. Far be it from us to do so. But it is much to be wished that their success was attained by methods which left the young heart pure and tender and chivalrous, and which did not rob it of the rare jewel of ancient Indian culture, the quality of reverence. The renovated polity of the future cannot lose it except at its peril."—*Servant of India.*

A stronger protest appeared in the *Times of India* from Mr. N. Tilak, a cousin of Mr. B. G. Tilak and an ex-member of the Home Rule League, who wrote as follows:

"One characteristic difference between the two parties of Indian politicians, the Extremists and the Moderates, is that while the former have little faith in the sincerity of Government, the very fact of Government sincerity is the great hope of the latter. 'With what judgment ye judge, ye shall be judged, and with what measure ye mete it shall be measured to you again.' The cardinal fact in the whole situation is that the Home Rule Leaguers have not yet realised their country's vital relation to the war. They are blind to the all-important fact that the time has already come to prepare seriously for the defence of their own country. Consequently they are under the delusion that whatever is done by the Indian people to help the cause of the Allies is done by way of obliging the British Government. The question with them is thus whether their countrymen should oblige Government or should receive in advance the price of the service they render for Government. To yield to so utter and so grave a misunderstanding of the whole situation would be the greatest possible danger to India in this critical hour. In expressing his opinion of the Home Rulers I think His Excellency the Governor meant this and nothing more."

. . . .

"We here in India are not sufficiently aware of the gravity of the situation, a complete knowledge of which would surely be enough to make us lay aside all petty considerations, bury deep all differences, and place ourselves and our resources at the disposal of our defenders without the least reserve and absolutely unconditionally. If the worst fears are realised with the Home Rulers having done nothing save raise their party cry, it will then not be Government so much as we, the Home Rulers' fellow-citizens, who will pronounce them to be India's worst enemies. The changed times give us a very clear message, which is that we should forget every self-centred problem and, summing up all the powers we possess, stand by our Government loyally and heroically. Times like these are simply putting us to the test, whether we are really fit for Home Rule, and, if we are fit, then to what extent. This great question of our fitness will be decided not by our own opinions, still less by our party creeds, but by the opinion of those British people who are determined to fight for victory till their last drop of blood is spilt and by the whole civilised world, which has become Britain's comrade in this war for justice, equity, and liberty. To secure the good opinion of liberty-loving Britain and the world we must rise above the turmoil of political agitation which at present rules our hearts."

Mr. Tilak added that he did not wish to be understood to mean that India did not look for any form of self-government. What was certain, however, was that the vast bulk of the Indian people did not want the Home Rule proposed by the Extremists.

"It is indeed," he said, "an extremely difficult hour

for those high-souled Brahmans, who, abhorring the course proposed by the Extremists in politics, are genuinely loyal to their country and their king. As for the non-Brahmans, they have only one idea, one purpose, one goal, and that is the safety, permanence, and continuity of British rule in India."

The intemperate political tendencies of the hour were further rebuked by a person who has since become conspicuous in a less happy connection. His antecedents had been remarkable.

Mohandas Karamchand Gandhi is now an elderly man, and belongs to the Hindu Vaishya or merchant caste. He is a native of Guzerat, in the presidency of Bombay, and has been called to the English Bar. Returning to India, he began to practise in the Bombay High Court, and was retained by a firm of his native town Purbandar to conduct a lawsuit in Natal.

While in South Africa [1] his sympathies were stirred by the disabilities suffered by his countrymen there, both indentured labourers and others.

He initiated strong protests, and in 1896 visited India, but returned to South Africa and assisted to organise Indian ambulances during the Boer War. Afterwards he enrolled himself as an advocate of the Supreme Court of Pretoria, arranging also for the purchase of a press and the starting of a newspaper. In 1906 the Government of the Transvaal enacted a law which required all Asiatics to register by means of thumb-impressions. The object was to prevent unlawful immigration. This law was stubbornly opposed by Mr. Gandhi and his followers on the ground that it degraded them. They combated its operation by

[1] I have taken the incidents of Mr. Gandhi's South African career from the only source available to me, a book called *Heroes of the Hour*, published by Ganesh & Co. of Madras.

passive resistance, refusing to register; and Mr. Gandhi himself underwent two short terms of imprisonment. The struggle, which lasted some time, excited the keen sympathy of educated India; and when in March 1912 Mr. Gokhale moved in the Imperial Legislative Council for the abolition of indentured emigration to Natal, the resolution was accepted by Government. After the accomplishment of the Union of South Africa, the British Cabinet, at the instance of the Government of India, endeavoured to procure repeal of the registration law; but repeal, when it came, was followed by the passing of an Immigration Act which was repugnant to Mr. Gandhi and his followers. At their invitation, and with the approval of the Home Government, Mr. Gokhale visited South Africa, but agitation continued for the removal of certain disabilities.

Another big effort of passive resistance and a strike of Indian labourers in the coal mines of Natal excited renewed sympathy in India, which was expressed by the Viceroy, Lord Hardinge, in a public speech. A Commission of Enquiry was appointed, and resulted in the removal of an obnoxious tax and other grievances.

Mr. Gandhi returned to India with a considerable reputation, and began to interest himself in affairs there. He first interfered in disputes between the indigo planters of Bihar and their tenants, championing the cause of the latter, and serving on the Commission appointed by Government to investigate their complaints. He then took up the case of the revenue-payers of the Kaira district of Bombay, who complained that the Government demand was too rigorous in view of scarcity.

His history gave him a unique position among the political classes, and latterly he had acquired a reputation among some persons of humbler position. To all he preached the doctrine that *satya griha* (insistence on truth, popularly translated as passive resistance) would conquer all difficulties. He was invited to and attended the Delhi War Conference. There he spoke briefly in favour of the loyal resolution moved by the Gaekwar of Baroda.

Now also, appealing to the Kaira people in whose affairs he had recently shown interest, he urged them to qualify themselves for Home Rule by helping the Empire. Again, at a Home Rule meeting convened in Bombay in order to protest against Lord Willingdon's speech of June 10th, he advised unconditional co-operation with Government on the part of educated India as more likely than anything else to bring Home Rule in sight.

The above criticisms and appeals did not affect the Extremist attitude; and when, on July 8th, the Reforms Report was published, the scheme which it proposed was promptly condemned by Extremist politicians and newspapers as inadequate and disappointing. The Moderates, however, welcomed this scheme, although they proposed to ask for some alterations; and as the Extremists persisted in their attitude of disdain, the Moderate leaders decided not to attend the special Congress arranged for discussion of the proposals, and resolved to call a subsequent conference of their own. Before, however, proceeding further with this narrative, it is desirable to give some account of the Reforms proposals. The Report was in two parts, the first headed "the material," and the second headed "the proposals."

The first part was a fine exposition of the situation; but interest, as was natural, mainly settled on the second part.

The most important proposal was the provision for

the major provinces of India (excluding Burma) of dyarchies or governments consisting of two wings, the first composed of a governor and two executive councillors, an Indian and a British official, appointed by the Crown, the second composed of a minister or ministers nominated by the Governor from among the elected members of the provincial Legislative Council and holding office for the term of the council concerned.

The Governor and Executive Councillors were to hold charge of the major or essential departments. These would be called " reserved."

The minister or ministers would take charge of other departments. These would be termed " transferred." The Government, thus constituted, would deliberate generally as a whole, but the Governor would have power to summon either wing for separate deliberation.

Decisions on the reserved subjects, and supplies for them in the provincial budget, would rest with the Governor and his Executive Council; decisions on and supplies for the transferred subjects would rest with the Governor and the ministers. The Governor was not to be in a position to refuse assent at discretion to the proposals of ministers. He was to be guided by an instrument of instructions issued to him on appointment by the Secretary of State in Council, or by the Secretary of State should the Council of the Secretary of State fail to survive reform. The Governor was, however, to advise his ministers, and could refuse assent to their decisions " when the consequences of acquiescence would clearly be serious."

Distinction between " reserved " and " transferred " departments would be drawn by a committee which would be appointed for inquiry into and report on this difficult question. The guiding principle should be " to include in the transferred list those departments which afford most opportunity for local knowledge and social service, those in which Indians have shown themselves to be keenly interested, those in which mistakes that occur, though serious, would not be irremediable, and those which stand most in need of development."

Provincial legislatures would be greatly enlarged and would contain substantial elected majorities. Election was to be on as broad a basis as possible, for the authors of the scheme did not intend that the result of their labours should be to "transfer powers from a bureaucracy to an oligarchy." The franchise and the composition of the various Legislative Councils would be determined by regulations to be framed on the advice of a committee to be hereafter specially appointed.

The provincial Governor was to be able to certify that a bill dealing with a reserved subject was essential for the peace or tranquillity of the province or for discharge of his responsibility for reserved subjects. The bill would then be referred to a Grand Committee of the Legislative Council, of which the Governor might nominate a bare majority. The bill as passed by the Grand Committee might again be discussed by the Legislative Council, but could neither be rejected nor amended except on the motion of a member of the Executive Council.

All provincial legislation would require the assent of the Governor and Governor-General, and would be subject to disallowance by His Majesty. The Governor could reserve provincial laws for the royal assent.

The annual budget would be laid before the Legislative Council. If the Council refused to accept the proposals for reserved subjects, the Governor-in-Council would have power to restore the whole, or any part, on the Governor's certifying that, for reasons to be stated, such restoration was essential either to the peace or tranquillity of the province or any part thereof, or to the discharge of his responsibility for reserved subjects. Except in so far as he exercised this power, the budget would be framed so as to give effect to resolutions of the Legislative Council. Standing committees of the Legislative Council were to be attached to all departments. Resolutions of the Council (except on the budget) would only have effect as recommendations.

Thus the system would imply arrangements by which one half of the provincial Government had independent charge of "reserved" subjects, the land revenue, the police, law and order, etc. Its policy in administering these departments would be ultimately one of which the British Parliament had approved. The other half of the Government would be in independent charge of "transferred" subjects, local self-government, medical and sanitary work, vernacular education, etc., its policy in regard to which would be one dictated by the provincial Legislative Council. Association was, of course, desirable between the two halves of the Government in so far as this was practicable without obscuring the responsibility of each half for taking its own decisions and for abiding by the consequences. The Governor, the Public Services, a common Treasury and Audit, would be the links between the two halves of these *provincial* Governments.

The entire field of provincial administration would be marked off from that of the Government of India which would preserve indisputable authority on matters adjudged by it to be essential for the discharge of its responsibilities for peace, order, and good government. As the popular element of the provincial Government acquired experience, transferred subjects would be added to and reserved subjects would be transferred until no reserved subjects remained, the need for an official element in the Government vanished, and the goal of complete responsible government was attained. Such transfers would be admissible at intervals of five years, when they might be considered on application from a provincial Government or provincial Legislative Council.

In the Government of India there was to be no dyarchy, but the Indian element in the Viceroy's Executive Council was to be increased.

The Legislative Council was to be replaced by a Legislative Assembly and a Council of State. The former would consist of about 100 members, and would be the popular body. The latter would consist of fifty members, exclusive of the Viceroy, who would be President with power to nominate a Vice-President. Not more than twenty-five members of this Council would be officials, but twenty-nine would be nominees of the President. The President of the Legislative Assembly would be nominated by the Viceroy. The Council of State would act as a second chamber. It would be possible on emergency to pass a bill through the Council of State in the first instance, merely reporting it to the Legislative Assembly. Ordinarily, bills would go first to the latter body. If passed, they would go on to the Council of State. If amended there, they would be laid before a joint session of both houses, unless the Governor-General in Council was prepared to certify that the amendments were essential to the interests of peace, order, and good government, including sound financial administration, in which case the Assembly would not have power to reject or modify such amendments. Resolutions of either the Council of State or Legislative Assembly would only have effect as recommendations. A council of Ruling Princes was to be established, and would be able to deliberate with the Council of State on matters of common interest.

Racial bars that still existed in regulations for the public services were to be abolished. In addition to recruitment in England where such existed, a system of appointment in India to all the public services was to be established. Percentages of recruitment in India, with definite ratios of increase, were to be fixed for all the services.

In the Indian Civil Service the percentage would be 33 per cent. of the superior posts, increasing annually by $1\frac{1}{2}$ per cent. until the position was reviewed by a Commission appointed by Parliament. Such a Commission would be appointed ten years after the first meetings of the new legislative bodies in order to examine the constitutional position both in the Government of India and in the Provinces. Similar Commissions would be subsequently appointed at intervals of not more than ten years.

The authors of the report expressed the view that "so far in the future as any man can foresee, a strong element of Europeans would be required in the public services." The continued presence of the British officer was vital, if the Indian people were to be made self-governing.

The authors very strongly condemned communal electorates as a very serious hindrance to the development of the self-governing principle. They would concede them, however, to the Muhammadans in provinces where the latter are in a minority, and to the Sikhs. In the case of the Muhammadans, they felt themselves bound by previous pledges. The Sikhs are everywhere in a minority, but supply a very valuable element in the Army.

The following principles underlie the main proposals above detailed:

(*a*) Indians must be educated and stirred into becoming a nation.

The present ideal of a small class must be generally adopted. It should be lifted up and held in front of all classes, races, and languages. It should draw all. The masses, who from the earliest ages had been absorbed entirely in their private affairs, and accepted ruler after ruler provided that he was strong enough to govern and protect them, must be educated into taking a share in a system of parliamentary government. The address to the Viceroy and the Secretary of State from the Deccan Ryots had described the sole purposes of ordinary persons of the tenant class to be "commerce, agriculture, menial service, and so on." If we add to these purposes attendance on religious fairs and occasional litigation, the description is complete. The authors of the Reforms scheme decided that contentment with such a limited horizon was pathetic, and must be disturbed in order that nationhood within the Empire might be achieved.

(*b*) The required goal must be achieved by prearranged measured stages. Every five years proposals would be admissible for the transfer of some Government department to the direction of a minister. Every ten years a Commission from England would see how things were going, and, if they were satisfactory, would presumably recommend a further advance.

The proposal for five years' transfer was abandoned subsequently. The whole idea that it is a promising arrangement to transfer departments of government in India to popular control by measured stages was entirely novel.

(*c*) From the very first, Government responsible to

the various legislatures would be conceded to a definitely marked extent. The object was to give the electorates which would now be created and their leaders a genuine sense of responsibility. To secure this, the responsibility would be clear-cut and unmistakable.

The adoption of the first two principles clearly involved the undertaking of a very difficult and critical enterprise, the results of which cannot be foreseen. The last objective is obviously desirable, provided that it can be attained without damaging the ability of the British Government to secure order, progress and content in India. The Report did not notice the obstacle which the nature of the Hindu religions and social system offers to the establishment of democratic government. Nationalists talk as if this obstacle did not exist. But it does exist in a very solid form, although it is a delicate matter for discussion in a published Government Report. The marked ascendancy which it confers on the Brahman is the reason for the strong desire of non-Brahmans in Madras for separate communal representation. Theirs is by no means the only community that craves this privilege. In fact, it may be said that if the scheme of reform insists on representative government without some degree of communal representation, it will in actual working be far from agreeable to large bodies of the population of India. Whatever may be the case in the future, at present the great majority are accustomed to regard themselves as members of such and such a community, sect, or faith, and if they are to learn to think differently, they should not be hurried. Widely diffused education and not abrupt intervention is the real remedy.

The authors invited reasoned criticism, official and non-official. The proposals would be examined by the

Local Governments, who had not seen them in their matured form. This examination ended in a condemnation of dyarchy by the large majority of Local Governments. Five heads of provinces proposed an alternative plan for unified government with an official majority of a Governor and two Executive Councillors (one an Indian) against two ministers. The ministers would not exercise the separate clear-cut responsibility in certain departments contemplated by dyarchy, but would exercise a joint responsibility in all departments.

Reasoned criticism of the Montagu-Chelmsford proposals took time to mature. But two noteworthy manifestos appeared with little delay. The first was a pronouncement issued by the Bengal Moderates, the text of which contained the following passages:

"Till a few days ago it looked as though the two schools of political thought in the country might yet come together in compromise, and that a united Congress could consider and pronounce a verdict on the official proposals of reform. The cry of total rejection with which they were greeted in some quarters on publication weakened somewhat after a few weeks were over, and a general disposition to consider details and offer specific criticisms manifested itself. Unfortunately, however, it has become apparent from writings in certain organs of the "home rule" press, manifestos issued here and there by that party, and the proceedings of the conferences held in various provinces within the last few weeks, that their attitude is still hostile. Disappointment and dissatisfaction are the notes invariably struck; the ideals that responsible government should be introduced at the very start and widened by successive stages, embodied in the Imperial Cabinet's declaration of August last, are unheeded if not expressly set aside; and the modifications demanded amount to a practical rejection of the official scheme in fundamentals. We are constrained to say, therefore, that the Extremist attitude is still one of rejection though thinly disguised. To make good this criticism, it is necessary to examine at some length the manifesto signed by Mrs. Besant and several other persons in different parts of the country and the resolutions passed by the recent Madras special provincial conference. To those who have watched how the Home Rule Leagues and their branches have captured the various Provincial Congress Committees in the country and the All-India Congress Committee, there is now little reason to doubt that the Special Congress to be held in Bombay will repeat, with perhaps a few alterations, the resolutions of the Madras conference.

. . . . . .

"The speeches of the Chairman of the Reception Committee, and of the President of the special session of the Madras Provincial Conference, held early this month, clearly indicate the spirit in which the reform scheme is looked upon by the Extremist Party. Mrs. Besant has chosen to characterise the scheme as 'leading to a line beyond which its authors cannot go—a perpetual slavery which can only be broken by a revolution.' Mr. Vijayraghava Chariar described the scheme from the chair of the Conference as 'a monster fondling of *Round Table* politicians,' and the attempt to secure support for such a contrivance as 'simply ludicrous, if not disingenuous.'

. . . . . .

"Now there is good reason to believe that Moderate views are held by much larger numbers than generally appear on the surface. But the very nature of their views disposes them as a class to be more acquiescent and less demonstrative than the others. If a referendum could be taken on the subject of the official scheme of reforms, not only among those who habitually give vocal expression to their political thoughts, but among all in the country who may be brought to form intelligent opinions on the issues involved, it is not improbable that the majority would be found to be on our side. However that be, owing to the activity, as has already been mentioned, of the Home Rule Leagues and their branches, it is certain that in all Congress organisations we have been reduced to a minority."

For all these reasons they decided not to attend the special Congress to be held in order to discuss the Reforms.

The second notable manifesto was a statement issued by the Secretary of the European Association on behalf of his Council.

"Until," he wrote, "it can be roughly ascertained what proportion the potential electors bear to the whole population, on what classes of subjects the electorate is tolerably qualified by education and the sense of the public good to pronounce, and in what spirit the electorate may be expected to deal (*a*) with special European interests in India and (*b*) with those of classes too backward to share in the franchise—until all this can be ascertained with some approach to accuracy, it is impossible to say dogmatically what powers can be entrusted to the representatives of the electorate. The eminent authors of the report, however, have left the whole question of an electorate to be settled by a committee to be appointed hereafter. In these circumstances the Council of the European Association must express itself with some reserve on the essentials of the scheme.

. . . .

"The Council has been struck in perusing the report by the failure of Mr. Montagu and Lord Chelmsford to realise the importance of the European non-official community in India. In many passages of the report it is tacitly assumed that the European official and the Indian non-official are the only parties to any political settlement, and when the report does expressly refer to the European non-official community, as in paragraph

344, it is mainly to offer some respectable platitudes for consideration.

"The Council of the European Association is emphatically of opinion that European non-officials are entitled to substantial representation as a community in the Provincial and Imperial Legislatures in addition to the representation already given through Chambers of Commerce, Trades Associations and Planters' Associations. Representatives of those specialised bodies naturally cannot receive any general political mandate from their constituents, and that is a strong reason for according an adequate measure of communal representation to Europeans. But there is a further reason in the fact that so long as representation is merely through a Chamber of Commerce and sectional bodies, a considerable number of Europeans engaged in the legal, medical, journalistic, and other professions, or resident where specialised bodies do not exist, are denied all representation.

"The hostility of the report towards communal representation for Indians, other than Muhammadans, and in the Punjab Sikhs, appears to the Council to be without justification. Nationhood can never be achieved by placing minorities or a backward majority under the heel of a clique excessively intolerant in social relations and avid of political power. And even if it were otherwise, the problematic future blessing of nationhood would not compensate the Indian masses for their suffering during the transitional period. Immense differences exist between various sections of the population in race, religion, culture, tradition, and vocational bent, and practical recognition of these differences is a condition of success in any political development. To initiate representative Government by means which deny representation to many classes of the population is inconsistent. Communal representation may not be equally necessary in all provinces, and it may not be permanently needed, but at any rate in the early years of the experiment it is essential. For if minorities and backward classes are thrown back on nominated representation, how are they ever to acquire the capacity for the use of the franchise which the authors of the report desire to evoke? . . . European opinion and sober Indian opinion may be prepared to support a marked increase in Indian control over policy if the execution of policy remains largely or very largely in British hands. On the other hand, European opinion and sober Indian opinion may be willing to support a rapid increase in the Indian element in the public services if the inspiration of the policy remains mainly British. But to effect these changes simultaneously, to alter hastily the racial composition of the public services, and to do this as if each of the changes could be rightly decided upon without reference to the other, is not statesmanship."

Shortly after the publication of the Reforms Scheme, a report of a different nature was published in India.

At the instance of the Government of Bengal, who were much concerned at the difficulties encountered in coping with revolutionary crime in their province, the Government of India, with the authority of the Secretary of State, had appointed a committee of five:

"To investigate and report on the nature and extent of the criminal conspiracies connected with the revolutionary movement in India;

"To examine and consider the difficulties that had arisen in dealing with such conspiracies, and to advise as to the legislation, if any, necessary to enable Government to deal effectively with them."

The President of the Committee was the Honourable Mr. Justice Rowlatt of the King's Bench; the members were the Honourable Sir Basil Scott, Chief Justice of Bombay; the Honourable Mr. Justice Kurnaraswarni

Sastri of the Madras High Court; the Honourable Mr. P. C. Mitter, Pleader of the Calcutta High Court and Member of the Bengal Legislative Council; and the author of this book.[1]

The Committee sat in Calcutta and at Lahore, and examined a number of witnesses, official and non-official, as well as a great variety of records of trials and other documents. In April they had submitted a unanimous report to the Government of India, which gave a full account of the origin and growth of revolutionary conspiracy in India, tracing the ramifications of the movement and the interconnection of its varying phases in different provinces. The Committee also submitted recommendations regarding the legislative measures required for coping with the difficulties encountered in dealing with the movement. Publication of the Report was announced on July 19th. As was to be expected, the book was hailed with showers of abuse by the Extremist Press. The Moderates generally reserved comment.

The country at large was in no way disturbed by all these political events. The people generally were interested in the abnormal delay of the rains and in rising prices. So far the war period had been marked by good harvests; but in 1918 the monsoon broke down disastrously. The high prices, first of salt and afterwards of cloth and oil, caused considerable hardship as the months advanced; and for one of the people who in the least understood the Reforms proposals, there were many thousands who, as the rains persisted in holding off, looked anxiously for Government measures to enable them to buy salt, oil, and cloth at prices within their means.

The days of civil officers were occupied by heavy routine duties and extra war work. Recruiting for the

[1] We were all entirely unknown to each other.

Army and for labour corps,[1] collection of supplies and comforts for troops, all progressed with zeal and rapidity. Attention, too, was riveted on the battle-fields of France. Now and then officers who had taken part in the great struggle returned to speak of its vicissitudes. A letter published in August by the *Pioneer* newspaper gave the impression which affairs in that month, before the definite failure of the monsoon, conveyed to one of these observers.

EUROPE AND INDIA—A CONTRAST

[BY ONE WHO HAS RETURNED FROM THE FRONT]

"From the darkness and gloom of the West, over the whole of which the realities of war and the shadows which all real things cast around them are much in evidence, it is like life from death to arrive in this wonderful, peaceful, well-fed happy country of India, where the war appears to have made so little appreciable impression and, where it is possible even in these days, when the fate of the nations of the world is trembling in the balance, to discuss politics as though political discussions and academic wranglings were the panacea for all the ills that man is heir to.

"What a favoured country this is! Contrast its condition with Europe to-day. The whole of Belgium, except a tiny piece at the south-west corner, is in the hands of the Germans, who have wantonly destroyed the beautiful towns and glorious buildings which had been handed down to us as a priceless heritage from the past, and which can never again be constructed, for the master minds and hands of the periods which produced these heirlooms of the world have gone, producing in turn hard commercial master minds which, though

[1] Even before September 1917 India had sent about twenty labour corps to Mesopotamia and twenty-five to France. Also she had despatched overseas about 60,000 artizans, labourers, and specialists of various kinds and 20,000 menials and followers. Many more were sent later.

capable of doing many things for the amenities of mankind, cannot build as those built of yore, for the soul of man has, in some mysterious manner, changed, and building for love, to the glory of God, and for the edifying of humanity, is not the outstanding feature of the period in which we are playing our part.

. . . .

"In Europe food and the very necessaries of life are rationed, as the supply of many commodities is not equal to the demand—a condition of things brought about by the removal of men from productive employment and using them for the destruction of the enemy of civilisation, who, like the Huns of Attila from whom they are descended, are carrying out the order of the German Emperor addressed to them in the same words as he spoke to his soldiers when sending them to China to quell the Boxer rising, 'Kill and destroy. Spare not. Leave the women and children only their eyes to cry with.'

"Compare the conditions described with those we find around us here—work is proceeding very much as usual. Certain commodities are expensive, but, being not necessary in every case for the sustenance of life, need not be purchased. Food is plentiful, and, though not as cheap as it was before the war, is within the reach of all, and can be procured without food tickets, which it is necessary for every one to have in Europe. Productive employment is seen on every hand. Works of utility are being constructed, though not of the same magnitude as during the piping times of peace, and on every hand there is evidence of that sense of security and order which the Britisher, with his slow but sure methods, ensures for all, and which results in producing the greatest good for the greatest number."

Great issues were at stake in Europe and Asia; but while the Empire was fighting for its life, the more advanced Nationalists remained absorbed in their own pursuits. The resources of the famous Buckingham and Carnatic Mills at Madras had been placed at the disposal of Government for assistance in the provision of essential war material. A statement published by Messrs. Binny & Co., the secretaries and treasurers of these mills, attributes the labour unrest which characterised the year 1918 to the unfortunate political situation in Southern India and to the anti-European sentiments propounded by certain politicians. It quotes four relevant passages from the paper *New India* in support of this contention. It states that a Labour Union had been started with representatives whose primary object was politics. This Union met more or less continuously throughout 1918. At its meetings the workmen were told that they were treated worse than beasts of burden. At one meeting, held on April 29th, they were informed that a variety of Madras leaders would explain to them the various political, social, and economic questions which touched them nearly. The report of the directors for the half-year ending December 31st, 1918, contains the following account of the results of these meetings:

"Both mills were entirely closed for twenty working days in all during the half-year. It was noteworthy that the mills singled out for attack were mills under European management, engaged in work of military importance. The directors trusted that the methods employed in Madras might not be followed or allowed in other parts of India. If political changes were to be sought for in this manner, the development of the resources of the country by manufacturers would be seriously retarded, as the investment of capital, European or Indian, would be prejudicial. The artificial fostering of race hatred might have disastrous results for Indian industries. From this it is not a long step to class hatred and to conditions of anarchy."

At the end of August special meetings of the Congress

and Muslim League, while admitting the Montagu-Chelmsford Scheme to be an advance on present conditions, declared it, as a whole, disappointing and unsatisfactory. They stated in effect that they would reject the scheme unless it embodied certain other demands which they specified. The Moderate leaders did not attend the Congress.

Early in September the Imperial Legislative Council assembled at Simla. On the 6th of the month the Honourable Mr. Surendranath Banerjee, leader of the Moderates, moved the following resolution:

"This Council, while thanking His Excellency the Viceroy and the Secretary of State for India for the Reform proposals, and recognising them as a genuine effort and a definite advance towards the progressive realisation of responsible government in India, recommends to the Governor-General in Council that a Committee consisting of all the non-official members of this Council be appointed to consider the Reforms Report and make recommendations to the Government of India."

The mover expressed strong approval of the Reforms proposals, criticising only those which related to the Government of India and the absence of dyarchy there. He concluded by inviting his countrymen to grasp with alacrity and enthusiasm the hand of fellowship and friendship held out to them, and "in co-operation with British statesmen to move forward to the accomplishment of those high destinies which, under the Providence of God, are reserved for our people."

The resolution was warmly supported by other members. Among British non-officials, however, the representative of the Bombay Chamber of Commerce said that he was not yet in possession of the considered opinion of his constituency; and the representative of the

Calcutta Chamber of Commerce, the late Mr. W. A. Ironside, complained that the proposals practically ignored the European non-official community.

A very few Indian non-officials expressed either limited satisfaction or dissatisfaction with the proposals; but only two finally opposed the resolution. The proposed committee sat and submitted recommendations which showed that the dissatisfied members had exercised no small influence over its deliberations. As, however, the author of this book took part in these memorable sessions, he can say from personal observation that the attitude of non-official members generally was one of friendly cordiality and offered promise of a brighter future. An additional war contribution of £45,000,000 was offered to His Majesty's Government, and even a debate on the Press Act produced no bitterness, while a resolution by a non-official member recommending that consideration and disposal of the Report of the Sedition Committee be kept in abeyance, and that a thorough inquiry into the work of the Criminal Investigation Department be undertaken by a mixed committee of officials and non-officials, was rejected by 46 to 2 votes.

In view of the very different debates of the following sessions on the same subject, it is interesting to note that of the six non-official members who spoke in addition to the mover, all condemned the proposal that consideration of the report should be kept in abeyance, one saying that this proposal was inopportune in view of attempts made in England to use the Report as an antidote to the intended Reforms. He added that not only was the proposal inopportune, but that it was calculated to injure the successful passage of the Reforms Bill through Parliament. One member, subsequently a bitter opponent of the resulting legislation, strongly commended the Report; and while three specially reserved opinion upon the legislative proposals, only one condemned them. The debate passed off with entire good humour and general harmony.

On September 9th and 10th, while the Council was sitting, serious riots with loss of life occurred in Calcutta.

For some time that section of the Muhammadan community of Calcutta which manifests an interest in public affairs had been agitated by the course of events outside their province, particularly by the war and its effects upon their co-religionists in Turkey and Asia. Their feelings had been worked up by newspaper effusions, and had previously been deeply stirred by the Arrah riots. Latterly the lower classes of all cities had suffered from high prices.

At the end of July an unwisely worded article had appeared in a paper relating to the presence of certain African Muhammadans in Paris. Originally published in England, it was reproduced in Calcutta without mischievous intention. It was misinterpreted, and an incorrect translation of an expression which appeared in some vernacular newspapers gave rise to an impression among many Muhammadans that insult to the tomb of the Prophet was intended. Violent and inflammatory language was used at various meetings held during August, and more than one speaker called upon the followers of Islam to avenge this insult to their faith. Towards the end of the month a leaflet was widely distributed which called upon Muhammadans in highly provocative language to attend a mass meeting to be held for the protection of Islam on September 8th, 9th, and 10th. Reference was made therein to religious insults, and it was urged that it was necessary to take steps to prevent attacks and 'accursed occurrences. It was stated that Muslim religious leaders would attend from all parts of India.

The Local Government could have no doubt that harangues would be delivered at the proposed meeting which, in the existing state of public feeling, would lead to a grave breach of the peace. The promoters of the meeting were, therefore, amicably requested to abandon it; and on their refusal, followed by the circulation of a second leaflet which was couched in still more inflammatory language and contained provocative references to the Arrah riots, Government decided to prohibit the mass meeting. The religious leaders who had arrived from other parts of India were directed to return to their homes; but before they went a few of the more influential were invited to see the Governor, who explained the situation to them. They endeavoured to persuade the reception committee to abandon the meeting. Efforts were, however, made to induce reconsideration of the Government's decision, and a crowd set out to march on Government House. The police were stoned and finally compelled to fire. The European Deputy Commissioner of Police was stabbed in the neck, and some cloth shops were looted. The Indian Defence Force was called out, and picketed the city on the night of the 9th. About midday on the 10th a larger mob assembled and began to plunder shops. A small military detachment in the vicinity was constrained to fire. The agitators called mill-hands to assist them, and the operatives of three large mills refused to do their work. A foreman, too, was brutally attacked and badly injured. Then a mob of about 2,000 persons endeavoured to force their way into Calcutta. A large number carried formidable clubs, and were led by fanatics shouting and dancing, their bodies smeared with mud. Further firing was necessary to prevent this mob from forcing their way into the city. The riots then subsided, but further sporadic firing took place.

A further reminder of the fanatical fury that can blaze out suddenly in India for slight material reason was given on September 18th by a religious riot at the village of Katarpur in the Saharampur district of the United Provinces. There thirty Muhammadans were killed, sixteen were injured, and a number of houses were burnt down by Hindus determined to prevent cow-sacrifice.

The murders were brutal and unprovoked. The rioters were led and instigated by Hindus of the better classes. One hundred and seventy-five Hindus were convicted after a long and patient trial by a tribunal of high authority; eight were sentenced to death, 135 to transportation for life, and two to seven years' rigorous imprisonment. The judges strongly animadverted on the nervous weakness of the Hindu sub-divisional magistrate.[1]

Criticisms of the Reforms Scheme accumulated. The more important are contained in a parliamentary blue book lately published. On November 1st the Moderates held a separate conference at Bombay. The President condemned the perverse attitude of the Extremist leaders, but considered that the proposals relating to the Government of India should be more advanced. If the whole of what was recommended was not given, if the proposals in the Report were in any way "whittled down," there would be grave public discontent "followed by agitation, the magnitude of which it would be difficult to exaggerate."

It was resolved that dyarchy should extend to the

[1] Within my own experience another Hindu magistrate once behaved admirably in a similar but less grave situation.

Central Government, although the Viceroy had particularly stated at the September Sessions of the Legislative Council that neither he nor the Government of India was prepared to go beyond the proposals contained in the Report. The Conference was attended by about 500 delegates, a figure far smaller than either the average Congress audience or the recent special Congress audience. It is probable that the attendance was materially affected by widespread influenza; but it consisted only of invited visitors, as fears had been entertained of possible wreckers. There is no doubt that the Moderate leaders were in a difficult position, and were encountering bitter opposition from antagonists far more able to catch the ear of the students, journalists, and junior members of the Bar who so often sway political audiences in India. They were, however, aware that in fact they represented many educated Indians of means and position, who feared and shrank from the strife of politics and abuse of newspapers. Had, indeed, such persons seized the opportunity and come forward in any number to steady the course of politics at this critical time, the record of the next few months would have been different. But they stood aside.

Unfortunately the monsoon failed badly; and in October and November the country was visited by a severe influenza epidemic which caused widespread suffering. The conclusion, however, of the Armistice and the triumph of the Allied cause were welcomed throughout the country. The Maharaja of Bikanir and Sir Satyendra Sinha[1] were deputed to England to represent India at the Peace Conference.

Political excitement subsided for a brief space, but broke out again at the usual December meetings.

[1] Now Lord Sinha.

Fervid orations were delivered at these gatherings. The principle of self-determination must be applied to India. Political prisoners and internees must be released. Repressive legislation was not the remedy for revolutionary crime. The Press Act must be repealed. The declaration of August 20th, 1917, was cautious and cold. The Montagu-Chelmsford proposals fell far short of the Congress-League Scheme. There must be fiscal freedom for India. The principal resolution passed at the Congress expressed the view that, so far as the provinces were concerned, full responsible government should be at once granted. Mr. Sastri, the only Moderate politician of importance present, moved an amendment proposing a fifteen years' time limit for the grant of full provincial autonomy. He was supported by Mrs. Besant, but the amendment was lost. Another resolution passed was to the effect that non-official Europeans should not be allowed to form separate electorates on the ground that they represent the mining or the tea industries. If they were allowed such representation, it should be merely in accordance with their numerical proportion to the population of their province.

A third resolution decided that the final authority in all internal affairs should be the supreme Legislative Assembly as voicing the will of the Indian nation.

A fourth resolution nominated Mr. Bal Gangadhar Tilak, Mr. Gandhi, and Saiyid Hassam Imam, lāte President of the Bombay Special Congress, as the representatives of India at the Peace Conference.

Another resolution condemned the proposals of the Sedition Committee, stating that if these were accepted, they "would interfere with the fundamental rights of the Indian people." This resolution was moved by Mr. Bipin Chandra Pal, who, in his own reported words, had "earned high distinction" in the pages of the Committee's Report. The resolution was carried unanimously.

In a closing address the President appealed for Hindu-Muslim unity.

The Congress had included some "tenant-delegates." The proceedings generally were characterised by a correspondent of a leading Moderate journal as "enthusiasm run riot." He added:

"One looked in vain for sobriety, restraint, and good sense; there was a notable tendency toward rabid extremism. . . . There was a tendency towards impatient idealism rather than practical statesmanship, towards indulgence in catch-phrases rather than sound thinking dispassionately done. And the worst of it was that it was not merely the rank and file which suffered from these defects; the leaders showed these weaknesses in an even greater degree."

The President of the Muslim League reminded British statesmen that it was politically unsound to indulge in heavy drafts on the loyalty of a subject people. India had retrograded in material prosperity under British rule. The British administration had not promoted or widened the sources of national wealth in India, and all the available wealth had been actually drained out of the country by the system of administration. Self-government was necessary. He referred to the Calcutta riots and the cases of certain Muhammadan internees, two of whom have since been, by order of the Government of India, committed to jail for endeavouring to induce Muhammadans to assist the Amir of Afghanistan in the recent hostilities. After asserting Muhammadan loyalty to the British Crown, subject to fidelity to the dictates of their faith, the President, Mr. Fazl-ul-Haq, concluded in the following words:

"I will not, therefore, be surprised if they take this opportunity finally to dispose of Turkey and her problems in Europe, and herein lies food for the amplest reflection. As the years roll on, the position of the Mussulmans in India becomes more and more critical, and demands our most anxious thought and care. In my humble opinion we should invoke divine help and guidance in all sincerity and meekness of heart; above all, we should renounce any lurking spirit of strife and quarrel with other communities, and seek their help and assistance in our troubles and difficulties. There are some Mussulmans who think that intolerance of non-Muslims is a point of bravery, and that a contrary feeling betokens cowardice. I have even come across Muslims who take a particular pleasure in assuming a militant attitude towards non-Muslims, as if devotion to Islam demands that we should always be on the warpath irrespective of consequences. All this is not merely morally reprehensible, but politically a grievous blunder. We are daily drifting towards a position when we shall have to tackle one of the most obstinate and powerful bureaucracies known in history. We shall then need all our strength, and also the help and co-operation of our non-Muslim brethren. Experience has shown that we can have this help and co-operation for the mere asking. Shall we be wise and strengthen our arms by an alliance with our brethren, or shall we be foolish and weaken whatever strength we possess by internecine quarrel and strife? We have to decide with the future of our community in the palm of our hands, and, please God, let us decide wisely."[1]

Resolutions were passed regarding the desirability of maintaining the control of the Sultan of Turkey as the true Khalifa over the Holy Places, deprecating the Katarpur riots, supporting self-determination, and other

[1] Another passage in Mr. Fazl-ul-Haq's speech referred to "the hurling of the hordes of Christendom against the bulwarks which the heroes of Islam had raised for the protection of their faith."

matters. In determining the political relations of the Empire for the future, resolute attempts must be made to effect complete reconciliation and lasting accord between the Empire and Muslim States, based on terms of equity and justice.

The All-India Home Rule League also met, with Mrs. Besant in the chair. Their rules were amended. Their object would be to support and strengthen the Congress, and to carry on a continuous educative propaganda on the necessity of Home Rule for India.

It was so evident, however, that both the Congress and the Muslim League had been captured by the most headstrong sections of each body, that Mrs. Besant thought it advisable to point out in her newspaper that India depended on England for her safety, writing that "apart from ideals and sentiments, this is the plain brutal truth, and no amount of shouting can alter it." For this reason stages toward responsible government were necessary, not that India was unfit "in all home matters" for immediate self-government.

There can be no doubt that among the younger members of the political classes in towns, some of the speeches and resolutions of these December meetings did infinite harm, inflaming still further racial animosity and inordinate expectations, preparing the way for serious trouble sooner or later.

CHAPTER VII

THE SEDITION BILLS AND THE "PASSIVE RESISTANCE" RIOTS

On May 22nd, 1919, the Secretary of State for India told the House of Commons that one of the causes of the recent troubles in India, which had resulted in the loss of nine European and 400 Indian lives, was the Sedition Act, which had caused widespread—he would almost say universal—opposition. He added that he was convinced that as passed, as now on the Statute Book, the Act was necessary, ought to have been passed, and could not have been avoided.

It is obvious that the Act in question, and the objects which it was meant to serve, call for clear explanation. I have already referred to the Report of the Sedition (Rowlatt) Committee, and have shown that in September 1918 the Imperial Legislative Council saw no cause whatever for postponing consideration thereof. The Council then did not expect that before it again assembled the war would have been decided. The conclusion of the Armistice impressed on the Government of India the desirability of early action to supply by legislation a measure which would take the place of the Defence of India Act, when, six months after the conclusion of peace, that Act would become inoperative. This conviction was mainly due to the needs of the province of Bengal.

The findings of the Sedition Committee were that in

all the main provinces of India within recent years, bands of conspirators, energetic and ingenious, although few in number, had caused discord or committed crime with the object of preparing the way for the overthrow by force of British rule. Sometimes revolutionary plots had been isolated, and sometimes they had been interconnected. In Bombay the conspiracies had been purely Brahman. In Bengal the conspirators were young men belonging to the educated middle classes. They had committed a long series of murders and robberies, which had only ceased when a considerable number of suspects were interned under the Defence of India Act. Their propaganda had produced a number of murders and robberies in their own province, and had penetrated to Bihar and Orissa, the United Provinces and Madras, where it failed to take root, but led to sporadic crime or disorder. In the Punjab returned emigrants and others had attempted to bring about a bloody rebellion in the critical month of February 1915. There, again, the situation was only retrieved by employment of the Defence of India Act. The fact was that the ordinary statute law was unable to cope with conspiracies rich in ramifications, extending over enormous tracts of country largely devoid of roads and railways, among peoples crowded, ignorant and credulous.

The Bengal conspirators, although a small fraction of the enormous population of that province, spared no pains to attract educated youths to their ranks from schools and colleges. In this they were remarkably successful. They organised and conducted for years a campaign of revolutionary propaganda, of burglary and robbery committed with the object of extracting money for the purchase of firearms and the financing of murderous enterprises which were to prove stepping-stones to a violent upheaval. Gradually they established a terrorism which made evidence of their doings exceedingly hard to obtain. All the time they were working mainly in the small towns and villages of a vast water-country, largely destitute of good communications, or in a big capital city and its suburbs, under cover first of all of the Partition agitation and then of a constant current of newspaper hostility to Government. The following extracts from the Report show the nature of their crimes and the frequent impunity with which those crimes were committed. The first is from the narrative of the year 1915:

"It remains to mention three murders which occurred in Eastern Bengal this year. On March 3rd, Babu Sarat Kumar Basu, the head master of the Zilla School at Comilla, was shot dead while walking with his servant. The servant was wounded in the stomach. A Muhammadan who pursued the murderers received two shots in the chest, and a woman was accidentally struck by a bullet from one of the pistols. Five empty Mauser pistol cartridges were found upon the scene. The head master's servant eventually died. The victim of this murder had come into antagonism with political parties in Bengal in 1908, and shortly before his murder had had occasion to report to the district magistrate about two students concerned in the distribution of seditious pamphlets. None but political reasons can be assigned for this murder."

The Report goes on to mention the murder of a police officer who was shot with his child by four or five youths armed with Mauser pistols. The next illustration belongs to the record of two years later:

"Another dacoity in 1917 remains to be specially mentioned. It was committed in a goldsmith's shop at No. 32, Armenian Street, Bura Bazar, Calcutta, at about 9 p.m. on May 7th. Two young Bengalis entered the shop and asked to see jewellery. Then four young Bengalis entered the shop and began firing wildly with pistols. Two brothers of the owner, who were in the shop, fell mortally wounded. There were also in the shop an assistant and a servant, who were both wounded, two women, one of whom escaped and the other hid under a bench, and a Muhammadan who escaped. The dacoits decamped with jewellery to the value of Rs. 5,459, and some of them drove away in a taxi-cab that they had in waiting."

In neither of these cases was a single conviction obtained. There were many such cases.

The panic which the Revolutionaries managed to inspire in the minds of members both of the educated and uneducated classes is well exemplified by unimpeachable testimony entirely independent of the Committee's report. On December 11th, 1916, Lord Carmichael, then Governor of Bengal, said in a speech:

"Only a few days ago I spoke to one of you, one who has influence, one who has eloquence, and who knows how to use both, and who, I believe, hates the crimes as much as I do; he told me that if he were to go, as he would like to go, to certain places in Bengal, and were to denounce the crimes publicly as he would like to denounce them, he would do it at the risk of his life; and I told him that this is not a risk which he ought lightly to undertake, and is certainly not a risk which I ought to ask him to undertake."

In a farewell speech the same Governor remarked in the same connection:

"The Defence of India Act is what has helped us. I am only saying what I believe to be absolutely true when I say that the Defence of India Act has helped to defend the young educated men of Bengal as nothing else has defended them—not their own fathers, not their teachers, for they were ignorant, not their associates, nor they themselves, for they were blind to the danger."

Mr. Justice Beachcroft and Sir N. G. Chandravarkar stated as follows in their Report referred to later on and completed some time after the publication of the Report of the Sedition Committee:

"The records before us conclusively prove that the revolutionary organisations are secret conspiracies which have spread into different parts of the province, entered homes, schools, and colleges, and have reduced their secrecy of operations almost to scientific methods. They have pledged their members to the closest secrecy of their movements on pain of instant death by murder in the event of disclosure; that is one of their rules, and every attempt has been made to give effect to it. Before the Defence of India Act was brought into force, the fair trial of a person accused of revolutionary crime had been rendered practically impossible by the murders of approvers, witnesses, police officers and law-abiding citizens suspected by revolutionaries of having given information to, or otherwise assisted, the police in the detection of revolutionary crime. A situation of terrorism was created, the current of truth and justice was disturbed, so as to prevent a fair, open, and impartial trial in the ordinary criminal courts, with the result that approvers and witnesses would not come forward to give evidence openly lest they should be assassinated."

The Committee took pains to present the facts for each province in clear narrative form. They carefully described the nature of the evidence on which their findings were based, and they were rewarded by the result. Their conclusions of fact withstood unshaken all the storms of abuse and controversy by which the report was subsequently assailed.

They had been requested to advise as to the legislation, if any, necessary to enable Government to deal effectively with such conspiracies when the Defence of India Act ceased to operate. In compliance with this request, they prepared two concluding chapters. The first recited the difficulties that had arisen in dealing with revolutionary conspiracies. It showed how the ordinary machinery of the law had failed to cope sufficiently with revolutionary crimes in Bengal. Legal evidence as to the authorship of particular crimes, the ownership of arms and other matters bearing on the identity of robbers and murderers, had again and again been unobtainable owing to the size and character of the country, the ignorance and timidity of the people, the comparative paucity of the police, the length of the trials which were habitually spun out by the cross-examination of witnesses upon every conceivable matter with a minuteness unknown in England. Moreover, a widespread and extraordinary terrorism dominated many of these unfortunate persons. Of this terrorism the Committee gave striking examples. They also pointed out that not until 1908 had the Government of India attempted to strengthen the law in order to enable it to meet the difficulties that had arisen in dealing with revolutionary crime. Conspiracy had then enjoyed two years' start. As the measures of 1908 were found inadequate, the Press Act of 1910 was passed. In the intervening two years, newspapers had continued to vilify British rule, and pamphlets of a fanatical and bloodthirsty character had been circulated. Thus it was that a soil was prepared on which anarchy flourished and criminal organisations were able to enlist a constant supply of desperate youths.

The last chapter of the report advised certain measures of legislation. The Committee pointed out that their instructions were applicable to the state of circumstances in which the difficulties referred to had been encountered. These difficulties had been for the present circumvented by special temporary legislation, the Defence of India Act and certain ordinances, but when these lapsed on the conclusion of the war, the old obstacles might or might not revive.

"We do not think," ran the report, "that it is for us to speculate nicely on these matters. We must, of course, keep in view that the present war will have come to an end, but we cannot say with what result or with what ulterior consequential effects or possibilities of consequential effects upon the situation. On the other hand, the persons interned under the Defence of India Act will be due for release, and the terms of imprisonment of many dangerous convicts will be coming to an end. Further, there will, especially in the Punjab, be a large number of disbanded soldiers, among whom it may be possible to stir up discontent. Nevertheless, if we thought it clear that the measures taken against the revolutionary movement under the Defence of India Act had so broken it that the possibility of the conspiracies being revived could be safely disregarded, we should say so. That is not our view, and it is on this footing that we report."

The Committee pointed out that before the war, in 1911, special preventive legislation had been considered advisable, and that in 1914 it had been recognised that the forces of law and order, working through the ordinary channels, could not cope with the situation in Bengal. They showed that the whole history of the endeavours of the Government to deal with revolutionary crime was a history of extreme unwillingness to recognise the potency of the terrorism exercised by the revolutionaries, and of reluctance to deprive any man of his liberty without an open and regular trial. Even the powers conferred by the old Regulation III of 1818, which enabled deportations or detentions of persons as state prisoners, were hardly ever resorted to. In fact, it was only when Government was forced by a developing and extending anarchical organisation from position to position that early in 1914 it contemplated a substantial number of internments. Even then no action was taken until the war broke out and, by adducing other considerations and greatly encouraging revolutionary crime, compelled prompt and effective remedy in the shape of the Defence of India Act.

Thus it was the suggestions which the Committee put forward contained hardly an idea which had not, in one connection or another, been the subject of critical discussion, although they did not reproduce as an assembled whole any scheme previously submitted.

The Committee proposed punitive and preventive measures,[1] the former in order better to secure the conviction and punishment of offenders, the latter to check the spread of conspiracy and the commission of revolutionary crime. They expected far more from the latter than from the former. Among the former were a few suggested amendments of the substantive existing law. These were to be permanent changes. Emergency measures, both punitive and preventive, were also proposed. The Committee pointed out that as the powers which they suggested must be ready for use at short notice, they should be on the statute-book in advance. This fact, too, was calculated to have some moral effect, as those who meditated renewal of an anarchical movement would thus know what they would have to encounter. To postpone legislation till

[1] The proposals have been frequently criticised, under the apparent impression that to suggest political concessions lay within the province of the Committee.

the danger was instant, was to risk a recurrence of the futile discussions as to possibilities of action which marked a period of years before the war. Emergency measures, that is, measures to be applied upon a notification by the Governor-General in Council declaring the existence of a state of affairs justifying such application, should therefore be framed and enacted. These powers would be both punitive and preventive, the latter to be of two degrees of stringency, as it was desirable that mild measures should, if possible, be taken first.

The notifications would be capable of application to particular provinces or to smaller areas. The principal measures recommended were provisions (*a*) for the trial of seditious crime by three judges of the highest grade and status, without juries or assessors who were liable to be affected by public discussion or deliberate terrorism; (*b*) for investing a provincial government, on emergency, with powers of internment similar to those which could be applied under the Defence of India Act, but modified by checks in the shape of local investigating and visiting committees.

Internments should be either a mere restriction of movements or a complete temporary deprivation of liberty, as the revolutionaries varied widely in character, some merely requiring to be kept from evil associations and others being irreconcilable desperadoes.

Emergency powers would only be used upon a notification by the Governor-General in Council declaring that a state of affairs justified such a course of action, except in the cases of revolutionaries involved in crimes committed before the expiration of the Defence of India Act and of desperate characters whose automatic release on that occasion could not be contemplated. Finally the Committee invited attention to the proof in their narrative that there were bodies outside India conspiring to promote seditious violence in that country. During the war armed insurrection had been plotted between these bodies and revolutionaries in India, with the encouragement of the enemies of the Empire. Although it was impossible to forecast post-war conditions either within or outside India, a situation should be contemplated in which, while India was peaceful, conspirators from abroad might enter the country to promote disorder. Provision was needed for such a contingency and to prevent revolutionary crime, when once established anew in any province, spreading to others and necessitating an extended proclamation of emergency measures. The Committee considered whether the Act enabling the employment of the emergency measures above described should be permanent or temporary. They decided that this was a question of policy upon which they would express no opinion.

In January 1919 the Government of India announced their intention of proceeding with the legislation recommended by the Sedition Committee on the opening of the February sessions of the Imperial Legislative Council. They published two draft Bills to be permanent in operation which embodied the Committee's recommendations. One Bill included the alterations proposed in the permanent law. The other, which was by far the more important, detailed the emergency legislation. It should be noted that in the interval between the publication of the Report and the close of the year 1918, the Government of Bengal had published a report received from a committee of two, Mr. Justice Beachcroft, a Calcutta High Court Judge of established reputation, and Sir Narain Chandravarkar, an ex-High Court Judge of Bombay, well-known in progressive

Indian circles. This committee had been appointed to examine and report on the cases of 806 *détenus* (100 State prisoners dealt with under Regulation III of 1818, 702 internees restrained under the Defence of India Act, and four persons confined under the Indian Ingress Ordinance). The Committee reported on August 31st to the following effect:

> "Our study and examination of the cases have impressed us with the correctness of the conclusion arrived at in their Report by the Sedition Committee 1918, presided over by Mr. Justice Rowlatt, as to the alliance and interconnection of all the groups, formed into one revolutionary movement with one common object, viz., the overthrow of His Majesty's Government in India by force. All the individual cases stand so closely interconnected as parts of one whole that they form, both as to the personnel and acts of crime, one continuous movement of revolution which must be regarded as living and prolonged in all its parts until the movement is completely extinguished."

The Committee recommended the release of six only of all the above enumerated *détenus*.

The publication of the new Bills in January was the signal for widespread and intensified Extremist condemnation of the Rowlatt Report and its proposals. The Moderate leaders, too, declared against the proposals. Even Sir Narain Chandravarkar announced that no legislation of the kind intended was required, as revolutionary effort would probably become extinct on the enactment of the forthcoming constitutional Reforms.

Before and after the Imperial Legislative Council met, speakers at public meetings and newspaper editors endeavoured to persuade the country that in announcing these Bills Government was endeavouring to erect a monstrous engine of tyranny and oppression. At Madras, the chairman of a meeting said that legislation had been proposed which gravely imperilled the elementary rights of every British citizen, and this at a time when Indians had given special proofs of their loyalty. Another speaker said that this legislation was an attempt to invent crimes. A third speaker accused Government of wishing to arm itself with a precautionary measure which would enable it to deal with the agitation which would follow on the passing of an unsatisfying measure of Reforms. Should, however, the Reforms be unsatisfying, a worse mutiny than 1857 would result.

At a Home Rule League meeting in Bombay an orator said that the provisions of the proposed Bills were designed to filch away liberties. Determined steps must be taken to prevent the Bills from becoming law. At a mass meeting in Calcutta the President said that against the British Crown there was no revolutionary party, but discontent was bitter against the bureaucracy. The Bills made it unsafe even to think freely. They took away all right to personal liberty. Another orator compared the proceedings of the Government to the action of Nadir Shah (who sacked Delhi and massacred its inhabitants). He was at any rate honest, but the Government was not even honest in its tyranny. A Calcutta newspaper accused the Government of being blinded by *zid* (enmity), of driving the people mad "without rhyme or reason."

In Lahore the first act of a tragic drama was a protest meeting held on February 4th by the "Indian Association," at which speeches were made by persons who were two months later to be called to account as leaders of open sedition and violence. One orator informed two Punjab non-official members of the Imperial Legislative Council that if they supported the Rowlatt Bills they would be regarded as enemies of their country and India would know the reason why. Gross travesties of the Bills were circulated among the ignorant and credulous lower orders in various large cities. It was only later that the Government of India appreciated the degree of mischief that had been thus accomplished.

The Imperial Legislative Council commenced sitting at Delhi on February 6th.

In his opening speech the Viceroy explained the necessity for proceeding with the Bills, as the

very important powers which had enabled the public peace and order to be preserved during the war would shortly cease to operate and must be replaced by adequate substitutes. The sudden release from restraint and control of the forces of anarchy could not be contemplated. The reaction against all authority which had manifested itself in many parts of the civilised world was unlikely to leave India entirely untouched, and the powers of evil were still abroad.

He was sure that special measures were necessary not to the maintenance of His Majesty's Government in India, but to the safety of the lives and property of its citizens. He therefore recommended the two Bills "to the very earnest and careful consideration of Council."

Sir William Vincent, the Home Member, introduced the second and more important of the Bills, that which related to the conferment of emergency powers. He pointed out that the Bill was aimed at seditious crime, and not in any sense at political movements properly so called. It was not nearly as wide as the Defence of India Act, and could be used against none but seditious activities. He explained the provisions of the Bill. It had not been undertaken without anxious consideration. Government had no desire to restrict liberty of person further than they were forced to by a sense of duty. He moved that the Bill be referred to a Select Committee, and stated that the Government would be perfectly open to consider such modifications as would not render the machinery ineffective for dealing with the evil which they sought to combat.

Two amendments were moved. The movers asked that the Bill should not be referred to a Select Committee at this stage, but postponed for consideration by the new councils which would come into existence after the passing of the coming Reforms Bill. They made it clear, however, that their objections were to the Bills themselves. These, if persisted in, would produce a tremendous agitation.

The amendments were supported by all the Indian non-official members. It was said that the Bill if passed into law would produce "untold misery," that it was "abhorrent and shocking," that it was "opposed to the fundamental principles of law and justice." When Government undertook a repressive measure of this kind, the innocent were not safe. It was possible to pay too high a price for the extinction of wickedness. Peace in administration, valuable as it is, might be sought in wrong ways. It was desirable to offer satisfying methods of political emancipation. These would cure the general atmosphere that feeds anarchy. The anarchist would then naturally die, even if untouched by the long arm of the law. The non-official members of the Council had consented to such repressive measures as the Press Act and Defence of India Act, but would not accept this Bill. No measure of the kind could be supported unless after the Reforms had come into effect it were found that revolutionary conspirators were still at work.

The Bill was supported by several official members, who pointed out that the real issue was, should the Government take adequate measures for protecting its subjects and loyal servants from bloodthirsty and seditious crime. Dangers were clearly visible which were not lessened by the triumph of Bolshevism in Russia, even though such triumph might be partial and temporary. The leaders of the revolutionary movement had not vanished from the earth. It was clear, from a recent debate in the Bengal Legislative Council, that they not only existed, but would renew operations when opportunity offered. Their designs had been furthered all along by the absence of determined persistent non-official opposition to their propaganda of racial hatred. Indian parents had a right to expect that the State would take effective steps to prevent the depravation and ruin of their sons. It was incumbent on Government to do its best to guard the lives and homes of its loyal servants. The facts were admitted by honourable members, and the case was not one for application of the principle, "Wait (helplessly) and see!" The Government would indeed wait, but it would wait armed and ready. There had been gross exaggeration of the possible effects of the Bill. Consideration of it could not be postponed, as a law must be ready to take the place of the Defence of India Act. In regard to the argument that the Bill poorly rewarded India's war effort, the Home Member pointed out that this war effort would have been impossible had not order been preserved. The Revolutionaries, against whom the Bill was directed, so far from helping in the war, had conspired with the King's enemies and done their best to ruin the Allied cause.

Both amendments were lost, although supported by the votes of all the Indian non-official members. And before going further, it is desirable to explain briefly the reference to a recent debate in the Bengal Legislative Council. On January 21st, 1919, a private member of that body had moved that the Council should recommend to the Governor in Council the immediate release of all internees. During the debate the Honourable Sir Henry Wheeler said, on the part of the Government:

"We have, unfortunately, the best reasons for going on with whatever checks have been imposed by the measures taken under the Defence Act. Men are still abroad who were known to be leaders in the revolutionary movement; they are still actively engaged in enlisting boys for their own ends and endeavouring to foment trouble; and simply because sedition has been checked for the moment, we should not be justified in assuming that it does not exist."

The resolution was lost.

The Government undertook to make the Act a temporary instead of a permanent measure, in the hope that the Reforms proposals might do something to remove the danger now experienced from anarchical conspiracies. The Act would operate for three years only. In order to make it more apparent that the application thereof would be strictly confined to the activities of revolutionary and anarchical conspirators, they called the measure a Bill "to cope with anarchical and revolutionary crime." Lastly, they promised to consider any other modifications which non-official members might wish to put forward in so far as they could do this without rendering the Bill ineffective for the purpose for which it was designed. The promise was strictly fulfilled. The Bill went through most careful and considerate examination in Select Committee, and returned to Council modified in every reasonably possible particular. But while the action of the Government was eminently conciliatory, the non-official Indian members remained obdurate.

Outside the Council, Extremist leaders and journalists spared no pains to incite bitter agitation. They were joined, unfortunately, by Mr. Gandhi, who sent to the Press a pledge signed by numerous persons of his way of thinking, declaring that if the Sedition Bills became law they would "civilly refuse to obey these laws and such other laws as a committee to be hereafter appointed might think fit." They further affirmed that in this struggle they would "faithfully follow the truth and refrain from violence to life, person, or property." This, however, was going too far for the Moderates. It was pointed out at once in a leading Moderate paper that the principle involved in the pledge was extremely dangerous and might lead anywhere, and on March 15th the Moderate leaders at Delhi issued a manifesto expressing disapproval of passive resistance. They did not, however, alter their own attitude toward the Bill, and the Extremist agitation continued.

We must return to the Legislative Council.

The Home Member had decided to republish the minor Bill, which was to be a piece of permanent legislation, and thus to postpone consideration thereof. Debates on the main (Emergency) Bill recommenced on March 12th and concluded on March 18th. Numerous amendments were moved; numerous speeches were made; and finally the Bill was passed after keen debates. Again there were prophecies, almost minatory, of agitation, and the measure was opposed by all the Indian non-official members. Before proceeding further it will be useful to notice two underlying ideas which inspired many of their arguments. The first was that in proposing to curtail personal liberty and intern without trial, the British Government was trying to do in India what it would not try to do in England. The second was that the police and the Executive could not be trusted safely with the powers committed to them by the Bill. In answer to the first, it was pointed out that England is a small country, endowed with excellent communications, and inhabited by a homogeneous community which differs widely from the great masses speaking diverse languages, for the most part extremely credulous and simple, who dwell together in the vast continent of India. It would be impossible for any gangs of conspirators to organise and keep going in Great Britain an elusive, potent, and enduring system of robbery and terrorism of the sort which had been so successful in Bengal and had attempted operations in other provinces. But if anything of the kind were attempted in Britain, and if the ordinary law were inefficacious because witnesses were terrorised and policemen were shot, it was certain that remedies would be applied as drastic as, and probably more drastic than, the Bill before the Council. Moreover, different as conditions are in England and India, the greatest reluctance had all along been shown by Secretaries of State and the Government of India to the undertaking of this kind of legislation. It was only under compelling necessity that the Bill had been devised.

As to the second argument, the fact remained that when in the preceding year the cases of 800 persons, interned or detained as State prisoners in Bengal, were investigated by the judges of the highest calibre, only six were recommended for release. Under the provisions of the Bill non-officials would be members of the investigating committees in all cases of internment. It was thus obvious that particular precautions had been taken to prevent any mistakes whatever in future. The Beachcroft-Chandravarkar Report bore remarkable testimony to the cautious work of the police in revolutionary cases. Revolutionary crime was, the Report explained, collective and continuous in its operation. The risk of exposure of dishonest police work was greater in revolutionary than in ordinary crime. And as regards the powers proposed for provincial governments and their executive subordinates, it was certain that these powers, which could only be exercised after a special notification issued by the Supreme Government itself, would only be applied for with the greatest reluctance, and would be used with extreme caution under a fire of bitterly hostile criticism.

In winding up the debate, the Home Member expressed an earnest hope that the passive resistance movement would not materialise. For Government to yield to such a movement would be to abdicate its authority. Sir William Vincent thanked the Moderate leaders for the manifesto which they had issued condemning Mr. Gandhi's declaration. He concluded :

"My Lord, I have now very nearly done. I have only a word or two to add. The conscience of the Government in the matter of this legislation is quite clear. We are acting from a deep-rooted conviction that we are doing what is right. We have proposed the law to meet what we know to be a terrible danger. We have provided numerous safeguards in it so as, so far as is possible, to prevent any injustice occurring under it. We think that many members of this Council know in their heart of hearts what this danger is, and how formidable it is to peaceable residents in parts of the Province.[1] My only regret is that I have failed to convince more Honourable members of the necessity for this law, and this is a matter of greater regret because

[1] *Sic* according to the official report of the Debate.

I feel it may be partly owing to some fault or deficiency in my presentment of the case."

As the Sedition Committee's Report showed, the atmosphere which swelled the ranks of the Bengal revolutionaries and facilitated their operations was largely created by newspapers and literature which constantly argued that British rule was tyrannical and ruinous. The astute authors of the revolutionary paper *Yugantar* had, thirteen years before, perceived that, in their own words, to give force to their movement, "the nature of the oppressor must be painted in bright colours and placed before the common people"; and constantly the leaders of the party of violence have devoted close attention to drawing what support and assistance they could, not only from their own publications, but from the contents of ordinary newspapers. A well-known revolutionary pamphlet shows how the "foreign department" of a big revolutionary association insisted on the importance of a regular study of the newspapers as essential for a recruit's training.

There can be no doubt whatever that the bitter diatribes against the Sedition Bills both in and outside the Imperial Legislative Council, supported by the false versions of their scope and meaning which were spread abroad, presented a remarkable opportunity to the enemies of the British Government. The following passage from the judgment of the Court,[1] which subsequently tried the Lahore rioters, gives a clear picture of the manner in which the opportunity was used.

"There may perhaps have been some few persons who believed that the Rowlatt Bills, if enacted, were liable to abuse, and doubtless a good many more were roused to opposition by the speeches in the Imperial

[1] The Court was one established after martial law had been enacted. It was a court of three, the senior a Chief Court judge.

Council and the campaign in the press, but the bulk of the city population do not read newspapers and would have remained in complete ignorance, not merely of the objections to the Bills, but even of their existence, unless other steps had been taken to educate them. . . . But even of the educated few, hardly any one appears to have read or considered the Bills for himself, and it was not the business of any one to combat all or any of the lies and misrepresentations which were in circulation. It is true that at one meeting Gokal Chand did give reasons of a legal and technical kind for his objections to the first of the two Bills, but the class of persons who attended the Lahore meetings did not go there to hear legal arguments and did not carry them away. What they learnt generally was that in spite of the opposition of the whole of India, and in particular of a saint named Gandhi, who, they were taught to believe, was the Rishi of the Hindus and the Wali of the Muhammadans, an alien government was trying to pass, and did pass an exceedingly harsh law which threatened the liberties of the humblest individuals; and that unless all classes and religions united against the Government, there was no hope of averting the imminent peril. This teaching was enforced with all the arts of demagogues, who were unsparing in their abuse of a government which, they said, was meting out tyranny in return for loyalty and sacrifice. . . . It was commonly believed that all and sundry, though innocent of all crime, would be arrested at the will of the police and condemned without trial; that all assemblies of more than three or four people would be prohibited; and that in some mysterious way even the women and children would be made to suffer."

While preparations were thus sedulously made for certain trouble, Mr. Gandhi, at the head of his committee of disciples, proclaimed a general closing of shops and suspension of business activity for March 30th. Subsequently he altered the day to April 6th; but on the former date occurred the first of a succession of tragedies more grievous in their nature and results than any that had befallen India since the days of the Mutiny.

An unfortunate consequence of the transfer of the headquarters of the Imperial Government from Calcutta to Delhi has been that the Viceroy and his Councillors, Executive and Legislative, have left a big, cosmopolitan and partly Europeanised city, where even if one section of inhabitants becomes disaffected and gives trouble, it is balanced and countered by other sections, to dwell among a comparatively small, ignorant, and backward population of little variety, easily impressed by fiction and exaggeration. The people of Delhi had been attentive to the recent controversial debates, and from subsequent occurrences it would seem that care was taken to intensify the impressions which they had received.

The Legislative Council had broken up, and the heads of the Government of India had left Delhi, when on the morning of March 30th the shops of the city were closed as a protest against the passage of the Sedition Bill. Some shopkeepers who opened were induced to close again, and crowds in the streets exerted themselves to persuade drivers of cars to take their vehicles home, leaving passengers to walk. About 1.30 p.m. a crowd assembled outside the railway station, and some members thereof entered and attempted to prevent the railway contractor who was supplying food to third-class passengers from carrying out his duties. He was told that he must recognise the *hartál* (stoppage of business). On refusing, he was assaulted. Two of his assailants were arrested, and the mob invaded the station in order to rescue them. The building was cleared by the police and some troops. A small party of British infantry was requisitioned from the Fort. The mob were driven off, throwing stones and bricks, but could not be dispersed; and finally the additional District Magistrate and Superintendent of Police, who were in charge of the police and military, considered that the further postponement of sterner measures would only lead to serious bloodshed. Two rounds of ammunition were fired and two rioters fell. Then the crowd broke; but, later on, heavy stoning of the police and of a small party of British infantry necessitated further firing. It was announced that eight men had been killed and twelve or thirteen were being treated for wounds at the civil hospital. Three days later a poster was discovered in the city inciting to murder. For some days shops were closed. Railway traffic, too, was obstructed.

These incidents were the prelude to disturbances in other cities of India; Mr. Gandhi had endeavoured to visit Delhi, but had been arrested and sent back to Bombay. He had been directed to remain in his own Presidency. The news of his arrest occasioned violent disturbances among the mill-hands at Ahmedabad, with whom his influence was particularly strong. A mob of these people set fire to and burnt Government offices, cut telegraph-wires, assaulted Europeans, beating a police-sergeant so severely that he died. In the neighbourhood a trainful of troops was derailed. At the town of Viramgaum an Indian Government official was burnt with kerosine oil. In Bombay itself Mr. Gandhi's Committee had advised that for the time being the laws regarding prohibited literature and registration of newspapers might be civilly disobeyed. Forbidden literature was sold, but no riots occurred. In Calcutta riots resulted in loss of life and injury to police officials. There, however, all was speedily over, and no disturbance occurred anywhere else in Bengal, the province which was the main cause of the anti-sedition legislation, but for which there would have been no such law-making. But by far the most widespread and tragic occurrences took place in the Punjab. These incidents are about to form the subject of report by a special committee,[1] and I shall confine my narrative to some salient facts. The measures taken to suppress particular outbreaks are under investigations.

Of the population of the Punjab, 55 per cent. is Muhammadan, 33 per cent. is Hindu, and 11 per cent. is Sikh. The most martial section is the Sikh, which, during the war, with less than one-hundredth[2] of the population, supplied about one-sixth of the fighting forces of the Indian Empire.

The Report of the Sedition Committee shows how, in the year 1907, certain agitators belonging to the educated classes endeavoured to stir up trouble in the Punjab. In that year the Lieutenant-Governor reported to the Government of India that in certain towns an active anti-English propaganda was being openly and sedulously preached. His report ran: "In Lahore, the capital of the province, the propaganda is virulent, and has resulted in a more or less general state of serious unrest." He held that some of the leaders looked to driving the British out of the country, or, at any rate, from power, either by force or by the passive resistance of the people as a whole, and that the method by which they had set themselves to bring the Government machine to a standstill was by endeavouring to stir up intense racial hatred.

In 1907 these men effected little; but the snake was merely scotched, and in 1909 a stream of seditious

[1] So are the occurrences at Delhi and Ahmedabad.

[2] This was the proportion in September 1917. Afterwards special efforts were made with marked success to stimulate recruiting in the United Provinces, and the Punjab proportions may have altered.

literature issuing from Lahore necessitated preventive measures. A bomb-outrage was contrived in 1913, and in the same year a Lahore Muhammadan journalist published disloyal and inflammatory articles regarding a religious riot at Cawnpore. Early in 1914 the Turkish Consul-General came to Lahore to present to the principal mosque a carpet sent by order of the Sultan as a token of gratitude for subscriptions sent to the Turkish Red Crescent funds. He was followed a fortnight later by two Turkish doctors of the Red Crescent Society.

Early in the war some Sikh returned emigrants from America committed a number of outrages, and, together with a Hindu belonging to the Bombay Presidency and a notorious Bengali revolutionary, planned simultaneous risings in various cities of the Punjab and other provinces. Amritsar and Lahore were successively the headquarters of this conspiracy, which would have brought untold calamity on India in February 1915 had it not been discovered and frustrated by the vigilance and energy of the Punjab authorities. The Sedition Committee Report tells how the plot was baffled, and how a state of incipient lawlessness and anarchy, which might well have caused irreparable damage to Great Britain, in a most critical hour, was terminated by the resolute and courageous administration of the Lieutenant-Governor, Sir Michael O'Dwyer. Since 1915 all had been quiet in the Punjab. The contributions of the Province to the fighting forces of the Empire had been remarkable, and the Provincial Government had felt itself strong enough to release a number of interned suspects. The Sedition Committee, however, note that they had received sound "admonition" from the following words of a Sikh official witness who appeared before them: "There are thousands of persons who have returned to India with revolutionary ideas,[1] and only those against whom we had definite information were interned or restricted. The majority have perfect liberty."

With many of the inhabitants of the Punjab the interval between thought and action is short. If captured by inflammatory harangues, they promptly give trouble. Unfortunately, too, in March 1919 they were suffering from bad harvests. Prices were very high, and the towns were full of economic discontent. Among the fanatical Muhammadan lower orders rumours were current that unjust treatment had been meted out to Turkey. The opportunity was favourable for the enemies of the Government for another reason. It was widely believed that the war had left Great Britain weak and exhausted. Two leaders in one of the subsequent riots cried aloud that the British Ráj was extinct, and other evidence attests the currency of ideas of this kind. The following passages from an April letter to the Press, written by a loyal Muhammadan gentleman, explains the use to which the occasion was put:

"It has been with feelings of the acutest pain and distress that I have been persistently hearing and receiving reports from almost unknowing and illiterate shopkeepers and neighbours, that Government has recently passed a Bill, under which powers have been given to the police to arrest any four persons talking or standing together in the bazar or before a shop, and that, therefore, the people are being asked by the so-called knowing leaders to practise *hartal* as a mark of protest against this kind of legislation. The laws referred to in these absolutely unfounded reports and black lies, that are being so sedulously spread, are obviously the Rowlatt Bills recently enacted as laws. No educated man, howsoever politically minded, will, for a moment, contend that the Rowlatt Bills are legis-

[1] See Appendix V.

lation of this kind, empowering the police to raid any house inhabited by four or five persons or to arrest any four or five persons assembled together in the bazar or in the 'baithaks.' Who, then, is responsible for wholly false and mischievous misrepresentations of this kind, and why are these being so freely and recklessly made? The answer to the latter question is plain. Mr. Gandhi has unfortunately passed a message for the closing of all shops and the suspension of all business activity on Sunday, the 6th instant. The politically minded folk, who by an ironic stroke of evil fortune arrogate to themselves the right of being the mouthpiece of this loyal and contented, but, in the language of these people, this Extremist province, feel that a demonstration on Mr. Gandhi's lines must take place on the date appointed, else their reputed influence with the people outside will suffer. So they decide to have a *hartal* in the province on the date fixed, and, in order to bring this about, inflame the unknowing and illiterate by spreading mischievous reports of this kind. But themselves they lurk behind, and dare not come in the open. How many among these politically minded persons in this province have taken Mr. Gandhi's vow, and if they have not, probably so because Mr. Gandhi's propaganda is the absurdest ever launched in the history of political freedom, then why are they misleading the ignorant shopkeeper and tonga-plyer by all kinds of false and unfounded misrepresentations, and at their expense bringing about a false and spurious demonstration? If the political workers in the Punjab believe that the Rowlatt Bills are nothing in the shape of what they are being represented to the ignorant public, and I have no doubt that no man in his senses will have the courage or unfairness to say otherwise, then do they not owe it a duty to their province and their conscience to publicly contradict these mischievous rumours, which are being spread in the interest of Mr. Gandhi's agitation?

"So much to the political workers of this province. I

have a word also to say to those who, possessed of material stakes in the peace and orderly progress of this country, have as much a right to political opinions as any set of fictitious workers. Why are they sitting with their hands folded, passive observers of a scene which should wake them to a sense of their duty? Passive resistance, let there be no misunderstanding, is active resistance, and they must condemn it with as much violence as they would condemn an open revolution. I would, therefore, appeal to all public associations in this province to address themselves immediately to the task which is their supreme duty at this hour, and unhesitatingly condemn this direct challenge to British laws, which spell the veriest justice and the freedom which results from their obedience." . . .

On April 6th, the date fixed by Mr. Gandhi, there was a complete suspension of business in Lahore.[1] A procession had been forbidden, but a crowd collected and threatened to become unmanageable. An advertised meeting was held, and was addressed by various speakers. The authorities were carefully watching the situation, and no disturbance occurred. Business was resumed on the 7th. On the 9th the annual Rám Naumi (Hindu religious) procession was held. Speeches were made advocating Hindu and Muhammadan unity. On the afternoon of the 10th news arrived of disturbances in the city of Amritsar and of murders of Europeans. The arrest of Mr. Gandhi had also been announced. A fresh suspension of business was started. Shops were shut, often by no means willingly. Leaflets and posters had prepared the way, and crowds insisted on a general closure. In the evening a large mob tried to invade the European quarter, wrecked the telegraph office, and was only dispersed by firing. On the morn-

[1] I have carefully consulted the judgments of the Courts that tried the Lahore and Amritsar rioters.

ing of the 11th a mass meeting of Hindus and Muhammadans was held in a famous mosque. This was an unprecedented occurrence, and provoked very strong subsequent Muhammadan censure. On breaking up, the meeting degenerated into a disorderly and mischievous rabble. A crowd marched through the streets shouting, among other cries, that the King was dead, and destroying pictures of their Majesties. On the 12th it was necessary to disperse another riotous crowd by firing. The shops remained closed, and were not opened until the city was placed under martial law.

The disturbances at Amritsar had been still more serious. Two leading lawyer agitators had been deported on the morning of the 10th by order of the Local Government. This led to an immediate suspension of business. A mob collected and attempted to enter the civil lines, where they at once attacked the telegraph office. It was necessary to fire before they could be turned back. Sections then went to the railway goods shed and murdered a European guard. In the city they burnt and plundered the National Bank, murdering the British agents in charge thereof. They sacked another bank, murdered the agent, burnt the town hall and the Indian Christian Church, attacked buildings, and violently assaulted other Europeans, including two ladies. But for the action of some loyal Indians they would have done more. They destroyed telegraph wires and tore up railway lines. Some degree of order was restored; but the country round was greatly disturbed, and on the 13th, in Amritsar, a prohibited meeting was attended by a large crowd. This was dispersed by rifle fire with heavy casualties.[1] At Kasur, in the neighbourhood, on the 12th, a mob, worked up by speeches delivered on that and the

[1] This was the Jallianwala Bagh affair now *sub judice.*

previous day, invaded and wrecked the railway station, attacked an incoming train, murdered two warrant officers, assaulted and injured two other military officers and two corporals, assaulted a European railway official and his wife, all passengers in the train, burnt the post office and a judicial court, and were finally dispersed by fire from the police. The Court that tried the accused men found that of them, two had shown mercy to the railway official, to his wife and children, but that the safety of these persons was due to the intervention of an Indian gentleman, Mr. Khair-ud-Din, examiner of accounts.

Martial law was declared in Lahore and Amritsar on the 15th. But disorder had spread to other towns and to villages adjoining towns. Wires were cut; railway lines were breached; two churches were burnt; Government property was attacked; Europeans were assaulted. By the 17th martial law was in working order in four districts. Afterwards it was extended to a wider area. By degrees order was re-established. From April 10th to the 17th railways and telegraph systems had been subjected to repeated and organised attacks. Isolated railway strikes had been engineered; two passenger troop-trains were derailed, in one case with loss of life.

During the disturbances a number of railway stations were attacked and either destroyed or damaged.

Mr. Gandhi from Bombay regretted that when he embarked upon a mass movement he underrated "the forces of evil." He was, however, convinced that Satyagraha (insistence on truth, *alias* passive resistance) had nothing to do with the violence of the mob. Nevertheless, he advised his Satyagrahi followers temporarily to suspend civil disobedience and to assist the Government in restoring order.[1] In his opinion "there

[1] Mr. Gandhi also personally assisted in restoring order at Ahmedabad.

were clever men behind the lawless deeds, and they showed concerted action." Mr. Gandhi, however, possesses plenty of intelligence himself, and can hardly have failed to notice either the rapid exacerbation of racial feeling which followed on his propaganda or the probability of results such as those actually achieved. But, after so much tragedy, even in May he contemplated a resumption of civil disobedience in July, and has since been reported to advocate this remedy for the Khalifat question.

Mrs. Besant, who was shocked by recent developments, and had vigorously opposed Mr. Gandhi's action, declared that the Rowlatt Act had been largely changed by the Legislative Council. There was nothing in it that a good citizen could object to.[1] She had combated the passive resistance movement on the ground that it would lead to a general disregard of law and consequently to riots and bloodshed. She admitted the existence of revolutionary movements in certain parts of the country, and considered it the duty of all leaders to assist the Government in putting down violence. These utterances gave great offence to many of her former followers.

A glance at the map of India will show that no province but the Punjab was seriously affected by these disturbances, although there were riots in a very few cities of other provinces. By far the gravest of these

[1] It would appear that subsequently, after arriving in England, Mrs. Besant forgot this declaration. In a pamphlet headed "The Case for India," published in London by the Home Rule for India League, she thus referred to the Rowlatt legislation. "The Rowlatt Act, nominally aimed at Revolutionaries, may be put into force on the mere opinion of the Governor-General in Council that any movement has a tendency in a revolutionary direction, and we know, by the administration of the Defence of India Act, how the most legitimate political movement can be thus suspected. Once in force in any district, the liberty of every individual in it lies at the mercy of the Local Government."

riots was that at Ahmedabad. There were many meetings of protest against the Sedition Bill in towns throughout India, for fantastic ideas of its provisions were everywhere circulated. But the greater part of these meetings dissolved harmlessly enough. They were convened by persons who had no wish to instigate violence.

The Punjab disturbances closely resembled in character the violent outbreak at Ahmedabad, but were much more extensive and determined. How far this circumstance was due to careful and deliberate preparation will be determined by the Disorders Committee. Newspapers have denounced Bolshevist intrigue as the malignant inspiration. But I have shown clearly that we need not go so far to find at least some seeds of the terrible calamity that overtook a province with so fine a war record. A mass of inflammable material had accumulated, and we shall know later what actually produced the conflagration.

Although the area of the riots covers a very small place on the map of India, this conflagration was of the gravest nature, and, had it not been speedily arrested, would have spread with incalculable results. It would seem that only the prompt proclamation of martial law saved a rapidly developing situation of extreme moment.[1] Even as things were, the outbreaks encouraged invasion from Afghanistan and involved incidents of the deepest tragedy. Their eventual consequences are not yet apparent.

The riotous mobs were, so far as present information goes, mainly composed of low-class and disorderly ele-

[1] Three farewell addresses presented to Sir Michael O'Dwyer at Lahore on May 12th by deputations from the Hindus, Sikhs, and Muhammadans of the Punjab, bore grateful testimony to his administration. Each alluded specially to these disturbances.

ments from cities and from villages adjacent to lines of railway. There was also some admixture of students. All had been worked on and excited by political agitators. It is important to see who stood by the British whole-heartedly in this hour of need.

For solid assistance the Punjab Government was indebted to its own ruling chiefs and to the Indian Army and police, all of whom maintained the reputation for steadfast loyalty which they had borne throughout the war.

The landholders, too, generally stood by the authorities. A strong manifesto was issued by their association bitterly condemning the passive resistance movement, and exhorting all members of the community to assist Government to restore order. So far it appears that only a few Sikhs joined the rioters. The attitude of the Sikh community generally was loyal. In the words of Sir Michael O'Dwyer, "Sikh gentlemen, Sikh soldiers, and Sikh peasants, at the risk of their lives, saved European ladies who had been attacked, conducted to places of safety others who had been in danger, and rescued wounded British soldiers from the roused fury of the mob." Other Indians, too, acted in a similar manner.

The Moderate politicians at Lahore did all they could to assist Government after the disturbances had broken out, but had not endeavoured to counteract the scandalous lies that had long been previously circulated regarding the purport and provisions of the Sedition Act.

In view of its material bearing on the lamentable course of events, the attitude of the Moderate leaders generally, from September 1918 to May 1919, in regard to the Sedition legislation and the subsequent riots, calls for a brief review.

It may clearly be inferred that when the report of the

Sedition Committee first came before the Imperial Legislative Council in September 1918, the non-official members as a body were prepared to accept it as a convincing exposition of facts, and to consider its recommendations in a fair and reasonable spirit. They had no idea then that for the Government to act on those recommendations would mean ingratitude for Indian participation in the war. It had not then occurred to them that to take effective means to suppress a noxious and dangerous form of crime practised by a very small section of the population could spell failure to recognise the loyal and gallant services of many thousands and the attitude of the country at large. This imagined connection was a subsequent, most unhappy, inspiration, born of outside pressure and newspaper diatribes. After the September debate the Government had reason to suppose that immediate legislative action was desirable on every ground. And even when they produced their Bills and met with unanimous opposition, they might well hope that, by all concessions possible, short of practical surrender, they would be able to secure the support of the Moderate section of the Opposition. They spared no pains to accomplish this. Surrender they could not. They were face to face with indefeasible obligations. Had they abjured these, they would have run away from their duty to protect the rising generation of educated Indians from ruinous influences and to safeguard the lives and property of innocent persons and loyal public servants. They would have abandoned the future of India to intimidation by the most violent and unscrupulous section of political opinion.

It is impossible to suppose that the leaders of the Moderates on the Legislative Council did not clearly perceive this. They were well aware of realities in

Bengal, and of the absolute need of the help which it lay in their power to give to a Government which had by initiation of, and perseverance in an advanced Reforms Scheme established a peculiar claim on their co-operation. They knew that so far from not caring to enlist political support in their contest with revolutionary conspiracy, Lord Chelmsford and his advisers had all along, from the very commencement of that contest, been at elaborate pains to ensure it. Two high-caste Hindus, one a Congress man, had been appointed to the Sedition Committee itself, a committee of only five members. That committee's Report had conclusively demonstrated what, indeed, was perfectly well known already, that desperate diseases require effectual preventives, as well as "satisfying methods of political emancipation." There can, in short, be no doubt that the Moderate leaders were under no delusion. Nor were they blinded by racial passion. What did they do?

They promptly repudiated Mr. Gandhi's movement, but in other matters remained generally passive. They did nothing to counteract the false impressions that were spreading abroad of the purport and contents of the Sedition Bill. If they spoke of it, they denounced it. When the riots began, they blamed the rioters, but devoted their main energies to censuring the measures of suppression adopted by the Government. Martial law should be abrogated; the Sedition Act must be repealed; a policy of surrender must be at once adopted. From January onwards they yielded to a rising tide and failed to act in a manner which would have inspired confidence in their ability to take a courageous line in that difficult future to which India is committed. It is certain that unless they can take and keep such a line, they will never bring into active politics that large class of well-disposed, educated, silent opinion which was alluded to in the Bengal manifesto quoted in my last chapter and should count for so much.[1] Only a persevering decided lead for good or bad will ever win the day in Indian politics. One Moderate, however, had, before the Delhi Sessions, spoken out boldly regarding the prevention of revolutionary crime. At the January debate of the Bengal Legislative Council, already alluded to, Mr. P. C. Mitter, an ex-member of the Sedition Committee itself, had said:

"These murders and dacoities took place, and they have ceased as soon as vigorous action was taken under the Defence of India Act. I am not here to deal with the question whether any change of the Defence of India Act is necessary or not, because the particular proposition before the House is whether these persons ought to be released or not. If the ordinary laws of the country are not sufficient in dealing with crimes like this, and if the extraordinary powers under the Defence of India Act really stamped out the crimes which were a disgrace to society—crimes which every patriotic Indian ought to feel sorry for—and if the operations of the Defence of India Act have to a great extent stamped out these crimes, then how can any responsible public man suggest to nullify the results of such action, and to let society go back to that state of anarchy in which it was before such vigorous actions were taken? I entirely endorse the view put forward by the honourable mover that we have a responsibility to our people and to ourselves. I only hope that that responsibility will enable us to see that it is our duty to protect innocent people from being shot down, and to see that the man, who by the fruits of his industry has made some money, is not ruthlessly pillaged. It is not a question of amnesty or mercy, but it is a ques-

[1] See page 168.

tion of the necessities of society, and if necessities of society require that certain persons, who are nothing better than a cancer to the body politic, should be treated in a particular way, it is necessary in the interest of the body politic to treat them in that way. I do hope, My Lord, that if we are to realise our responsibilities, if the Reform Scheme is to be a reality for the future well-being of our country, I do hope that gentlemen of the position of the honourable mover will try and come up to that standard of responsibility for which I am pleading."

Had the Moderate leaders on the Imperial Legislative Council acted in the spirit of these stirring words, there would have been no colourable pretext for the allegation that the Bills were humiliating to the loyal citizens of India. Neither the Bolshevist nor the Afghan invader could have pretended that India was united in opposition to a Bill passed for the prevention of revolutionary crime. The Government would have received the support which it had a right to expect from all well-disposed sections of Indians, and the only persons who would have felt aggrieved would have been those men who for years have steadily laboured to sow the seeds which sooner or later were sure to bring forth a crop such as that which was reaped in April 1919.

CHAPTER VIII

A SUMMARY OF EXISTING CONDITIONS

BRITAIN is pledged to establish a democratic system of government over two-thirds of India, the most conservative country in the world. These two-thirds possess a population composed of various races following various religions and speaking various languages. The great majority of these people, whose numbers are equal to two and a half times the population of the United States, are extremely ignorant and entirely unused to any form of political ambition. They are engrossed in their private and caste affairs. Britain does not mean to restore British India to the descendants of the chiefs and kings whom she succeeded. Nor does any class of Indians ask for such a restoration. She does not purpose to set up parliaments which will merely represent the literary and pacific, the present political classes. Such parliaments would crumble to pieces as soon as they ceased to receive constant British support. Her aim is to hand over eventually the direction of domestic affairs in British India to parliaments springing from, and effectually representative of, all classes. If this goal be eventually reached, if India gradually develops into a loyal, prosperous, well-governed, and self-governing country within the circle of the British Empire, a great service will have been rendered to humanity. But many and great difficulties lie in the way, and if these are to be successfully encountered, stock should be taken of the actual conditions under which the first stage of the journey is to be attempted. These will best be appreciated if we trace briefly the course of Indian political progress on Western lines, and the attitude of the British Government toward such progress.

There is ample proof that the gradual extension of British rule in India was welcomed by the majority of the population. Especially was it welcomed by the masses, by the agriculturists, who found themselves assured of reaping the fruits of their labours, shielded from plunder and violence, and protected from arbitrary exactions; by the low castes and outcastes, who found themselves equal to Brahmans even, in the eye of the law, and often the objects of charitable or missionary effort. It is, indeed, through the influence of the spirit of British rule that these people have learnt to respect themselves as they never respected themselves before. British rule was also acceptable to the majority of the very classes who now so frequently expatiate on its defects. Indeed, these classes, with the exception of the strong Brahman element which they contain, own their own present prominence to British rule. They would lose it at once if Britain withdrew from the country.

The Mutiny was a rebellion of discontented soldiery encouraged by the representatives of some fallen dynasties. Many of the East India Company's regiments became persuaded that we had ceased to pay regard to Indian religions, customs, and ideas; they thought that our power was illusory or had declined. So they rose and were followed by those elements in the ordinary population which are always ready to take advantage of internal commotion. The villagers generally fought among themselves. The population of Oudh, recently annexed and in the centre of Hindustan, followed the lead of its large landholders, whom we had foolishly endeavoured to displace summarily in pursuit of the idea that they were grasping middlemen. We profited by the lessons of the Mutiny. We did not alter our system of government, for that had not been called in question. But we discarded some of our maxims. We no longer annexed ruling states on account of misgovernment or the failure of heirs by blood of the reigning house. We respected the titles of *de facto* landlords. We reassured all Indians of our intention to interfere in no way with their religions, and we strengthened the British Army in India. For the first time we associated Indians with us in legislation. These were men of rank and few in number, for the people of India had always considered that there should be a well-defined governing class and a governed class. With them religious prestige, valour in arms, pride of birth, were the things that mattered.

It may seem that we were late in seeking such association; but before we blame our fathers, to whom both India and ourselves owe so much, let us remember that when, aided by Indians, they built up an empire out of confusion, the country had, as was frankly stated by an Indian professor at the Industrial Conference of 1909, "ever been foreign to democratic and representative institutions such as those dominant in Western countries." We may note, too, that until the time of the Mutiny the British were constantly busy with wars waged for the protection of their territories or their allies, with organisation and construction, with improving the communications of a vast continent, with arranging and classifying land tenures, with introducing that education which, in the words of Dadabhai Naoroji was "to pour a new light on the people of

India," with framing a system of just and intelligible laws, with maintaining and enforcing order. When we see how troubled and anxious were the years of the Governor-Generals from Warren Hastings to Lord Canning, we rather marvel at what was achieved than are surprised that the achievements were accompanied by omissions and mistakes. If British rule in those years was autocratic, it attracted the good will of the great majority of its subjects, was organised on the immemorial pattern of Asia,[1] was carefully controlled by laws, and in the interests of peace, security, and unity, was the only form of government practicable in the India of that time.

After the Mutiny, reconstruction and improvement for years absorbed the energies of British administrators. A new India, developed by British capital, enriched by British commerce, and fostered by British education, gradually took shape; and in that new India the paramount position of the British seemed at first perfectly natural. It was this position that secured the greater happiness of by far the greater number. All the classes of Indians whose sole objects in life are commerce, agriculture, labour, or other ordinary material pursuits, were contented. Their attitude of mind is shown by the introductory article to the record of the proceedings of the second Congress summarised in my Chapter II.[2] They cared for no change in a form of government which prevented others from robbing them and "by its system of civil jurisprudence" afforded them opportunities of enriching themselves. They did not understand that anything was wrong, nor did they know what could be done to improve their prospects. It may be said of all these classes, which form the large majority of the people of India, that

[1] See Appendix VII. [2] See pages 37-8.

although they had few representatives on legislative councils, they were informally consulted by Government officers regarding any law-making which was likely to affect their interests, that in these officers they found impartial arbiters and friendly advisers.

But there was a very small, though growing, minority with wider ambitions. Certain sects of Brahmans had lost their ascendancy in things political, and longed to recover it. The clerical and professional classes in towns found that prices were rising, that all but successful lawyers or Government servants of distinction must content themselves with moderate prospects and moderate incomes. They read Western newspapers and watched the strife of British politics and events in the rest of the world outside India. Sometimes they sent their sons to England. Sometimes they were assured that behind them in the early years, before the foreigner came, lay the golden age of India. British rule seemed uninteresting, and the memories of previous oppression had grown faint. The courts of the old rulers, with all their defects, had offered frequent spectacles, unexpected chances, and sometimes remarkable preferment. An ambitious man might push or intrigue himself into a post of power and thus provide for all those relatives who hang so heavily on many an Indian householder. There were no codes or regulations; there were no British ideas of inflexible impartiality; there was no colour-bar.

To such discontents were added ideas imported from British politics, as well as a certain racial resentment. Altogether a more interesting outlook was desired; and when the Congress movement started, it soon met with warm support. Gradually the annual December oratorical festivals took the place of fairs and caste-gatherings, as the relaxations of many of the English-educated classes. The leaders at those festivals spoke in louder and bolder tones. The only Indian journalists belonged to their fraternity.

I have endeavoured to show in this narrative why the British Government was cautious in responding to a demand for a parliamentary system from so small a fraction of the general population. The ambition for a larger share in the executive administration was understood more easily. From time to time efforts were made to meet it. But the reduction of the small British official element in a vast continent which not long before had been the scene of a violent struggle could not be lightly contemplated, for even now, unless this element be substantially maintained, Indian executive and judicial officers will often, in times of political or fanatical unrest, find themselves in positions where social and religious pressure will make it difficult for them to do their duty. They are subject to attacks by which British officers cannot be reached. Moreover, it must be frankly said that without an effective staff of British officers the intentions and policy of the British Government will be liable to serious misconstruction.

The public services, however, have been and are being gradually Indianised. Constitutional reforms, too, in the direction of associating a popular element with the Government, were instituted in April 1892. For long these seemed sufficient; but social forces were shifting. The leadership of the great landed proprietors, so strong in 1885, was steadily declining. They were becoming impoverished by constant litigation. They persistently neglected to educate their sons properly, and clung desperately to the ways of their fathers, relying on the shelter and protection of the British Government.

The clerical and professional classes, on the other hand, were steadily progressing in influence. Popular voting in a limited measure had come with district and municipal boards; newspapers were increasing; popular oratory was beginning. Indian lawyers were growing in numbers. Many were unable to find sufficient employment. The restlessness of these classes was enhanced by the unpractical character of much of their education, by the maxims which they drew from English history and literature, by some measure of religious and social unrest, and by a scarcity of commercial and industrial openings. This restlessness gradually increased, until it was fanned into a flame by a violent political agitation and developed a revolutionary element. It was largely met for a time by the Morley-Minto reforms. But the events attendant on a world-wide war, and nationalism widely preached, have taken political ambitions in tow, and have lately dragged them along at an unprecedented pace.

It may be said of both Moderates and Extremists that they greatly underrate certain considerations which the British Government must face even in these days of widely preached "self-determination," and even if, in the words of Mr. Lloyd George, "the world is rushing along at a giddy pace, covering the track of centuries in a year." It is certain that the educational and social conditions of the great body of the Indian peoples have not largely advanced since the year 1908, when those reforms were announced which were so gratefully received and did in fact open the way to a speedier prominence of the political classes than had till then been contemplated by their most sanguine leaders. Hindu society is still divided into castes and sub-castes, to a great extent rigidly separated from each other by customs, occupations, and social status.

With very few exceptions they neither intermarry nor can eat together. There are still in India many millions of wholly ignorant cultivators and labourers who carry on most of the work of the country. India is still "a vast continent inhabited by 315,000,000 of people sprung from various racial stocks, professing a variety of religious creeds, in various stages of intellectual and moral growth."[1] In short, however rapid may have been the recent progress of Indian political ambitions, disaster must come should Britain refuse to look at Indian political problems from the plane of reason. They cannot be decided merely by reference to abstract principles.

As regards British attitude toward Indian progress in the past, testimony is available in the speeches of the Presidents of the memorable political meetings of 1916.

"There is," said Mr. Jinnah on the part of the Muslim League, "first the great fact of the British rule in India with its Western character and standards of administration, which, while retaining absolute power of initiative, direction, and decision, has maintained for many decades unbroken peace and order in the land, administered even-handed justice, brought the Indian mind, through a widespread system of Western education, into contact with the thoughts and ideals of the West, and thus led to the birth of a great and living movement for the intellectual and moral regeneration of the people."

Mr. Mazumdar for the Congress carried the story on.

"It was this government," he said, referring to the Government of the Crown after the Mutiny, "which, actuated by its benevolent intentions, introduced, by slow degrees, various reforms and changes which gradually broadened and liberalised the administration, and restored peace and order throughout the country.

[1] See page 122.

In its gradual development it introduced, though in a limited form, self-government in the local concerns of the people, admitted the children of the soil to a limited extent into the administration of the country, and reformed the Councils by introducing an appreciable element of representation in them. It has annihilated time and space by the construction of railways and the establishment of telegraphic communication. It has established a form of administration which in its integrity and purity could well vie with that of any other civilised country in the world, while the security of life and property which it conferred was, until lately, a boon of which any people may be justly proud."

It is obvious from the quotations contained in Chapter IV that these two gentlemen said other things of a less appreciative kind; but what can be more significant than such clear admissions? That Britain has been cautious in responding to Indian aspirations for progress on Western democratic lines may at once be admitted. She had good reason to be. That she has been wilfully obscurantist and ungenerous may be promptly denied. And if now she hesitates, uncertain as to how best to legislate for radical changes, she does so because the warning conveyed by the adage "Marry in haste and repent at leisure" applies with peculiar force to law-making which will profoundly affect the whole future of both countries.

The present system, the system of administration responsible only to the parliament of Great Britain, has carried India through the Great War so successfully as to vindicate itself effectually from many of the reproaches frequently levelled against it. It does not, however, satisfy the aspirations of the Indian Nationalist; and as he generally belongs to the middle or professional classes, it is useful to note that his grievance against it is often economic. His standard of living is rising, but the cost of living is rising too. He thinks that he is impoverished, and that his country is drained by foreign rule. His reasoning is based on the following facts:

The number of English-educated men is too numerous for the public services and the legal profession. Although the services are increasingly manned by Indians, they can never provide for the number who crave admission. The Bar is overcrowded, and while offering large fortunes to some, yields to many a bare pittance. Other possible callings are the medical and scholastic. There is a widespread need of good doctors and of efficient enthusiastic teachers. But of these the quantity is limited. Physicians of the old school largely retain their patients, and the Indian medical graduate has no idea of working up a rural practice. Schoolmasters of the ordinary kind are over-plentiful, poorly paid, and frequently discontented with a profession which they only adopted as a last resource. Industrial enterprise is, so far, scarce in the interior of India, and many youths have received an education which disinclines them for business and commercial callings. All marry young, whatever may be their prospects. Hindus are compelled to do this by religious obligations. All read in the newspapers that foreign rule is the cause of their difficulties and their poverty. They are told that it causes severer famines, although no statement can be remoter from fact; that it is responsible for epidemics, although these spring from the climate and the insanitary habits of the people.[1] Too often their own

[1] The meteorological authorities inform us that within the past 250 years no change can have occurred in the climate of India. Failures of the monsoon were as great before as since fifty years ago, and must inevitably have produced famines far more desolating than those which have occurred since the introduction and extension of railways, and since the whole science of famine relief has been developed by the British,

narrow circumstances dispose them to accept these reiterated assertions. There can be no doubt that the spread of revolutionary ideas in Bengal schools and colleges is partly attributable to the miserable salaries of many of the teachers in these institutions. The views of such men are coloured by grinding poverty and deleterious literature. Sometimes they take to journalism and eke out a scanty living by diffusing the ideas which they have imbibed.

The legal and learned professions contain many members who are poor and feel acutely any rise of prices.[1] Outside these callings are many middle-class youths who have received English education, often at considerable cost and sacrifice to their parents, but are unable to obtain university degrees or similar hall-marks. They have to look outside law for a livelihood, and cannot obtain well-paid educational posts. The bent of their training has unfitted them for agriculture, the great business of the country, even if they come of an agricultural stock. They are unwilling to accept salaries which content relatives who have not learnt English at all. Industrial employers expect them to begin at the bottom of the ladder. This they are often extremely reluctant to do. But they too have married young, and are constrained by necessity. Sometimes they find their way into newspaper offices. Sometimes they obtain ill-paid clerkships. Generally they take what they can get, often persuaded that were it not for alien rule they would be better off.

The British Government has again and again endeavoured to combat epidemics and the causes of epidemics. Few executive officers of long district experience have failed to take part in prolonged combats with plague or cholera.

[1] The author some years ago visited a school in Bengal where a teacher of long service and proved efficiency could only afford cooked food once a day. Similar privation was common.

The difficulties of the professional middle classes have been enhanced by a great rise of prices accompanied by a growing preference for European comforts and methods of living. If things are ever to be otherwise, if all these young men are ever to know kinder fortunes, prudential considerations must be allowed a voice in their matrimonial arrangements, their education must broaden and improve,[1] and their prospects of industrial employment must expand. No such expansion, however, can be anticipated until Indian money grows far more venturesome. It seldom finances industrial enterprises which are not conducted by Europeans. It often remains persistently in barren seclusion.

Within the past four years no less than 1,200,000,000 of rupees have been drawn from the Indian mints. Sir James Meston, the Finance member of the Government, remarked in March 1919 that, unless this continuing panic were checked and the hoarded coin were restored to circulation, the whole basis of Indian currency and exchange policy would be reconsidered. It is the shyness of Indian capital, especially in regard to Indian enterprise, that leaves so many inlets for the foreign money and foreign enterprise often lamented by newspapers and politicians on the ground that the profits therefrom leave the country. But the young men of India are seldom told this. On the contrary, they hear such complaints as the following:

Some years ago an enlightened gentleman of Bombay, while frankly admitting that India owes her railways and thereby her new nationalism to English capital, went on to grumble, because so much of that capital was extracting petroleum from Burma, coal

[1] The recommendations of the Calcutta University Committee have prepared the way for radical reform.

from Bengal, and gold from Mysore. The profits of this enterprise, he explained, went away from India, and Indian interests would best be served if the gold and petroleum were left underground to await the indigenous enterprise which would come with progressive regeneration. Lord Curzon thus referred to murmurs of this kind:

"When I hear the employment of British capital in India deplored, I feel tempted to ask where without it would have been Calcutta? Where would have been Bombay? Where would have been our railways, our shipping, our river navigation, our immense and prosperous trade? And why should a different argument be applied to India from any other country in the world? When Great Britain poured her wealth into South America and China, I never heard those countries complain that they were being ruined. No one pities Egypt when a foreign nation resuscitates her trade and dams the Nile."

In fact, India "has benefited enormously by her commercial development in British hands."[1] But far more remains to be achieved. India has a great reserve of strength in her large command of raw material, but Europe has now far less capital to spare. If Indian capital be not forthcoming in larger measure, India will not develop industrially as she should, and substantial expansion of employment for her educated youth cannot be anticipated. Incidentally we may note how necessary it is that reasonable calm should prevail in politics if Indian capital is to require less coaxing forth and outside money is to be attracted at a cheap rate of interest. As regards the competition of British with Indian capital we may quote the remarks of an acute critic:[2]

"Is it true that the resources of the country are

[1] Montagu-Chelmsford Report. [2] Mr. William Archer.

being exploited, or nearly so, by Europeans? When one has seen the palaces of merchants and manufacturers round Bombay and Ahmedabad, and the Calcutta mansions of the landlords enriched by the permanent settlement of Bengal, one has a little difficulty in compassionating these 'hewers of wood and drawers of water.' Almost all of the 200 to 250 cotton mills (mostly in the Bombay Presidency) have been built by Indian capital, and if the sixty to seventy jute mills in Bengal are mainly in European hands, that is certainly not because Bengalis have no money to embark in such enterprises. It is true that coal mines, tea plantations, and gold mines are, for the most part, owned by Europeans; but Indian capital and enterprise are largely employed in the production of silk, paper, timber, flour, in oil pressing, and in carpet weaving. It is not the fact that European enterprise has elbowed Indian enterprise aside; it may rather be said to have flowed in where the lack of Indian enterprise (far more than the lack of Indian capital) left gaps for it to fill; and it is the fact that Indians are year by year securing a larger share of the import and export trade of the country."

To discuss the whole subject of the alleged drain would be beyond the scope of this chapter. I have shown why India has required the foreign capital for which she has had such excellent value. Another grievance often reiterated is the amount of the sums sent out of the country in pensions and private remittances to England. For these India has had her return in the work of British officials who have not spared themselves in her service. Were it not for the labour of these men, for the protection which the presence of the British in India has afforded to the country, the foreign capitalist would not have lent his money at the rate which he has accepted, nor would the local financier have done as much as he has done.

The Indian student hears much of the loss which India has sustained from the commercial policy of the East India Company and from the competition of the organised and scientific processes of British industry. He is seldom aware of the efforts which the Indian Government has made or is making to help agricultural development by a system of co-operative banks and credit societies, to stimulate and broaden education, to encourage industrial development. If he hears of such endeavours at all, he is frequently informed that they have been undertaken for some selfish purpose. Let us hope that with action on the report of the recent Industrial Commission a clearer understanding will come and a better era will begin. It has been justly said by His Excellency Lord Chelmsford that "no reforms will achieve their purpose unless they have their counterpart in the industrial sphere. A great industrial advance, reacting strongly on social and educational conditions, is a condition precedent to the development of healthy political life in this country."

But "man does not live by bread alone," and the rise and spread of Indian national sentiment is one of the most remarkable phenomena of our time. Nourished originally by the Congress movement, sometimes expressing itself in bursts of racial feeling, it took definite shape in 1905. But we can see its earlier influence in such passages as the following from the diary of Mr. Romesh Chandra Dutt, once a member of the Civil Service and afterwards a Congress leader. Describing a night spent at the North Cape with other tourists, during an expedition to Norway and Sweden in 1886, he wrote:

"I will not conceal the pain and humiliation which I felt in my inmost soul as I stood on that memorable night among representatives of the free and advancing nations of the earth rejoicing in their national greatness. Champagne was drunk on the top of the hill, and Germans and Frenchmen, Englishmen and Americans, pressed us to share their hospitality. I accepted their offer with thanks on my lips, but I felt within me that I had no place among them."

It is easy to conceive how the victories of Japan over what used to be one of the proudest European nations must have intensified such feelings.

Since 1905 nationalism has gradually expanded, generally blending in some measure with racial feeling. The Morley-Minto Councils operated to weaken social barriers and stimulate co-operation, but have been powerless to arrest or even check nationalist tendencies; and away from the Council-rooms, in the cities and towns, among the English-educated classes, these are now, partly through the influence of the Press, partly from the general unsettlement of the times, and partly as a result of increasingly frequent "constitutional agitations," far stronger and more combative than they were in 1908. It is only natural that Indian agitators should seek to better the instruction which they often receive from British politics, but unfortunately agitations in India, however legally flawless, are generally sustained by methods which sharply exacerbate racial feeling and have already led more than once to lamentable disorders. Almost always it may be said of such movements that even if they attain some immediate object, they leave a widened breach between peoples who have great need of each other, and that they produce a train of unforeseen and undesired consequences. This is perfectly well known in India; and the effect of some bitter lessons of the past may be seen in the prompt repudiation by the Moderates of Mr. Gandhi's passive resistance movement. But, unfortunately, of late years, for various reasons, the idea has found growing favour that, if an agitation be sufficiently loud and menacing, it will achieve success. The disastrous results of the agitation over the Sedition Bill, and the manner in which that movement was used for criminal purposes by the enemies of the State, may induce a greater reluctance to light fires which can by no means be extinguished at will.

We have our own defects and national peculiarities. Much of the resentment of the Indian political classes is social, and lies deep in the colour-line which has been drawn with rigour in some British colonies and is still drawn in India, at times unavoidably. India was a land of caste and social cleavages, of a severity unknown in Western countries, long before the British ever saw it. It is still a land of such divisions, and would remain one if the British left it. It is true that educated Indians have had some reason to complain of social barriers, and avoidable incidents occur from time to time which breed bad feeling.[1] But the existing wall of reserve has been buttressed largely by the extreme sensitiveness and racial dislike often cherished by Nationalists themselves. Only recently a very able Indian politician frankly admitted this, stating that some Nationalists desired that no Indian of prominence should be associated with Europeans even in social matters, and "mixing up wish with reality, indulge in day-dreams from which perhaps the European might be absent." He reminded his audience that in the India of the future the European would be present as well as the Indian. If all politicians would regard prospects in this sensible light, and if they would fashion their ideas accordingly, they would find plenty of response from the British side. And we ourselves, at this crisis

[1] The Press can do much to improve relations.

of the world's history, cannot wonder either at the sensibility of the political classes or at their natural appetite for posts and power. It is easy to see why, although they have been sheltered by a strong Imperial system from a world-wide storm, they meditate little on the benefits of such protection and much on the least agreeable of its accompaniments. It is comprehensible that, in their own words, they want to be in their own country "what other people are in theirs," that they think that they would hold their heads higher in the world under a national government of their own. These are ideas which in themselves appeal to Englishmen whether resident in India or elsewhere. Both sides must approach the questions raised thereby from a practical point of view. Such approach would be far easier if more Indian Nationalists showed a disposition to allow for existing facts, for the hard-earned position of Britain in India, for the heavy and compelling responsibilities which that position entails. "Britain," said the Maharaja of Ulwar, at the Delhi War Conference, "has wished India well, and has guided her destinies for 160 years." This is a true saying. The guidance has been through Britain's sons in India, who, aided by Indians, have established and maintained order, have dealt with obstacles, have taken risks, have worked indefatigably for progress. Necessity has trained them to consider what is really practicable in the interests of all communities. If their point of view were better understood, we would hear less of the doctrine that, unlike Britons at home, who are amiable philanthropists, Britons in India are specious oppressors.

This doctrine is ever the result of Extremism, the origin of which was, as I have shown, clearly described by Mr. Gokhale. Its history, its vicissitudes, its achievements have been traced in these pages. At this moment it pursues constitutional methods, as these promise more fruitful results. Moreover, it has of late years attracted many adherents who have no taste for any but declamatory tactics. It includes, however, some men whose plans the future will disclose. For the present they wear the label "loyalty to the Crown, but impatience of bureaucratic government." Loyalty to the Crown is indeed a potent and valuable factor in India, but, professed by such persons as these, is simply a mask. Their aim is to reduce British rule to impotence as soon as possible by any methods that seem to promise success. The Sedition Bill legislation and its sequel afforded a notable opportunity to sober politicians of isolating such people. The opportunity was lost.

Mr. Jinnah, addressing the Muslim League in December 1916, quoted a passage from the speech of the Prime Minister on the Irish situation, and remarked that every word thereof applied almost literally to conditions in India. Mr. Lloyd George had said that in attempting to settle the Irish difficulty he had felt all the time that he was moving "in an atmosphere of nervous suspicion and distrust, pervasive, universal, of everything and everybody. . . . It was a quagmire of distrust which clogged the footsteps of progress. That was the real enemy of Ireland."

Mr. Jinnah's audience understood him to mean that advanced Indians are the victims of undeserved suspicion. It is true that the restrictions on military service, recruiting for which had till then been confined to the martial castes and classes, have encouraged this belief; and persons prominent in politics have, since the inception of a revolutionary movement, sometimes been watched by the police in a foolish and obtrusive fashion. This was sure to happen when the latter were faced with grave outbursts of political crime. But trust is, after all, a plant of spontaneous growth. The British Government wishes to trust every section of Indians, and, not least, the section which, unless peaceful progress be definitely and violently arrested, must in time leaven many others. Should it be compelled to distrust particular leaders of this section, such distrust must be in the highest degree unwelcome, and can easily be removed by those concerned.

In any case, however, there remains another suspicion, and that is an Indian suspicion. It is the idea, often fostered by the Press, that the policy of the Government, even when definitely progressive, is, in fact, dictated by racial exclusiveness, by needless and selfish caution. Racialism among Indians derives much of its strength from this suspicion which has wrought considerable mischief. It has obstructed a much-needed reform of secondary education with the theory that the real design is to limit the numbers of the restless English-educated. It has hindered measures of supreme importance to the public welfare, and has thereby advertised the necessity of retaining safeguards against such hindrances. For the latter reason Progressives might be expected to work for its removal, but hitherto there have been few signs of the approach of so bright a dawn. In September 1918 there was an indication of a change of view. There had been similar indications when the Morley-Minto Reforms were announced. Those had passed. This, too, passed. It yielded to the idea that there is a royal road to democratic government in India which is blocked by inconsiderate selfishness.

And yet it has often been seen that when members of the political classes meet British officials with open minds, either because there is no antagonism of views or because politics are not in question at all, things go well enough. Indians, too, of these classes who enter Government service work contentedly, and have often shown a fine spirit of loyalty in difficult circumstances. So far, indeed, is it from being the case, that there is an immovable barrier between them and the British officers with whom or under whom they serve, that intercourse is generally pleasant and sometimes ripens into warm regard. May these circumstances be harbingers of better things to come! We might be sure that they would be were it not for the preaching of racial hate.

We have discussed the economic condition of the political classes, and the influence on these classes of nationalism and racialism. We must now turn to the landlords, a far more numerous class which contributes very largely to the revenues of the country. The future depends, in no small measure, on the degree to which the landlords will adapt their ideas to the requirements of the new era. Their influence in a great agricultural country must always be powerful. In parts of India the influence of the proprietors of large estates has weakened for reasons indicated on a former page. But where, as in the United Provinces and the Punjab, there are quantities of yeomen farmers living on the land in close touch with, and often belonging to the same caste as, their tenants, the influence of landlords is still very strong indeed. A quotation from a speech by Sir Michael O'Dwyer shows clearly its value during the recent war. In the Imperial Legislative Council he said:

"Take one cardinal feature of the Punjab. We have no great territorial aristocracy like other provinces, but we have what is perhaps even more valuable. We have over most of the province a large class of landed gentry or prosperous yeomen living on the land, in close touch with the rural masses of whom they are usually the recognised leaders, and an invaluable support to the administration. Over all the province we have that splendid body of stalwart peasant proprietors, Muhammandas, Hindus, Sikhs, whose energy and enterprise, guided by a government in which they have never lost confidence, have built up the prosperity of the Punjab, and whose loyalty and sturdy valour have built up the fabric of the Indian Army. These are the two classes to which the Punjab Government has looked, and never looked in vain, in times of stress and difficulty; those are the two classes to which we owe almost exclusively the magnificent contributions which the province is now making in men and materials. In recognising the services of the province during the war, it is only just and reasonable that those classes should receive first consideration."

The Government of the United Provinces, too, has mainly to thank the landlords for the success of its war-efforts.

In Bengal only are the territorial proprietors materially interwoven with the professional or literary classes, and there they manifest more interest in politics than they do in other provinces. But in landlords generally, conservative and cautious instincts are naturally dominant. Their attitude toward the recent disturbances was very apprehensive, as was shown in an eminent degree by a circular appeal by 300 landlords of Bengal issued in May 1919.[1]

There are, of course, in all provinces among the territorial aristocracy, men who sit on the Legislative Councils and interest themselves in politics, but these are by no means as fluent in speech as the lawyer-members, and have so far played a part there which corresponds in a small degree with the real power of the order to

[1] Addressed to their tenants.

which they belong. It can never be the interest of the landlords to desire weak government, even if it be national government, and they do not desire it. They are well aware of their stake in the country, and know that, in the words of a letter written last April by the Maharaja of Darbhanga to two large land-holding associations, their "very existence depends" on the protection of property and the maintenance of law and order which they "have been enjoying and continue to enjoy under the British Government." For this reason the Maharaja went on to urge the associations to exert themselves to the utmost "in quieting down the unrest which stalks through the land, and render the utmost possible assistance to the State in preventing disorder and removing root and branch the causes which have brought into existence this dreadful state of things."

It is true that some of the more important landlords are attracted by the vision of a self-governing India in the future, and others find it convenient to swim with the Nationalists. But in practice landlords, as a class, have never wished that the British Government should cease to be able to protect and arbitrate. They desire this less than ever now. Politics are to their minds a game which can pass into somewhat bitter earnest. They are conscious of being inadequately prepared for it. Their attention has hitherto been directed far more to their tenants, to litigation, and their private concerns than to anything else. The adjustment of their relations with the former has often been a matter of no ordinary complexity, for disputes regarding the landed tenures of India require careful study and impartial arbitration. Experience shows that for such arbitration they prefer British revenue officers.

The landlords, although very numerous, are the

minority of the rural population. The majority consists of peasant proprietors, under-proprietors, and tenants of various grades.

The cultivators generally are so far untouched by the Nationalist propaganda. Some have been approached by persons who tell them that they are exploited and impoverished;[1] their corn is, to their injury, exported from the country; their money is drained away in salaries spent by foreigners in Europe; their condition can be bettered only by Home Rule. So far, such appeals have effected little more than a promise of unrest in odd places and a delegation of tenants to the last Congress, the history of which would probably be instructive. As was stated by Lord Curzon in 1909, what the agricultural masses require of a government is, that it shall worry them for money as little as possible; shall assist them generously in times of famine, floods, or other calamities; shall settle their disputes without fear or favour; shall protect them from the exactions of the worst kinds of landlords, money-lenders, or legal practitioners. At present they value British administration because its main effort is to supply these requirements. If untouched by insidious suggestions, they confide in its integrity, its freedom from susceptibility to intrigue or secret influence. Of many individual British civil administrators they have kindly recollections. Never was the demeanour of the country people of the Author's own provinces more conspicuously friendly toward British officers on tour than it was in the early months of the war, when some hearts were failing for fear of the future. Nor is it easy to think that the enthusiasm manifested by the masses on the occasion of the visit of their

[1] The recent report of the Foodstuffs Commissioner and Mr. Dalton's report of 1910 on the rise of prices in India testify strongly to the contrary.

Majesties the King and Queen, sprang from those who were dissatisfied with their Government or unaware of the goodwill and honest purpose of His Majesty's servants.

These people, who when let alone are contented, friendly, and industrious, but when captured by those who wilfully or recklessly pour jars of paraffin upon their ignorance and credulity, can break out into fanatical fury, are to be trained to co-operate in affairs in order that they may take their part in the democratic India of the future. Let us not forget that they have been correctly described in the Reforms Report as "illiterate peasants whose mental outlook has been coloured by the physical facts of India, the blazing sun, the enervating rains." We stand on the threshold of a new era, but cannot anticipate that such physical facts will alter or that they will cease to operate on the minds of these many millions. It remains to be seen how far they will avail themselves of the political education which they are to undergo. If this political education implies the continuous and self-sacrificing effort on the part of the educated classes which was preached by Mr. Gokhale in 1909 and by Lord Sinha in 1915; if Indian Nationalism is so genuine and healthful a creed as to be able to inspire living patient service of a true and noble kind, all will be well and the co-operation of British officers is amply assured. But it may be said, both of the cultivators, and of the labourers and lower orders in and near towns who have been lately so seriously affected by Extremist agitation, that if incidents of this education are to be persuasion of tenants to withhold rent at discretion, of peasant-proprietors to withhold revenue, of mill-hands and labourers to beware of British employers, of all to cultivate racial hatred and distrust; if the minds of the ignorant masses are to be warped, as the minds of the better-educated youth of the country have to a considerable extent already been warped in what are called political interests; then, indeed, the last state will be worse than the first, and incalculable mischief is in prospect. Such mischief can only be averted by determined co-operation between the sober elements of Indian society and the officers of Government, strengthened, should occasion demand, by convincing proof that Britain will not abandon to hostile disorder the Empire built up by British and Indian valour and effort.

It appears that where the low castes or depressed classes are articulate, where they have organised associations, as in Madras and Bombay, they view coming constitutional changes with apprehension. From addresses lately presented to the Viceroy and Secretary of State, it appears that they fear what they anticipate would mean a régime of class legislation and repression, and consider that British rule alone, in the present circumstances of India, can hold the scales even between creeds and castes. Yet in the Joint Congress and Muslim League address to the Viceroy and Secretary of State presented at Delhi on November 26th, 1917, it was claimed that these associations had made many representations in favour of the amelioration of the condition of the masses and had "pressed for the removal of all disabilities and distinctions based on racial and religious grounds." As far as representations and resolutions go, this claim is well founded, and behind these representations and resolutions lies a genuine sentiment. There is testimony to this in the eagerness with which opportunities for social service are sometimes seized by youths of the political classes, and in the existence of associations for the purpose of philanthropic work among the lower orders. The forerunners in such paths were the Christian missionaries. But a great deal more than resolutions or sentiment, or the societies that, amid the gravest obstacles, cultivate the advancement of social reform, will be required before material impression can be made on the usages of centuries. Not only are about 50,000,000 of Hindus treated as untouchable by the higher castes of their own faith, but in parts of Southern India they are even regarded as unapproachable. They are not allowed to enter the temples or use the village wells. Before British rule they were serfs. Now, though legally free, they are outcastes in a sense hardly appreciable in a Western country. Thus it is that in addresses to the Viceroy and Secretary of State they have expressed the strongest distrust of the Home Rule Leaguers; and thus it is that the President of the Indian National social conference held at Calcutta, less than two years ago, reminded his audience that while "gorgeous visions of a United India" were filling the political imagination, "loud protests of indignation were being raised by classes and communities amongst us which we can no longer ignore."

The authors of the Reforms Report desire that both the agricultural masses and the depressed classes may ultimately learn the lesson of self-protection. Special assistance is to be given to them if under the new régime they fail to "share in the general progress." Such assistance will be certainly needed, although the Honourable Mr. Surendra Nath Banerjee has informed the Parliamentary Joint Committee that the influence of caste was on the wane, and that the Brahmans themselves, as well as the educated classes, desired its disappearance. Since the large majority of Hindus of the higher castes, and particularly of Brahmans, consider the caste system to be, as it undoubtedly is, the very foundation of the Hindu religious and social edifice, Mr. Banerjee must indeed have been transported by the atmosphere of democratic England before he embarked on so venturous an assertion.[1] Even Hindus who have received education in English, much as they may chafe under the rules and restrictions which caste imposes, widely as they may sometimes relax those rules and restrictions, would, if the caste-system really were on the verge of dissolution, inquire very anxiously indeed what could possibly take its place and what would become of Hinduism after its disappearance.

To the elements out of which, diversified as they are by varieties of caste, language, and religion, the self-governing India of the future is to be evolved, must be added numbers of gallant Indians who have been fighting in the Empire's cause. They belong to the agricultural and landholding classes, to the forces of conservatism. But since the commencement of the war they have been far more in contact with Western countries and Western ideas than ever before. It is not known how far they are attracted by the idea of government composed of indigenous parliaments. They have no previous experience or tradition of anything of the kind. But one lesson of recent years they have probably grasped. As was said by an Indian member of the Imperial Legislative Council:

"From the time when the memory of man runneth not to the contrary, India has attracted the cupidity of powerful rulers and states; from time immemorial her eternal mountains have witnessed the march of invading hordes, and her mighty rivers have flowed past the battle-fields of contending armies. The peace and prosperity of the country have been interrupted by long periods of rapine and plunder; and the soil of India has seen the rise of great and powerful empires."

[1] Further examined, Mr. Banerjee said that he referred to the educated Brahmans of Bengal.

There is little in the state of Asia or the world which gives assurance that things are now calm and peaceful; that the nations are satisfied with what they have got, or that the future of India will henceforth be a matter of interest merely to India and Great Britain. Never was it more certain that, in the words of the President of the 1915 Congress, "free from England, and without a real power of resistance, India would be immediately in the thick of another struggle of nations."[1]

We have considered the position of the Ruling Chiefs, and noted their devotion to the Throne and the generous loyalty of their response to the Empire's needs. We are given to understand by a few of the more prominent Hindu princes that they are in sympathy with the prospect of an increasingly democratic India. The future will show how far such an India will affect politics in their states.

We must remember the non-official representatives of Britain in India, and particularly those to whom India's commercial progress is mainly due. It is obvious that no constitutional settlement should be made which fails to give due weight and security to their interests.

We have, too, the indigenous Anglo-Indians, the Eurasians, the Indian Christians and other communities who stand somewhat apart from the general masses of the population. Hindu-Muhammadan relations at their best and at their worst have been illustrated by events of various kinds described in previous pages. Ordinarily they are placid.

We have seen that the demand for a parliamentary

[1] The traditional relations between Indian soldiers and their British officers are more easily understood from Younghusband's *Story of the Guides* than from any other book I know.

system came from a small section of India's many peoples, a section which pursues nationalist ideals and considers that British rule obstructs the realisation of these ideals. Partly for this reason the Nationalists are frequently moved by a racialism which has, in its extreme phase, produced a string of revolutionary conspiracies. Nationalist ambitions have been sharpened by economic pressure and by the present world-tendency to regard parliamentary government as the hall-mark of a civilised state. From the latter point of view, and because there is in true nationalism a source of uplifting inspiration, these ambitions must necessarily appeal to many thinking Indians outside active politics, but of these some are uneasy and by no means appreciate the uncertainty of the future. We cannot doubt, however, that unless they lead to recognised calamity, nationalist ideals will in years to come appeal to a constantly widening circle. Even now they dominate the Press, and have largely penetrated schools and colleges. The British Cabinet has responded to these aspirations in a definite and unmistakable manner.

Minimising difficulties which recently seemed insuperable to two Liberal Secretaries of State, they issued the declaration of August 20th, 1917, and proclaimed a policy of not only increasing association of Indians with every branch of the administration, but also progressive realisation of responsible government in India as an integral part of the British Empire. Progress is to be by stages; and the Viceroy and Secretary of State, in framing their proposals for carrying out the declared policy, have aimed at including in the very first stage by means of dyarchy, a measure of separate clear-cut ministerial responsibility. We have seen that the majority of local governments considered that dyarchy is unlikely to work without severe friction, and have framed alternative proposals. The choice between the two sets of proposals will shortly be made by Parliament.[1]

In order to fulfil the purpose of the Declaration, the authors of the Reforms Report propose to disturb the present usually placid contentment of the masses because such disturbance will be "for India's highest good." It is certainly a consequence of the terms of the Declaration, but implies facilities for politicians which, unless employed with loyal discretion, will do India much harm and make administration extremely difficult. Often they will be honourably and discreetly used; but when they are not, the brunt of any consequent troubles will fall on the Executive servants of the Crown, and more especially on the Civil Service and Police.

It is these services who supply the commissioners, district officers, and superintendents who, themselves a mere handful, are responsible for the maintenance of peace and order among millions.

Generally a district officer has no troops whatever to support him, but merely a force of civil police under a British superintendent. His charge consists of a population of all castes and creeds, numbering from about 1,000,000 to 2,000,000 or 3,000,000. He has not only to keep the peace, but to collect the revenue, to combat epidemics, to foster education, and to do all he can for his people in every possible way. His friend and adviser is the commissioner, a senior officer who is responsible to Government for the charges of several district officers. The district officer is assisted by Indian deputy magistrates and sometimes by a European Joint Magistrate. He exercises a general supervision over the work of the police, which is carried on

[1] This was written before recent Parliamentary legislation.

under the control of the superintendent. He presides over a very large Indian subordinate staff. Some district officers are Indians, and many more will be Indians in future.

It may be said of district and police officers that as things are, their responsibilities are heavy and their days are fully occupied. They often pass through anxious experiences, and, in order to carry out their duties, need to be regarded as representatives not of a moribund, but of an active and vigorous power. Yet it is certain that in the future they will have at times to contend with the impression that power is departing from the British Raj, for that is how impending changes and a gradually shrinking British official element must appear and will often be represented to the Indian masses. Only if responsibility changes the political spirit will executive officers receive much help from it in difficulties. Nationalists have hitherto regarded them as generally hostile to reform. The truth is that they have to deal with not only the political, but all classes and creeds, and wish to be able effectively to discharge their responsibilities. If they are inclined to linger in the old tents, it is because before leaving those tents they would like reasonable assurance that the new encampment will not develop into a troubled scene where the same results will be expected from their work, but the atmosphere around it will gradually deteriorate.

The Police have again and again been assailed by politicians because of the action which they have been compelled to take in dealing with and thwarting revolutionary crime. The English-educated classes have always been reluctant to acknowledge that the game of revolutionary politics must necessarily be perilous and rough for the players and their associates, that practised in India among vast masses of people who inhabit great tracts of country sparsely policed, it necessitates stringent and effective remedies which may inconvenience other than guilty persons. Nor have the Nationalists hitherto been able to see that as they so much dislike such repressive measures, it is desirable that they should themselves take determined steps to put an end to the revolutionary propaganda which has produced occasion for them. It is certainly no gratification to the Police or to any officers of Government to devote energies for which there is ample employment in other directions to the disagreeable and thankless task of fighting anarchical conspiracy.

British civil officers generally have good reason to be well aware of the enormous value of educated non-official co-operation, and their hearts warm to those from whom they receive it. They are proud that their mission is a mission of liberty and progress: and their sympathies would naturally incline towards Indians who, reading English history and literature, are attracted by the ideas of nationality and freedom which they draw from those inspiring pages. But there are other sources of inspiration; and when such ideas operate through a medium of sensitive and suspicious racialism, they produce something widely different from that co-operation which is essential for progress, and when forthcoming, slights all difference of colour, inspiring a mutual goodwill which makes all things possible.

The Extremists wish to push forward recklessly, regardless of obstacles or consequence, of sectarian and social divisions, of the dangers of racial conflict, of the ignorance of the great majority of the population, of the responsibility of Britain for the good government of India. They mean to press their views by the promotion of incessant agitation. The Moderates see the danger of precipitate changes, and know that progress worth having can only come through co-operation with Government and its officers. Their position is difficult, but they can establish it by trusting the strength which will be theirs with courageous resolution. Neither party allows sufficiently for the natural obstacles in the path of democratic progress in India or for British responsibilities to every class and race. Neither party seems to grasp adequately the difficulties of the coming years of transition, difficulties inevitable in any case, and augmented by the troubled state of the world. These difficulties are, however, understood by many thinking Indians and by the Services. In their opinion, whatever be the scheme of reforms, Government must preserve full weight and power for years yet. Without Britain, India would directly be torn by invasion; and, in the absence of a trained electorate that can protect itself and be said to represent sufficiently the educated intelligence of all classes of His Majesty's subjects, Britain cannot abdicate her responsibilities for India's domestic affairs.

It is not surprising in such times as these that the doctrines of Western democracy have carried the ambitions of Indian Nationalists on to adventurous lengths. As some declare for a future of perpetual agitation, we may note that premature Home Rule would mean an unhappy attempt at government by particular castes and classes. Genuine Indian progressives would, without that British support which has done so much to assist them all these years, be liable to succumb to the reactionary sectarian and social influences which they are even now reluctant to combat seriously. Clouds of confusion would gather rapidly; British interests and credit would suffer irretrievable damage; and the vision of a brilliant happy India, raised by the endeavours of all classes of her sons to a worthy place within the circle of the British Empire, would prove a delusive dream.

Thus it is that to many who have eaten the salt of India, who wish India well and desire to see her prosper and progress, it seems that a vital issue of the present is, Will the constitutional changes in prospect be such as adequately to maintain British supremacy, so long as that alone can carry on the work of the past and guarantee the well-being of the people whom we have known as the friendly companions of the best years of our lives?

Since this book went to the Press the revised Government of India Bill has become law. The King-Emperor has appealed to his people and to his servants in India for perseverance and mutual forbearance in treading the difficult path now definitely marked out. At present some circumstances are working for much bitterness. But we may trust that this bitterness will pass; that the danger which threatens India from Central Asia will, as always hitherto, promote domestic concord; that His Majesty's appeal will stimulate active perception of the public good. Never has the message been clearer that the interests of Britain and India are essentially the same.

THE END

APPENDICES

APPENDIX I

POLITICAL UNITY IN EARLY INDIA[1]

TWICE in the centuries before the Muhammadan conquests the political unity of all India was nearly accomplished; first in the third century B.C. by Asoka, and again in the fourth century A.D. by Samodragupta. Both these emperors had their capitals in Northern India, in the Gangetic plain.

"Harsha was the last native monarch prior to the Muhammadan conquest who held the position of paramount power in the north. His death loosened the bonds which restrained the disruptive forces always ready to operate in India, and allowed them to produce their normal results —a medley of petty States, with ever-varying boundaries, and engaged in internecine war. Such was India when first disclosed to European observation in the fourth century B.C., and such it has always been, except during the comparatively brief periods in which a rigorous central government has compelled the mutually repellent molecules of the body politic to check their gyrations and submit to the grasp of a superior controlling force."—*Vincent Smith's "Early History of India."*

[1] See page 28.

APPENDIX II

THE *ANANDA MATH*[1]

THE methods of the *sanyasis* in the famous novel of Bankim Chandra, *The Ananda Math* (Monastery of Joy), vaguely foreshadow the political robberies of the Revolutionaries of present times.

The *sanyasi* rebels against the rule of the Muhammadan Nawab Nazim of Bengal, which was supported by the East India Company, are described by Bankim Chandra as seizing public money by violence when they can and using it to finance their warfare. They are victorious against Mussulman sepoys, even though led by Englishmen. They bring Muslim rule to a close. Among the concluding passages of the book are the following:

"Satyananda," said the physician, "grieve not! In your delusion you have won your victories with the proceeds of robbery. A vice never leads to good consequences, and you may never expect to save your country by sinful procedure. Really what may happen now will be for the best. There is no hope of a revival of the true Faith if the English be not our rulers. The true Faith does not consist in the worship of 330,000,000 deities; that is only a base worship of the masses. Under its influence the true Faith, which *mlecchas* (barbarians) call Hinduism, has disappeared. The true Hinduism is based on knowledge and not on action" (To revive true religion, objective knowledge must be disseminated. It must first be imported.) "The English are great in objective sciences, and they are apt teachers. Therefore the English shall be made our sovereign. Imbued with a knowledge of objective sciences by English education, our people will be able

[1] See page 62.

to comprehend subjective truths. Then there would be no obstacle to the spread of the true Faith; it will shine forth of itself. Till that is so, till the Hindus are great again in knowledge, virtue, and power, till then the English rule will remain unaltered. The people will be happy under them, and follow their own religion without hindrance. . . . Where is the enemy now? There is none. The English are a friendly power; and no one, in truth, has the power to come off victorious in a fight with the English."

APPENDIX III

THE KHALIFAT[1]

MUHAMMADANS in India are rather sharply divided into Shias and Sunnis. According to Shias, the Prophet, who belonged to the Koreish tribe of Arabs, on his death-bed recognised his son-in-law Ali as his spiritual and temporal successor (Khalif). He was, however, in fact succeeded by Abu Bakr, another of his companions, whom he had deputed to take his place at the daily prayers. Abu Bakr was succeeded by Omar, and Omar by Othman. Both Omar and Othman belonged to the band of Muhammad's companions. Then Ali came in, and was murdered after a short lease of power. He left two sons, Hassan and Husain, grandsons of the Prophet. Hassan abdicated, and was succeeded by Muawiya, the representative of another tribe of Arabs. He was followed by Yezid; and Husain, rebelling against Yezid, was killed on the fatal field of Karbala.

The sad end of a grandson of the Prophet shook Islam to its depths, and is now yearly commemorated in the Muharram. It also apparently originated the Shia doctrine that Ali should have succeeded his father-in-law, and that therefore Abu Bakr, Omar, and Othman were not true Khalifs. But this doctrine was opposed by the Sunnis, the Muslims who hold by the sunnas or precedents. These basing their creed on the general allegiance of the Faithful, recognise the Khalifats of Abu Bakr, Omar, and Othman as well as the Khalifat of Ali.

The last of the dynasties of Arabian Khalifs came to an end in 1258 A.D. But about three centuries later the title was assumed by the Sultans of Turkey, as protectors of

[1] See page 73.

the Holy Places and the most powerful Muhammadan sovereigns in the world, although without pretensions of consanguinity to Muhammad. These claims have not been admitted by the Shias, but have been largely acknowledged by the Sunnis. The Shias are strong in Persia, but comparatively weak in India. The kings of Oudh were Shias. The Moghul Emperors were Sunnis. Both Shias and Sunnis intensely revere the Holy Places of Arabia, Mecca, Medina, and Karbala, and regard it as essential that these should be in Muslim hands.

APPENDIX IV

EXTRACTS FROM A REPLY BY HIS EXCELLENCY LORD CHELMSFORD TO THE PRESS DEFENCE ASSOCIATION [1]

GENTLEMEN,—I think you will admit that it is unusual for a Viceroy to receive a deputation of this nature, but when you sought permission to wait on me, I put aside precedent because I thought it well to meet you face to face to hear your representations and to give you a clear and frank answer to those representations. I presume at the time of making your request you weighed the fact that the Empire is in the throes of a life-and-death struggle, and that such a time is hardly the moment at which to raise even such an important matter as this. But you must not take my ready consent to receive you to mean that I considered the moment you had chosen opportune. I put aside, however, this consideration, though it has meant that precious time has had to be devoted to a matter which might well have awaited a more convenient season. I shall not dwell further on this point. I merely mention it because I want to show that in a matter like this I am always ready to meet those who feel they have a grievance to advance.

Let me make one more preliminary observation. You are here as representatives of the Press, to complain of certain legislation which embodies the attitude of the Government of India towards certain aspects of journalism. The function of the Press informing public opinion holds within its compass the possibilities of an ideal as high and noble as any that can be imagined. You have each and

[1] See page 136.

all of you the right to be proud of the profession to which you belong, and I find it a little embarrassing to discuss with you, however dispassionately, matters which may be taken to reflect upon the methods in which journalism is, or may be, or has been, conducted in India. You have yourselves placed me in that position, and I only ask you, if you find yourselves in disagreement with what I say, to acquit me of any discourtesy, and to realise that I am dealing with the question in the abstract, and not in any sense whatever are my remarks to be taken as having any personal application.

A Free Press

You have rightly abstained from addressing to me any elaborate argument in defence of the principle of a free Press. It is a principle that commands the instinctive adherence of every Englishman. I am an Englishman, and I can assure you that my education, my training, my inherited instincts, all bias me in this matter, and the bias is not against your case, but in favour of it. Anything in the nature of muzzling the Press strikes right across the grain of my whole being.

If, therefore, I find that so broad-minded an Englishman as Lord Minto found it necessary to pass an Act such as that of which you complain, that so staunch an apostle of liberty as Lord Morley approved of it as Secretary of State, and that my predecessor saw no reason to relax the restrictions it imposes, I venture to think that there must be a better case than you are disposed to admit in favour of this much-abused Press Act.

. . . . . .

The Operation of the Act

Turning to the second portion of your paragraph 5, your arguments would lead one to suppose that this Act had been worked by the Local Governments with great harshness and indiscretion, and I have had a careful search made of the records of the Government of India, but I cannot find that a single case of that character has been brought to our notice, and, on the other hand, the Government of India were careful from the first to issue instructions enjoining leniency and discrimination. In no single case has an appeal to a High Court against the Local Government's orders succeeded, and in the majority of cases the Court has definitely branded the articles complained of as objecttionable.

Perhaps it will make the case a little clearer if we look at the statistics of the operation of this Act since 1910. Take newspapers first: 143 have been warned once, and thirty thrice or oftener. Only three have had their first security forfeited, and not one its second. As regards Presses: fifty-five have been warned once, nine twice, and five thrice or oftener. Thirteen have had their first security forfeited; only one its second. I cannot agree with you that this evidences illiberal action on the part of the executive authority, and in this period, if your argument holds good, we should surely expect to find a steady diminution in the number of presses, newspapers, and periodicals. But what are the facts? The presses have increased from 2,736 in 1909–10 to 3,237 in 1915–16; newspapers from 726 to 857, and the periodicals from 829 to 2,927. And these figures do not support the theory that a journalist's career is as perilous as you suggest.

. . . . . .

Present Conditions

In paragraph 13 you claim that the Press is now honest and law-abiding, and that all necessity for restriction has disappeared. Is that not rather arguing in a circle? Because a river has been embanked and thus prevented from flooding the surrounding country, do the engineers say: "This river is now safe, and we will not trouble to maintain the embankment"? I do not think you can urge that because floods have been controlled the possibility of their recurrence has disappeared. The history of the Press in

India is against your theory. In 1878 a growing section of the Indian Press was expressing covert or open hostility to Government. The passing of the Act of that year exercised a restraining influence, but when it was removed there was a recrudescence of malevolent hostility. From 1884 to 1898 a section of the Press steadily grew more scurrilous, more malignant, more seditious, until the penal law had to be strengthened, in 1898, but even that was not sufficient. Misrepresentation and vilification of Government, and even overt sedition, went steadily on until the Newspapers (Excitement to Violence) Act was passed in 1908, and it was only when that proved inadequate that the Press Act of 1910, now under discussion, really checked the flood that was spreading over the land. Do not think I am framing an indictment against the Press of India as a whole or against journalism as it is now conducted. I am only recounting the facts that led up to the debates in the Legislative Council on the Act of 1910. Those debates did not touch the case of the many well-conducted and responsible papers then any more than I am doing now; but that the danger then was great and serious I do not think that you dispute, and if you say the danger has passed away I cannot agree with you; for so long as there are papers in India, as there still are, that in pursuit of their own ends think it right to magnify the ills from which she suffers; to harp upon plague, famine, malaria, and poverty, and ascribe them all to the curse of an alien Government; so long as there are papers that play on the weaknesses of impressionable boys and encourage that lack of discipline and of respect for all authority that has done so much to swell the ranks of secret revolution; so long as it is considered legitimate to stir up hatred and contempt in order to foster discontent,—I feel that any relaxation of the existing law would be followed, as surely as night follows day, by a gradual increase of virulence, until we should come back to the conditions that prevailed before the passing of the Act.

EXAMPLES QUOTED

There will be some that will hold up their hands in horror at the suggestion that such things as I have indicated are still to be found in the Press, but here is an extract that I should like to read to you: "The meaning of Imperialism is that a powerful nation thinks that it is justified in depriving a weaker people of their liberty, and retaining that people under their rule in perpetual slavery on the plea of civilising them and bettering their lot." Here is another: "If the Indian rulers had given effect to the terms of the Royal Proclamation of 1858, India would not have been converted into a land of permanent famine and pestilence and its children into a race of effeminate weaklings." What is this but to exaggerate the ills of India and to ascribe them all to Government? Listen to this; it is part of a long article: "The same feeling of pity possesses the populace when they stand face to face with political crimes committed by youthful and misguided idealists. They know that these young men come fully prepared for sacrificing their own lives in the discharge of the work entrusted to them. The gallows have absolutely no terrors for them. To send them to the gallows would not hinder, but, on the contrary, very materially help their criminal propaganda. This has been the universal experience of history in these matters. Those who are already in sympathy with this criminal propaganda will not be cowed down by their chastisement, but will rather look upon their punishment as martyrdom, and draw fresh inspiration from it for carrying on their work. Everybody except the official machinist and the purblind publicist understands all this."

Now, hear, not what I think about it, but what a High Court Judge has to say about this article: "This seems to me most pernicious writing, and writing which must tend to encourage political assassination by removing public detestation of such crimes. *New India* is presumably read by numbers of excitable young men animated (and not unnaturally) by the same ideal which the writer ascribes to the assassins, but which it is impossible for any right-minded person to connect with their crimes. Such young men are practically told that the assassins are pursuing the same ideal as themselves with singular courage and disregard of self, and that such criminals should not be punished, but convinced of the folly of their ways. The article presents the assassins to such young men, and to the public generally, in a far more favourable light than any ordinary person would have viewed them in, and, although it may not amount to incitement, it certainly seems to me to give encouragement to the commission of crimes which undoubtedly fall within section 4(1)."

I do not wish to detain you, but I must still give you a few more extracts. A poet writes:

"How long will the blood of the innocent people be shed, and how long will we writhe in agony?"

He prays God to release Indians from this miserable condition. He complains that they have lost their wealth, honour, and all good qualities. He inquires what can be worse than their present condition. Another poet says:

"When will the oppressions of the wicked cease in India; when will the enemies of Indians be crushed, and how long will this cruel oppression of the weak continue?"

Yet another:

"Slavery has deprived Indians of wealth, honour, and freedom, and has reduced them to destitution and starvation. What further harm is it going to cause to India? Will it drain their very blood? It has paralysed their limbs and muzzled their mouths. Why is it so mercilessly pursuing them? God gave equal liberty to all. Why then should accursed slavery be oppressing Indians?"

And here is one more:

"The arrest is legal, doubtless, but it is truly unlawful. The breaking of the sacred law of justice which holds society together when injustice is perpetrated, when crimes are committed legally, when innocence is no protection and harmless men are treated as criminals, then we live in a condition of anarchy no matter what legal sanction may cover the wrong-doer. Civilisation does not protect us. We should be better off in a state of savagery; for then we should be on our guard. We should carry arms and protect ourselves. We are helpless. We pay taxes to be wronged."

Stirring up Hatred and Contempt

What are these but stirring up hatred and contempt? Do you come before me to-day as journalists to say that you do not regret that such sentiments should have appeared in the public Press? Do you suggest that language like this can have no ill-effect, and that you are prepared to see such things said every day through the length and breadth of India? Are these, I would ask you, the writings of persons whose loyalty and good intentions and honesty of purpose are unquestioned, but who have unwittingly fallen into a trap which the Act has laid for them? Can I judge the tree except by its fruit? These are not extracts from the old files of 1910; they are cuttings from newspapers of 1916. If the terrors of the Act to which you have so freely adverted are not sufficient to prevent the publication of such stuff as this, will you tell me what would happen if the Act were repealed? Can you blame me if, with such publications before me—and I am afraid I could find you more in the same strain—I refuse to assent to your assurance that the Press of India has purged itself, and that the time has come to accord to it once again the freedom which should be its pride no less than its privilege?

APPENDIX V

SIR MICHAEL O'DWYER ON THE DANGER OF THE HOME RULE PROPAGANDA IN THE PUNJAB [1]

. . . . . .

THAT brings me to the question of the Home Rule progaganda.

Honourable Members will remember that some two months ago my Government passed orders forbidding two gentlemen who were prominently identified with that propaganda from entering the province. I took that action not because I desire to stifle or repress any reasonable political discussion, but because I was, and am, convinced that an agitation for Home Rule in this province on the lines advocated by the leaders of the movement, and as it would be interpreted by those to whom it would be addressed, would stir up the dying embers of the revolutionary fires which we have almost succeeded in extinguishing, and set parts of the province in a blaze once more. I desire to make the attitude of Government in this matter quite clear. Government, while opposed to any sudden or catastrophic constitutional change, recognises that among a large section of the community there is a growing desire, and a natural desire, for an increased measure of self-government.

His Excellency the Viceroy, in the Imperial Council on February 7th, formally stated that the "expediency of broadening the basis of government, and the demand of Indians to play a greater part in the conduct of affairs in this country, are not matters which have escaped our atten-

[1] See pages 137, 211.

tion." He added that proposals had been submitted to the Home Government, and asked the Council to remember that the consideration of certain constitutional questions affecting a portion of the Empire might have to yield place for a time to the more urgent task of so prosecuting the war as to ensure the preservation of the Empire.

But, gentlemen, the increasing measure of self-government by steady and orderly change for which this country will fit itself as education spreads, as causes of disunion diminish, and as large numbers of the vast population gain political experience, is something very far from the sudden upheaval, and the startling transfer of political authority into ignorant and inexperienced hands, which the protagonists of Home Rule contemplated in their extravagant demands. Such changes would be as revolutionary in their character, and, I believe, as subversive of the existing constitution, as those which the "Ghadr" emissaries endeavoured to bring about. Indeed, it is not without significance to find that the watchword of the thousands who participated in the dacoities of the South-west Punjab two years ago, and of many of the men who fomented the "Ghadr" Conspiracy on the Pacific coast, was *swaraj*, or Home Rule, and that the hundreds of emigrants who returned to the Punjab to spread rebellion in the province by fire and sword, claimed that their object was to establish Home Rule. It may be urged that this was the crude interpretation of a legitimate and constitutional ideal by ignorant men. That may be so; but what we have to consider is not the ideal in the mind of the political philosopher in his arm-chair or the journalist at his desk, but the ideal conveyed to the average man, and we have had positive proof, based on judicial findings, of several experienced tribunals, that of the thousands of Punjabis to whom the *swaraj*, or Home Rule, doctrine was preached in America, some hundreds at least set themselves as early as possible to realise that ideal by the sword, the pistol, and the bomb.[1] Take even a more convincing case.

[1] See pages 98, 187.

The so-called "Dr." Mathra Singh, who recently suffered the extreme penalty of the law, was one of the most active and dangerous of the revolutionary leaders. He was the expert bomb-maker; he was also a man widely travelled and of superior education, very different from the ignorant dupes whom he enmeshed in the conspiracy. Yet this man, though his hands were steeped in crime, asserted to the last that he was merely acting as an advocate of Home Rule. We have to judge men not by their words, but by their acts; we have to judge movements not by the ideals that perhaps inspire their leaders, but by the results they have produced, or are likely to produce, on the community. Applying those tests, can any reasonable man say that the Home Rule propaganda is one which could be preached in the Punjab to-day without serious danger to the public peace and to the stability of the Government?

One more remark before I leave this subject.

The case of Home Rule for Ireland is often cited as an argument in their favour by those who advocate Home Rule for India. At the risk of entering into the thorny field of Irish politics, I may say there is no analogy between the two cases.

The Home Rule movement in Ireland aimed at the restoration of the status—a separate legislature and a separate executive, though with limited powers—which Ireland had enjoyed for centuries down to the Union of 1800. The great majority of the Irish people supported the movement, and many of those who wished well to Ireland, even if they did not count on any material advantages from Home Rule, were inclined to favour the scheme on sentimental and historical grounds, and looked forward to the time when the softening of racial and religious asperities would enable all classes to combine for the restoration and the successful working of the system of self-government, which in one form or another Ireland had for centuries enjoyed. That was a lofty and a generous ideal. Unfortunately, the nearer it came to realisation, the greater became the practical difficulties; the old feuds and factions were revived with increasing bitterness and threatened civil war. A year ago one section of the supporters of Irish *swaraj* (the Sinn Fein, or *Swadeshists*), following in the footsteps of our Punjabi *swarajists*, allied themselves with the king's enemies and brought about an abortive rebellion. That was speedily suppressed, but it has left a fatal legacy of distrust and ill-feeling which all good Irishmen, whatever their creed or politics, deplore; for it has prevented Ireland from bearing the full share in the defence of the Empire. Well, gentlemen, the conclusion I would ask you to draw is this. If the Home Rule movement, after a hundred years of agitation, has so far produced no better results among a people fairly enlightened and homogeneous, in a country no larger or more populous than a single division in the Punjab, what result can we expect from it in this vast continent, with its infinite variety of races, creeds, and traditions, and its appalling inequalities in social and political development? What results would we expect from it even in our own province? In the matter of Home Rule, I fear the case of Ireland, in so far as it is analogous at all, conveys to us a lesson and a warning.

APPENDIX VI

DADABHAI NAOROJI

DADABHAI NAOROJI was a Parsi, born in Bombay in 1825. He came of a family of priests. He was a promising scholar of the Elphinstone College in that city. On reaching manhood, he at first devoted himself to educational work, and it is said that it was to his initiative that Bombay owed her first school for girls. In 1855 he proceeded to England as representative of Messrs. Cama and Co., and began to occupy himself largely in journalism and in bringing before the public advanced Indian views regarding political and economic questions. Subsequently he returned to India, and was appointed Diwan of the Baroda State. Resigning this post later, he served as a member of the Bombay Corporation, from 1881 to 1885, and rendered excellent service to that body. He was appointed an additional member of the Imperial Legislative Council, and was one of the promoters of, and partakers in, the First Indian National Congress.

In 1886 he left for England, determined to enter Parliament, and stood for Holborn. He was unsuccessful, and, returning to India, became President of the second Congress.[1] In 1887 he returned to England, and after some years was elected Member of Parliament for Central Finsbury. His election was hailed with much enthusiasm in India.

He retained his seat for three years, and, in 1893, induced Mr. Herbert Paul to move a resolution proposing that examinations for the Indian Civil Service should be held

[1] See page 38.

simultaneously in India and England. He also, with the assistance of Sir William Wedderburn and the late Mr. W. S. Caine, organised an Indian Parliamentary Committee. In 1895 he was appointed to the Royal Commission on Indian Expenditure, and did laborious service on that body. In 1893 he presided over the ninth Congress sessions, and received great ovations. In 1895 he lost his seat in Parliament, and afterwards devoted himself mainly to Congress propaganda. He was elected President of the memorable Congress of 1906,[1] but was unable to be present. His address was read out in that assemblage. He died at the ripe age of ninety-two, much respected.

[1] See page 66.

APPENDIX VII

THE REFORMS SCHEME: SPEECH BY SIR HARCOURT BUTLER, LIEUTENANT-GOVERNOR, UNITED PROVINCES, ON JULY 15TH, 1918[1]

I NEED not say more about man-power or war loan, but I have a few more words to say to you. I propose in the course of my present tour to deal in a spirit of hopefulness and, I trust, of helpfulness with some of the problems which have arisen out of this war. This afternoon I shall speak to you about the scheme of reforms which has just been published. It is early yet to appreciate fully the reception of that scheme. Some are favourable to it, a few seem hostile, many are reserving their opinion. You will not expect me to offer any opinion on the scheme itself. What I want to do is this. I want to impress upon you the enormous difficulties which beset this question of reforms. It is enormously difficult to graft the ideas of Western democracy on to an ancient social system of which a prominent feature is the institution of caste.[2] It is enormously difficult to harmonise the aspirations of a modern industrial Empire with the aspirations of an essentially spiritual and conservative land like India. It is enormously difficult again to devise a scheme which will suit the diverse masses of languages, opinions, creeds, and religious differences which go to make up India. But no difficulties have deterred or stayed His Majesty's Government and the Government of India. They have declared in the most unequivocal terms that there must be a real step forward in the direction of responsible government. The Secretary of State and the Viceroy have sought and heard opinions throughout the length and breadth of the land from repre-

[1] See page 226. [2] See page 166

sentatives of every class. They are in possession of an amount of information which no one else in India has. Whatever may be thought of their definite proposals, it must be admitted that never before has any inquiry been conducted with such anxious care to ascertain the wishes of the diversified and heterogeneous peoples of India. It is the duty of every man in this province who takes interest in public affairs to give this scheme the fairest possible consideration, and I believe that they will do so. They may want some details altered, they may want this or that proposal modified, but they will, I believe, lay their heads together in a spirit of constructive statesmanship, and see through co-operation and compromise some adequate solution of the problem. I regard it as absolutely essential that we should work together, because if this scheme fails or is rejected, we shall have to face a situation which will be difficult and delicate and might deteriorate. But I need not dwell upon this contingency, especially in this province. If you believe, as I think you must believe, that the Secretary of State and the Viceroy have made an earnest and honest and, may I add? a very able endeavour to deal with this difficult problem, then I beg you to go out and meet them half way, to put aside any preconceived ideas, to throw off catchwords and phrases, to stick closely to things and not to words, and to concentrate your thoughts on the future well-being of India. We have seen how precarious and perilous has been the course of reforms in China, in Persia, in Turkey, and now in Russia. May I quote to you the saying of an able Chinese statesman? "To speak in a parable; a new form of government is like an infant, whose food must be regulated with circumspection if one desires it to thrive. If in our zeal for the infant's growth we give it several days' nourishment at once, there is small hope of its ever attaining manhood."

THREE CARDINAL CONDITIONS

It seems to me that there are three cardinal conditions of healthy reform. The first is, that any reform must be a real reform, and must not be put out of shape and substance by too many safeguards, checks, and counter-checks. This is a canon of moral strategy. Reform must not be afraid of itself. The second condition is that any scheme of reforms in India must bear some relation to the reforms of the last fifty years. You have been told that the Minto-Morley reforms were doomed to failure and have failed. With all respect to those who hold this view, I must say that this is not my experience as vice-president of the Imperial Legislative Council, as Lieutenant-Governor of Burma, and as Lieutenant-Governor of the United Provinces. In my experience, and this was the expressed opinion of Lord Hardinge, the Minto-Morley reforms have been successful. They have been a valuable training to Indian politicians, and have prepared them for another forward move. The executive government has been far more influenced by the discussions in Council than is popularly imagined, and the debates have been maintained at a really high level. Occasionally time has been wasted, occasionally feeling has run high. Of what assembly cannot this be said? I was led to believe that in our Legislative Council I should find a spirit of opposition and hostility to Government. I have found, on the contrary, a responsive and reasonable spirit. Indeed, I go so far, gentlemen, as to say that it is the very success of the Minto-Morley reforms that makes me most hopeful in regard to the future course of reform. The third condition is that any scheme of reform that can hope to reach maturity must fit in with the general administrative system of the country. It is often not realised how exceedingly ancient and powerful that administrative system is. The British found it in being in India. Its roots go down to the time of Asoka. Remember that in the Eastern Roman Empire a system of scientific and bureaucratic organisation, animated by ideas very different from ours, kept back the tide of invasion from Europe for many hundred years. Only when you disturb an administrative system can you realise how far its tentacles have spread. I know there are some who think that all evils will come to an end if only democracy is substituted for bureaucracy. I ask them to think what things they mean when they use these terms. Except in the smallest communities such as the city states, democracy never has meant and never can mean direct government by the people or an electorate. Every modern democracy is dependent even in times of peace for its successful working on the services of a body of trained administrators; and the need for such services tends to become greater rather than less with the growth, extent, and complexity of the state's activities. In France, in America, and in England this truth is more and more realised and acted on.

Not least important is the spirit which animates and informs discussion. No reform can be achieved without some rise in political temperature. That rise may be greater now owing to the prolonged strain of the war. Let us see things clearly and quietly. Let us approach the scheme of reform with a desire to make the best of it. I can assure you that this Government will assist you in all reasonable endeavours to secure political, industrial, and educational progress; I have already instituted a reform which I believe to be far-reaching and beneficial. I refer to the reconstitution of the Finance Committee of the Legislative Council. They now meet monthly, and the more important schemes of provincial expenditure are referred to them for advice, and great importance is attached to their advice. This reform may be swallowed up in larger schemes, but it is an important and encouraging commencement. I entreat you, with all my heart I do entreat, to keep up hope. You have a proverb—"Dunya omed par qaim"—The world rests on hope. Be sure of this that a great responsibility rests on anyone now who is in a position to influence opinion, whether on a large or small scale, to create and develop an atmosphere of large progressive hope. You will not find the officials of this province unready to meet you half-way. Let us work together. Faith and action and the future are ours.

APPENDIX VIII

(a) AND (b)

SPEECHES AT THE DELHI WAR CONFERENCE,[1] APRIL 1918, BY H.H. THE MAHARAJA OF ULWAR AND THE HONOURABLE MR. W. A. IRONSIDE

(A)

BRITAIN AND INDIA: SPEECH BY HIS HIGHNESS THE MAHARAJA OF ULWAR AT THE DELHI WAR CONFERENCE

SPEAKING at the War Conference at Delhi held in April 1918, in support of the resolution endorsing the recommendations of the sub-committees and recommending them to the early consideration and adoption by the Government of India and His Majesty's Government, His Highness the Maharaja of Ulwar said:

"On an occasion so solemn and unique in the destiny of the Empire as the present, I rise to speak under a deep sense of responsibility. We have eagerly responded to the trumpet-call of the Empire at the present moment by assembling here, not because it is a bare duty, but because it is a privilege to assist in her hour of need the great country who has wished India well and has guided her destinies for 160 years. What is real friendship? What are the bonds of partnership? With the words of the gracious message of the Emperor of India ringing in our ears, with the Prime Minister's appeal fresh in our minds, is it likely, I ask, that the heart of India can lie dormant at this time? Is it possible to conceive that India is going to let this opportunity go by to prove, as she has proved in the past, that, according to her power and circumstances, she is true

[1] See page 152

to herself, and so is determined to be true to the Empire of which she forms an integral part.

"It was truly put once by one of Your Excellency's predecessors when talking to India; he said, 'You cannot do without us. We should be impotent without you.' If this is so, and it is so, then let this sacred union be a consecration at the altar of divine love for the advance of both countries to the highest purpose of life. India is proud of her connection with the country whose love of justice and liberty is now being practically tested on the anvil of the battle-field, and every blow is adding lustre and glory before the world to the steel foundations on which her structure is built. With such a country our destinies are bound, and with her we rise, with her we fall.

"Our Fatherland, like any other country in the world, has her domestic needs. She requires many adjustments of her present conditions. She aspires, and legitimately so, to strengthen, if possible, her position within the Empire, so that she may no longer go forth before the world with bent head. India is now eager to raise her head on an equality with her sister dominions, but Your Excellency and your Government know her wants, and you are aware of her urgent needs. If I like to think that for the present my country reposes these sacred charges in the trust of the British people, it is because we have a more urgent duty to fulfil. Trust begets trust, and we know if we can, with the mercy of Providence, succeed in doing what the occasion demands us to do for Old England, on whom we repose our confidence, she will not be slow to respond to our needs. The responsibility at this moment is ours, and when there is a silver lining to the clouds, the responsibility will be hers. For the present India is enthusiastically bent on sharing the glories in the common cause of the Empire which is being fought out on the battle-fields. In this vast gathering which readily assembled at Your Excellency's invitation, I see no British India or Native States before me to-day. It is one India, a united India with a singleness of mind and purpose. Two busy days have been spent by the members of this Conference in devising the best means for the adoption of urgent measures to meet the situation arising out of the crisis through which the Empire is passing at the present time. There are certain remedies which I may mention, particularly such as the free granting of the King's commissions to Indians, the raising of the pay of the Indian soldiers; the establishing of institutions in India as military training colleges for its sons, which have to be dealt with in the resolutions, and which, if applied in a generous spirit of trust, are calculated to produce instant results in accelerating recruiting.

"In cordially supporting the resolutions which cover these and other points, I would join earnestly in commending it for the early consideration of, and adoption by, the Government of India and His Majesty's Government.

"Before concluding I will say only a few more words. In this hall we hold the fair name and fame of India in our hands. Here we come to resolve to perform what we ought, and hence we go to perform without fail what we resolve. Our countrymen have their eyes fixed on us. The people will ask, 'What have you given?' and 'What have you asked for?' The answers can be summed up in one word—'trust.' I may not be a British Indian, but I am an Indian, and as such I say that, in this supreme hour of the need of the Empire, for the fair name of our mother-country this is the opportunity to close our ranks and to prove to the world that we can respond to trust and confidence in a manner which can become the envy of others. Then when sunshine comes again, and the clouds of war disappear, we shall have reason to look back upon a past on which we can await the verdict of history with legitimate pride and confidence. In the dutiful message which goes in reply to the message from the Throne we all combine in emphasising once again our assurances of loyalty and attachment to the person of His Majesty, and we send with it our prayers for victory."

(B)

Speech by the late Mr. W. A. Ironside, Representative of the Calcutta Chamber of Commerce at the Delhi War Conference, in the part of the European Commercial Community

After the flow of eloquence to which we have listened, I feel, Sir, that any endeavour of mine adequately to express, on behalf of the great community I have the honour to represent, an outward and visible sign of our desires and hopes, of our determination and our faith, must sound at least weak and ineffective but none the less genuine. Few of us have knowledge or experience in oratory and rhetoric, and we are not students of dialectics, but I am sincere in every word that I utter. We are proud in the claim that we are men and women of British birth, not merely, as some would say, strangers in a strange land. We are as much part and parcel of the Empire as though we lived in London or any other little corner of His Majesty's dominions. Every man and woman, Sir, places himself or herself unreservedly at your disposal; and order us, tell us what you require of us, what you want us to do, and there will, I assure you, be no faint-hearted response. Take of our man-power, take of our resources. We wish to range ourselves on equal terms with our people from the other parts of the Empire.

I am not going to descend to politics, but would like to take this great opportunity to assure my Indian neighbours and fellow citizens that the future welfare of India and her people, when the present great adventure has been finished and final victory attained, will be by frank and honest endeavour, in co-operation with them, our first concern. The men of my community in increasing numbers view India's necessities through different glasses, and are ready, when their hands are free of this sterner work, to take a hand in making her future.

Your Excellency, no words are necessary to spur us to greater effort. The heroic examples of our men and women are surely enough to those of us who are left. Our dearest and our best have died that England should live. The men of the *Vindictive* and her escort vessels last week left behind for us to follow an example for all time. They gave all for their country. So, surely, this is no time to place restrictions on our duty. The road to conquest must mean greater trials and sacrifices, but we will endure until the end, fortified by a great and abiding faith in justice and right and in the God of our fathers to bring us to final victory.

In my poor way, Sir, I have given you a message from the people of my community and race. You will not find us wanting to act our part and justify ourselves as true citizens of His Majesty.

Printed by Hazell, Watson & Viney, Ld., London and Aylesbury, England.